The Money Signal

CHICAGO STUDIES IN AMERICAN POLITICS

A series edited by Susan Herbst, Lawrence R. Jacobs, Adam J. Berinsky, and Frances Lee; Benjamin I. Page, editor emeritus

Also in the series:

Additional series titles follow index.

The Money Signal

*How Fundraising Matters in
American Politics*

DANIELLE M. THOMSEN

THE UNIVERSITY OF CHICAGO PRESS   CHICAGO AND LONDON

The University of Chicago Press, Chicago 60637
The University of Chicago Press, Ltd., London
© 2025 by The University of Chicago
Published 2025

34 33 32 31 30 29 28 27 26 25   1 2 3 4 5

ISBN-13: 978-0-226-84112-0 (cloth)
ISBN-13: 978-0-226-84114-4 (paper)
ISBN-13: 978-0-226-84113-7 (e-book)
DOI: https://doi.org/10.7208/chicago/9780226841137.001.0001

Library of Congress Cataloging-in-Publication Data

Names: Thomsen, Danielle M., author.
Title: The money signal : how fundraising matters in American politics /
    Danielle M. Thomsen.
Other titles: How fundraising matters in American politics
Description: Chicago : The University of Chicago Press, 2025. |
    Series: Chicago studies in American politics | Includes bibliographical
    references and index.
Identifiers: LCCN 2025000621 | ISBN 9780226841120 (cloth) |
    ISBN 9780226841144 (paperback) | ISBN 9780226841137 (ebook)
Subjects: LCSH: Campaign funds—United States. | Political candidates—
    United States | United States. Congress—Elections. | United States—
    Politics and government—21st century.
Classification: LCC JK1991 .T494 2025 | DDC 324.7/80973—dc23/eng/20250214
LC record available at https://lccn.loc.gov/2025000621

Contents

Acknowledgments

I remember thinking early on that this book would write itself. It most certainly did not. I am deeply indebted to the many people who propelled this book past the finish line. My first thanks go to those who were willing to be interviewed for the project. They took time out of their busy schedules to talk with me about their experiences running for office, covering congressional elections, and overseeing the data at the heart of the manuscript. Many others responded to a survey, and their collective insights had a profound impact on the trajectory of the book. I am very fortunate to have had the opportunity to work with Sara Doskow on the manuscript. I am grateful to Sara and Frances Lee for including it in the Chicago Studies in American Politics series and to the reviewers for their constructive and thoughtful feedback.

In addition, I thank the University of California, Irvine, and the Department of Political Science for supporting my research and kindly sponsoring a book conference. A dream team of scholars — Adam Bonica, Gary Jacobson, Frances Lee, Eric Schickler, and Lynn Vavreck — participated, and they saw a book that was sharper and bolder than the one in front of them. Their feedback transformed the manuscript and pushed me to think about money in a bigger way. The product is leaps and bounds better as a result, and I am beyond grateful for their generosity. Michael Tesler steered the conversation in fruitful directions and gave encouragement throughout the process. I also thank my colleagues who participated in the conference or provided support, including Matt Beckmann, Graeme Boushey, Simone Chambers, Jordie Davies, Sara Goodman, Mary McThomas, Davin Phoenix, and Sam Vortherms.

Many others generously provided input on chapters and papers and lent an ear at various points. Jim Curry is owed a special thanks for his incisive comments and willingness to revisit later drafts. Trish Kirkland,

Rachel Potter, and Lauren Ross have been cherished friends and sources of support at every stage. Nick Carnes, Michael Tesler, and Sam Vortherms made helpful suggestions on the candidate survey. John Aldrich read the entire manuscript and gave insightful comments as always. Ryan Mundy has been instrumental in this project, and his impact is visible throughout the book. Various parts of the manuscript have benefited from feedback from Steve Ansolabehere, Rob Boatright, Barry Burden, Dan Butler, Brandice Canes-Wrone, Nathan Cisneros, Jen Gaudette, Bernie Grofman, Laurel Harbridge-Yong, Hans Hassell, Seth Hill, Trish Kirkland, Josh Lerner, Neil Malhotra, Seth Masket, Nolan McCarty, Suzanne Mettler, Kathy Michelmore, Ken Miller, Kevin Munger, Michael Olson, Spencer Piston, Rachel Potter, Eleanor Powell, Steve Rogers, Jon Rogowski, Kira Sanbonmatsu, William Smith, Rochelle Snyder, Katelyn Stauffer, Michele Swers, Rein Taagepera, Dan Thompson, Sarah Treul, Jennifer Victor, Craig Volden, Simon Weschle, Alan Wiseman, Antoine Yoshinaka, and Hye Young You.

I also appreciate the invitations to present this research at conferences and talks. I thank seminar participants at Berkeley; University of Chicago; Columbia University; UC, Davis; Florida State University; UC, Irvine; UCLA; University of Michigan; University of North Carolina at Chapel Hill; Princeton University; UCSD; University of Tennessee; Texas A&M University; Vanderbilt University; Washington University in St. Louis; University of Wisconsin-Madison; Yale University; the SoCal Political Economy and Institutions Workshop; and the Women in Legislative Studies Workshop, as well as conference participants at the Congress and History Conference at Harvard/MIT, the Center for Effective Lawmaking Conference at the University of Virginia, and the Candidates and Competition Conference at Princeton University.

This project benefited from generous financial support from several organizations and institutions. UCI and the School of Social Sciences gave me the time and resources needed to complete the manuscript, and the Jack W. Peltason Center for the Study of Democracy provided additional funding. I was fortunate to spend a truly wonderful year at the Center for the Study of Democratic Politics at Princeton University where the seeds of this book were sown. QUery On Inc. awarded grant funding at a key moment and allowed me to focus on research and writing. The Negotiating Agreement in Congress Research Grant from the Social Science Research Council funded the survey of primary voters, and Sam Luks and Marissa Shih at YouGov were a pleasure to work with. I also thank the Center for Effective Lawmaking at the University of Virginia and Vanderbilt University for research support as well as the Hunt Alternatives Fund's Political Parity Project and the Campbell Institute at Syracuse University for initial funding at the outset of this data collection effort.

It has taken me more than a decade to collect the data used in this book. I want to express my gratitude to the army of research assistants across multiple universities for their help in collecting, cleaning, and validating the data: Sandra Aguilar, Emily Chen, Olivia Dinh, Noelle Doan, Alina Dunlap, Dina Eldawy, Taylor Evangelisti, Brendan Gilligan, Lailee Gole-sorki, Taylor Imperiale, Joel Kersting, Katherine Kleve, Dana Lechleiter, Mahteme Legesse, Maggie Mabie, Lindsey McCabe, Nurie Metodieva, Melina Much, Lex Perry, Raychel Renna, Saad Siddiq, Billy Silk, Daniel Stublen, Jen Sweet, Kelly Wulf, and Andrew Yam. Special thanks to Timur Ohloff for his hard work in the early days of the project and to Ryan Mundy and Savannah Plaskon for theirs closer to the end.

My final professional thanks go to those who have either made their data publicly available or generously shared their data. I am grateful to Gary Jacobson for sharing his invaluable congressional elections data that span this entire period and to Hans Hassell, Rachel Porter, Sarah Treul, Steven Pettigrew, Karen Owen, and Emily Wanless for data on prior office experience in various years. I thank Adam Bonica for his pathbreaking Database on Ideology, Money in Politics, and Elections (DIME), Rob Boatright for data on primary election dates and primary filing deadlines, Andrew Hall and Alexander Fouirnaies for data on term-limited state legislators, Carl Klarner for data on state legislative candidates, and Charles Stewart and Jonathan Woon for committee data. Peter Bucchianeri, Craig Volden, and Alan Wiseman generously shared both state legislative effectiveness scores and issue-by-issue effectiveness scores for members of Congress.

Other centers and agencies have been essential for this research as well. OpenSecrets, formerly the Center for Responsive Politics, generously shared sector-specific fundraising data, and Doug Weber and Alex Baumgart provided helpful research support. Last but certainly not least, I owe an enormous thanks to the Federal Election Commission. The longer I work with FEC data, the more I am in awe of the agency. I am especially thankful to Jason Bucelato for walking me through FEC data and answering my many questions. This project would not have been possible without the incredible efforts of those who work at the Federal Election Commission.

Books can feel endless, and I am most grateful to those who made life full and fun along the way. I first thank my parents, Kent and Rita, for their steadfast love and support, for the Midwestern values they instilled in me, and for working hard and leading by example. It is impossible to thank them enough. My sister, Carly, is an inspiration, role model, and academic star. I have looked up to my sister for as long as I can remember, and I am beyond lucky to travel through life with her at my side. I also thank the Nikkhah Mojdehi clan—Reza, Mahnaz, Mahsa, Jafar, Radeen, and Ervin—for bringing new joy to my world. My deepest gratitude is to my husband, Mohammad. He is without a doubt my better half. He has shared in this journey with me, eagerly engaging in too many conversations about money and measures and bringing love, warmth, and an unwavering optimism to each and every day. This book is dedicated to him.

CHAPTER ONE

The Meaning of Money

In 2019, former federal prosecutor and US Navy pilot Mikie Sherrill became the first Democrat to represent New Jersey's Eleventh Congressional District since 1985. Sherrill filed with the Federal Election Commission in May 2017, more than a year before the primary. In the months that followed, she reported impressive fundraising numbers, raising $250,000 in her first quarter and $500,000 in each of the next two. The incumbent, Republican Rodney Frelinghuysen, had been in Congress for twenty years and chaired the powerful House Appropriations Committee. The race was expected to be close, but Frelinghuysen took many by surprise when he announced his retirement in January 2018 (Corasaniti and Goldmacher 2018).

Sherrill continued to gain momentum. Her fundraising totals attracted local and national attention, and she raised nearly $3 million before the June primary.[1] Sherrill's top Democratic opponent, businesswoman Tamara Harris, fell far short in the money chase, and over half of the $700,000 in Harris's preprimary war chest came from herself. Sherrill skated to primary victory with 77 percent of the vote, Harris was a distant second at 14 percent, and three others each received less than 5 percent. By November, Sherrill's fundraising haul surpassed $8 million, and she won the general election by a comfortable fifteen points. While flipping party control of a seat is rare, Mikie Sherrill followed the conventional playbook: her pathway to office was paved through raising money.

The central argument of this book is that money is a widely used signal of viability and strength in American politics. Money matters because fundraising is a focal point for key political players, including candidates, donors, journalists, and party leaders. Candidates are keenly aware of their competitors' receipts, and they strive to report strong early totals to be seen as serious contenders. Donors direct their contributions to those with a track record of raising money. Journalists cite dollars in their coverage of campaigns to indicate electability and support. Party leaders set high benchmarks and reward better fundraisers with better positions in office. Fundraising prowess comes with a host of benefits on the campaign trail and in Washington.

Money is important for both material and symbolic reasons. Donations affect whether candidates can access infrastructure like staff and office space and purchase the goods and services that fuel their campaigns. But material resources are only part of the story. The use of dollars as a signal shapes the perceptions and behavior of relevant actors and observers. Early money is critical because it serves as a first impression and molds expectations about what is likely to follow. The money chase is the primary way to convey who is ahead or behind in the horse race, who is stronger or weaker as a candidate, and who has power and sway in office. We have to look beyond the ballot to capture the meaning of money in American politics.

Turning to dollars as a focal point changes how we think about the reach and influence of money. Most previous studies have examined the impact of money on votes at the ballot box or votes in office. This book suggests that the power of money is different. Money is used as a signal long before the election and well after the votes have been cast. The consequence is that an elite donor class structures the selection of our representatives by steering resources, attention, and momentum to some candidates over others. Fundraising demands have soared, and the impact of donors has become more and more entrenched. The broad influence of the donor selectorate on who runs and who wins raises serious questions for American democracy.

Scholarly Perspectives on Money

In studying money and politics, political scientists have looked for two main effects of campaign fundraising and spending. One is the effect of campaign contributions on the behavior of elected officials. A long line of work has cast doubt on the idea that money buys lawmakers' votes (Chappell 1982; Wawro 2001; Welch 1982; Wright 1985). In an article titled "Why Is There So Little Money in U.S. Politics?" Ansolabehere, de Figueiredo, and Snyder (2003) surveyed nearly forty studies on the effect of PAC contributions and found little evidence that money has much of an influence on votes. Others have shown that campaign donations are more likely to secure access to politicians, but mostly to friendly or allied lawmakers.[2]

The second is the effect of campaign spending on votes on Election Day. While the association between expenditures and victory patterns is evident, political scientists have been more skeptical of the direct effect of money because donors tend to give to likely winners. Challengers who spend more thus do fare better, and the main point of contention in prior work was whether and how much incumbents benefit as well (e.g., Abramowitz 1988; Gerber 1998; Green and Krasno 1988, 1990; Jacobson 1980, 1990). But these studies focused on vote totals in general elections, and money matters even *less* in general elections today as district partisanship has become paramount. Fundraising in primaries has received limited attention by comparison.[3]

Scholars have taught us a lot about the impact of money, but they have largely overlooked one of the most pervasive ways in which money infiltrates American politics. This book argues that the value of money is rooted in its widespread use as a signal and focal point. Congressional elections are low-information environments. Candidates and officeholders who raise large sums of money are viewed as viable and noteworthy, which results in a positive feedback loop where they are deemed more formidable to other candidates, more attractive to donors seeking to give their money efficaciously, more competitive to journalists who cover frontrunners, and more electable to party leaders who want to win majorities.

In the real world of politics, there is little ambiguity about the value of dollars. The ability to raise money is one of the main heuristics used to judge candidates, and fundraising is a top priority for those who want to win or retain power. Candidates certainly talk about the importance of money. One 2022 House candidate who raised over a million dollars before the primary told me in an interview, "The pressure to raise money is very intense and very consistent." He elaborated,

> The advice that you get all the time from the national party and from your consultants is that the only thing that really matters is raising money. That definitely gets into your head. The pressure sinks in every night when you go to bed. Either you think, I raised a lot of money; how the hell am I going to do that again tomorrow? or, I raised no money today; how the hell am I going to raise money tomorrow? It becomes the only thing you think about when you

go to bed, and it becomes the only thing you think about when you get up in the morning. That's the pressure I'm referring to.

This book invites a new way of thinking about the importance of money, one that moves beyond votes at the ballot box and votes in office. The insights have important parallels to classic work on lawmaker behavior. In his seminal research on Congress, Fenno (1977, 1978) wrote about how legislators create a presentation of self that is aimed at gaining the trust of voters. But this is not the only presentation that legislators make. The money chase is another stage on which candidates and lawmakers perform. This presentation of self is directed largely toward political elites. Fundraising is another way in which both candidates and officeholders attempt to leave the correct impression, at least to those who are following the money.

Design of the Study

I draw on a wide array of data to show how various actors and observers use dollars as a focal point. Significant attention is given to candidates and officeholders because requests for money start with them. I rely heavily on an original dataset of more than thirty-five thousand US House candidates who ran from 1980 to 2022. The dataset includes all fundraising reports filed by each candidate within the election cycle, which allows for the most comprehensive analysis of money across more than four decades. It also includes variables like prior political experience and district partisanship, so money can be examined alongside other factors. These data offer a new window into when candidates and officeholders raise money, how much they raise, and whether they drop out before the primary.[4]

I supplement these big-picture fundraising data with interviews with House candidates and an original survey of 2022 House candidates. The interviews are invaluable because they lift the curtain on fundraising, capture candidate perceptions around the value of money, and provide deeper insight into dropout decisions. The survey data further demonstrate how candidates view dollars and how fundraising demands structure their time on the campaign trail. A closer look at the perceptions and behavior of candidates highlights the ways that money is used and perpetuated as a metric.

Beyond candidates, I explore how donors, journalists, and party leaders bolster the value of money. Analyses of donors investigate how early donor support shapes future support, and I draw on a conjoint experiment of donors for additional evidence. I also collected new data on newspaper coverage of fundraising in a subset of five hundred House races, and I interviewed journalists who report on fundraising. While voters are unlikely to track fundraising, one chapter is devoted to the association between campaign receipts and election outcomes. Finally, I analyze the allocation of rewards in office to probe how fundraising continues to pay dividends after the election.

Clearly there must be some connection between fundraising and victory patterns for money to have the meaning that it does. Yet we cannot fully understand the impact of money if we only consider vote totals. We need to adopt a broader view—one that extends long before the election and well after the votes have been cast—to see how the meaning of money is created and reinforced. By triangulating a variety of data sources, the book sheds light on the mechanisms through which money exerts its influence. The widespread coordination around fundraising as a focal point is key to understanding why and how money matters.

"Everyone's Watching"

Nearly fifty years ago, Fenno (1977, 1978) detailed how legislators cultivate a unique style—a *home style*—in their districts. He outlined three ingredients of home style: how lawmakers present themselves to constituents, how they allocate resources, and how they explain their activity in Washington. This book extends Fenno's ideas about presentation of self to the fundraising arena. Fenno drew on Goffman's earlier work in this area. Goffman (1959) used the metaphor of theatrical performance to illustrate how people "make a presentation of themselves" and seek to mold the perceptions of others through their words and actions.

Whereas Fenno (1977, 1978) focuses on home style in the district, the goal here is to turn the spotlight on how fundraising numbers leave an impression as well. There is no physical act or speech, no deliberate or inadvertent expression. But fundraising is nonetheless a performance, one that conveys trust in the candidate and a willingness to put skin in the game and give money. In addition, most donations are not anonymous. A donation is itself a public endorsement, a financially and reputationally costly action on the part of the donor. Fundraising is a highly visible form of self-presentation with a wide reach and record that lasts. Moreover, the repeated filing of reports provides not just one but a track record of performances.

Fundraising data are readily accessible, and it is easy to know who has more and who has less. As one House candidate put it, "Because it's public, you're being compared to every other candidate. It's like a race. Everyone's watching, and you got the best time—or you're third or fourth." Another candidate went further: "Money is the lifeblood. It is how DC judges you, it is how stakeholders judge you, and it is the only way [DC] folks can compare the candidates." Quarterly and preelection reports are due at regular intervals, which further contributes to the hype around their release. Money is far simpler to monitor than speeches, debates, or endorsements, especially in the low-information environments that characterize congressional elections and primaries in particular.

Key political players use fundraising to draw conclusions and learn information. First, the national party places a large premium on fundraising. When asked about the attention that money brings, one candidate said, "[Money] is seen as a form of viability and legitimacy, both by the national party and by the press who track the 'horse-race-iness' of it all. You're more likely to get earned media if you can raise money and demonstrate that you're running a viable and legitimate campaign." Even successful fundraisers are in touch with the national party only after they report strong initial numbers. The party sets high fundraising targets of a few hundred thousand dollars per quarter.[5] I asked candidates if money is the only metric used by the national party. One said they also watch local endorsements, but money is "their main marker." Another agreed that "money is probably not the only metric, but it is certainly the main metric that they look at to establish legitimacy."

Following the money has become a staple of political journalism as well. Journalists often cite quarterly reports, reference FEC deadlines, and describe the state of a race through money.[6] Dollars are appealing because they are measurable, comparable across candidates, and fit easily into the horse-race frame (Graber and Dunaway 2017; La Raja 2007). One veteran political journalist explained why he covers fundraising: "There's very little way of saying, 'Here's a big field, and these are the ones that I think have a chance.' I take money seriously because it's one of the few metrics that I can look at that tells me who's in the game and who's not. In the absence of polling, what other way is there to separate the serious candidates from the ones who aren't?"

Candidates and their staff comb through fundraising records perhaps more than anyone. When asked whether they looked at FEC reports during the campaign, one candidate replied, "I basically lived on that website." Several noted that it is "technically illegal" to prospect donors from FEC records. Most used reports to gather information and see which donors were aligned with whom. One candidate said, "My team would look at [FEC reports], and they'd tell me so and so gave to [my top opponent]. We would hear about certain people who I knew or stood out. The campaign teams are definitely looking at those." She continued, "[Donors] are your clients in a way. You see what clients the company has and who your competitor has secured support from or contracts with."

Campaign strategies are crafted with an eye toward what fundraising conveys. Candidates time their entry based in part on their expected showing. One said, "The advice is to have a really, really strong first quarter because that puts you on the map."[7] Candidates also try to shape their early totals: "I did ask my vendors, 'Can I pay you in the next quarter?' so that I had a good cash on hand at the end of my first quarter. But it was a numbers game." Another described the "creative accounting" of his opponent, who "goosed the fundraising numbers" by reporting in-kind donations from family members as consulting services. Some spend nearly as much as they raise to report a large number, which recently came up on the podcast *Deconstructed*: "If you spend $95,000 and you bring in $100,000, you actually only netted $5,000. So why do it? The answer is that when you report to the public how much money you've raised, there's a hundred thousand dollar number there. . . . It allows you to look like a more intimidating candidate to the press, to your opponents, [and] to newspapers to garner coverage" (Grim 2022).

For officeholders, building a large campaign war chest is advantageous in other ways. The ability to raise money opens up a variety of professional opportunities. One dimension of leadership is fundraising for the party team (Lee 2009, 2016). Heberlig, Hetherington, and Larson (2006) find that members who redistribute money are more likely to be appointed to leadership. In addition, higher offices tend to cost more, and better fundraisers have an upper hand if they decide to run. Money helps for their own reelection too, since high-quality challengers are unlikely to run if they do not see a path to victory (Cox and Katz 1996; Levitt and Wolfram 1997; Jacobson 1989).

To be sure, candidates and officeholders raise money in part because of the material benefits it affords. But money also comes with other benefits that fuel perceptions of strength. One candidate differentiated between these, noting, "It is more difficult to overcome the perception power of money in politics than it is to overcome the purchasing power of money in politics." Early money has a particularly potent feedback effect, whereby those who post formidable totals are taken more seriously by journalists, other donors, party leaders, and potential and actual competitors. Candidates understand these benefits, and it influences their incentives and strategies on the campaign trail and in office. The perceptions around money provide new insight into why totals continue to soar.

Changes in Fundraising over Time

Prior to the passage of the Federal Election Campaign Act (FECA) of 1971, the lack of reporting requirements hindered our understanding of the association between money and election outcomes. After the data became available, it was clear that money is a good indicator of wins and losses. Figure 1.1 shows the average primary and general election victory rate of top fundraisers. Among all House primary candidates from 1980 to 2022, top fundraisers win 92 percent of the time; if unopposed candidates are excluded, they win 81 percent of the time. The average in opposed primaries reached a low of 71 percent in 1992, when a large number of incumbents lost, and a high of 86 percent in 2012. In general elections, top fundraisers win 92 percent of the time, ranging from 86 percent in 2010 to 97 percent in 2004. Yet top fundraisers fare the same today as they did in the 1980s.

What has changed, however, is the *amount* of money it takes to be the top fundraiser. Figure 1.2 shows the median preprimary receipts of the top-raising primary candidate and the median total receipts of the top-raising general election candidate (all in 2021 dollars). The increase is stark. Candidates today raise more before the primary than general election candidates did in the 1980s. Top fundraisers in opposed primaries raised $170,000 in 1980, compared to $960,000 in 2022—an increase of more than fivefold. What is more, the median includes primary winners who have no shot of winning in November. Early totals of top-raising general election candidates, who are likely to be elected, are higher: top general election fundraisers raised a median of $220,000 before the primary in 1980, compared to $1.3 million in 2022.

Total campaign receipts raised by general election candidates have hit record highs as well. In 2022, top fundraisers in general elections raised a median of $2.1 million for their congressional bids, or nearly four times

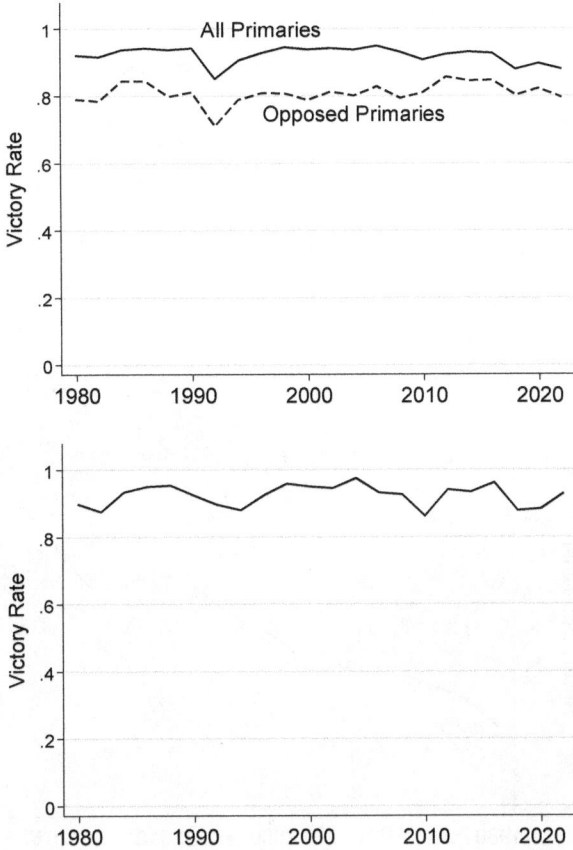

FIGURE I.I. Primary and General Election Victory Rate of Top Fundraisers
Primary elections (*top*), general elections (*bottom*)

Note: Average victory rate of the top primary and general election fundraisers from 1980 to 2022. Vote totals are from America Votes and the FEC; fundraising data are from the FEC.

the 1980 median of $550,000. In most years, there is a small but notice-able increase from the previous cycle. Totals have steadily risen in recent years, from a median of $1.5 million in 2016 to $1.7 million in 2018 to $1.9 million in 2020. While Democrats were more successful in 2018, top Republican and Democratic general election candidates raised similar amounts in recent years: in 2022, the median values were $2.0 and $2.2 mil-lion, respectively.

The influx of money in elections has altered what it takes to run for office. The *million-dollar* price tag of primary elections would have been

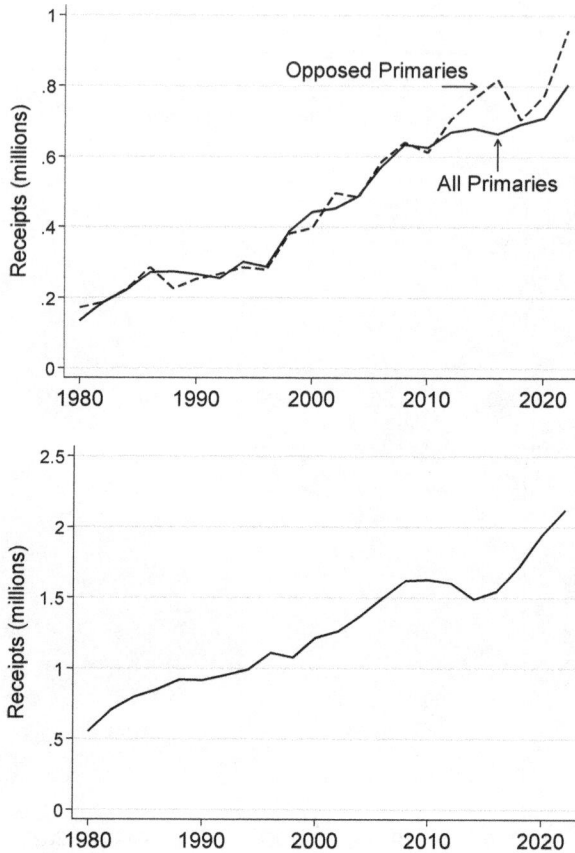

FIGURE I.2. Primary and General Election Receipts of Top Fundraisers
Primary elections (*top*), general elections (*bottom*)

Note: Median amount raised by the top primary and general election fundraisers from 1980 to 2022 (in 2021 dollars). Fundraising data are from the FEC.

unforeseen by the earliest reformers, who set total spending limits several times lower than this amount. Fundraising is a central part of campaigning in the contemporary era, and the amount of money that candidates raise has soared among incumbents, challengers, and open-seat candidates alike. Candidates are not shy about their distaste for fundraising. Incumbents widely bemoan the amount of time they spend dialing for dollars, with many attributing the diminished value of service to the constant need to fundraise. But those who want to win raise a lot of money, and they do so earlier and earlier in the cycle.

Increased Role of Primary Elections

Dramatic shifts in the arena of competition set the stage for why early money is increasingly important. Today, the vast majority of general elections are all but decided by the partisan tilt of the district (Jacobson 2015; Hopkins 2018). Figure 1.3 shows the number of House members elected from safe and competitive districts from 1980 to 2022. The number of lawmakers elected from safe districts has risen sharply, while the number elected from competitive districts has plummeted. In fact, in the 1980s and 1990s, more House members were elected from competitive districts than from safe ones. Now most legislators represent safe partisan districts. In recent congresses, more than three hundred House members, or 70 percent, are elected from safe districts where their party enjoys at least a fifteen-point advantage.

Voters are tethered to their party loyalties, and American politics has become what Sides, Tausanovitch, and Vavreck (2022) describe as increasingly calcified. Moreover, the stakes have increased as partisanship has become tied to issues around race and identity (e.g., Mason 2018; Schickler 2016; Sides, Tesler, and Vavreck 2018; Tesler 2016). The hardening of partisan attitudes and the nationalization of elections has coincided with a narrowing of majorities in Congress that Lee (2016) draws attention to.

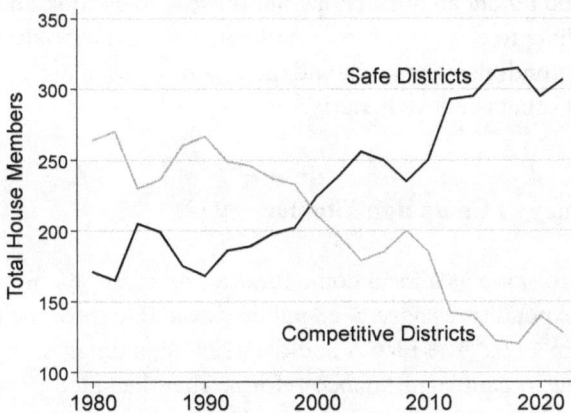

FIGURE 1.3. Members Elected from Safe and Competitive Districts

Note: House members elected from safe and competitive districts from 1980 to 2022. Safe districts are those where the legislator's party received more than 57.5 percent of the presidential vote, and competitive districts are those where the legislator's party received less.

Few general elections are up for grabs, and the limited number of credible opportunities for partisan pickups has exacerbated the need to win in those races. But for Congress as a whole, the bulk of Democratic and Republican lawmakers represent lopsided districts that consistently support candidates of one party or the other.

Primary contests are thus the arena where most representatives are selected. This shift in the nature of competition has prompted a growing body of research to examine the primary stage (e.g., Hirano and Snyder 2014, 2019; Porter and Steelman 2023; Porter and Treul 2025; Thomsen 2023; Woon 2018). Lawmakers elected in safe districts are most fearful of primary voters and primary challenges (Anderson, Butler, and Harbridge-Yong 2020; Boatright 2013, 2020). Much of the action today happens in the months leading up to the primary (Bonica 2017, 2020; Hassell 2018, 2023). The reliance on early money stems in part from these changes in the congressional landscape. Money is likely to matter far more in elections where there is no partisan cue.

The rise in safe-seat lawmakers and the increased role of primary elections provide an important backdrop for the argument and analyses in this book. The preprimary period is more critical than it used to be. Early money is seen as a valuable signal in an otherwise low-information environment. Observers can easily assess who leads and who trails. Other commonly used heuristics like partisanship are absent in primaries, and polling is rare in the early stages of a campaign. Few people pay attention to politics too far ahead of elections, but those who do look first and foremost to dollars to size up a race. Candidates and officeholders certainly behave as if fundraising matters, and the record highs in early fundraising suggest that others believe it matters too.

Transparency in Campaign Finance

For money to serve as a focal point, fundraising must be observable. Receipts and expenditures have been publicly available since the passage of the FECA in 1971.[8] The FECA and the 1974 amendments were a major development in campaign finance reform. They included provisions for limits on candidate contributions, expenditure ceilings for candidates and parties, disclosure requirements, and public funding for presidential campaigns. The act also created the Federal Election Commission, an independent agency that enforces the law and administers compliance. Some aspects of the FECA have since been overturned by the Supreme Court, but the FEC as an agency and the reporting requirements that govern elections are here to stay.

The establishment of reporting requirements is built on the idea that transparency tamps down corruption, and it is likely the case that transparency is normatively better than the alternative. Indeed, Wood and Grose (2022) find that transparency provides information to voters about the character of candidates, and this information affects voter and legislator behavior. Even candidates who lament the emphasis on money highlight other benefits of publicly available reports. One said, "It's important to showcase that some donors are on board and to see who your max top checks are and do that evaluation of, Are you pumping a bunch of your own money in? Is it small dollars? Is it all big dollars? Our average contribution at one point was forty dollars, and it looked like [my competitor's] average contribution was well over a hundred dollars. That's important for the public and for candidates [to know]." To be clear, the argument is not that receipts should be hidden from public scrutiny or that we should return to an era when reporting requirements were not enforced.[9] Moreover, a lot of attributes that voters care about typically are and should be available to the public—things like occupation, experience, policy positions, gender, and race, to name a few. Political observers use traits and cues all the time to draw inferences and make comparisons. Yet money is a good example of how different attributes have different levels of salience at different moments in time.

Campaign receipts and expenditures have been publicly available for fifty years, but money was not in the limelight to the degree it is today. For one thing, the political context has changed, with primaries now more central in the selection of officeholders. In addition, technological innovations, namely the rise of the internet, led to the widespread accessibility of fundraising data. In the preinternet era, journalists and other observers would write or call the FEC to inquire about reports. Since 2002, however, the costs of obtaining this information decreased when it went online. Detailed data are just a click away. These technological and political changes paved the way for money to take up the space that it does. The problem is that the outsized reliance on money has a host of negative consequences for elections and representation.

Problems with the Money Signal

The intense focus on money raises a number of concerns for American democracy. First, the short line between money and viability makes donors, rather than voters, the real selectorate that candidates appeal to. Candidates spend a lot of time cultivating support from donors. In these conversations, they craft messages and refine policy positions with donors, rather than voters, on the receiving end. Donors are unrepresentative in all kinds of ways.[10] They are older, wealthier, whiter, better educated, and more ideologically extreme than nondonors (e.g., Bafumi and Herron 2010; Barber 2016; Bonica 2014; Bonica and Grumbach 2023; Grumbach and Sahn 2020; Hill and Huber 2017; Pew 2018).

Worse yet, more money comes from a tiny slice of spectacularly rich megadonors. In the 1980s, between 10 and 15 percent of contributions in federal elections came from the top 0.01 percent of Americans; by 2012, more than 40 percent did (Bonica et al. 2013, 112). A survey of multimillionaires demonstrated that two-thirds donated in the prior year, and a striking 21 percent bundled other peoples' contributions, an uncommon activity even among donors (Page et al. 2013, 54). The preferences of the superrich unsurprisingly drift farthest from average citizens, and they are more conservative on a range of issues (Page et al. 2013; Page and Gilens 2020; see also Bartels 2008; Gilens 2012). And as Hacker and Pierson (2010a,b) detail, those at the very top have benefited most from government policies, making the rich richer at the expense of the middle class.

Second, the need to raise millions of dollars matters for who runs, who wins, and the makeup of political institutions. Carnes (2018) finds that the high price tag of running for office hits working-class individuals especially hard. Bonica (2020) shows that lawyers' early money advantage explains why they are so much more likely to win. One candidate similarly highlighted the connection between fundraising and the composition of Congress: "Campaign finance is a key reason why a majority of Congress is millionaires and why the demographics of Congress look the way they do. It's about access to capital just like businesses. You might have the best ideas in the world, but if you don't have access to funders, they're just not going to go anywhere. That's very similar, sadly, in politics and something that needs to change." Those who are not plugged into wealthy networks are at a serious disadvantage. One candidate said, "It's $100 here, it's $25 there. The majority of the people that I talk to can't afford to give me $2,900 [the maximum amount in 2022]." Others described the impact of asking for money from family and friends who are stretched thin: "If your brother makes $55,000 and you're asking for $2,900, that's a significant amount of money. Being able to build up the fortitude to ask your family for that amount of money or to even ask them for money at all takes a toll."

Third, the use of money as a focal point leads to unorthodox conceptions of representation. Electoral victories indicate approval within the lawmaker's district, but building a formidable war chest does not. What is more, officeholders increasingly rely on out-of-district dollars to fund their campaigns (Gimpel, Lee, and Pearson-Merkowitz 2008; Grenzke 1988). The consequences for representation are grim: Canes-Wrone and Miller (2022) find that members of Congress who receive a greater percentage of out-of-district contributions are more responsive to the national donor base. Whereas Mayhew's (1974a) reelection seekers improved their odds by advertising and claiming credit to constituents, fundraising outside of the district is a critical part of representation today.

A final reason to decry the emphasis on money is rooted in perceptions of democratic legitimacy. Majorities of Democrats and Republicans think that donors have more influence than ordinary Americans (Lessig 2011; Pew 2018; Primo and Milyo 2020). Donors unsurprisingly have a more optimistic view of legislator responsiveness: 37 percent of Americans say that their representative would help them with a problem if they contacted them, compared to 53 percent of those who donated money and 63 percent of donors who gave more than $250 (Pew 2018). They are probably not wrong, either. Kalla and Broockman (2016) find that senior policy officials make themselves available between three and four times more often to those who purported to be donors. The collective belief in donor influence undermines basic principles of democratic government.

We have to lean out from money in order for the emphasis on fundraising to change. Getting there will be difficult without dramatic reforms like spending limits for candidates, parties, and outside groups. For the past few decades, the Supreme Court has ruled that spending limits violate the First Amendment's protection of free speech. Adherence to this doctrine is likely to persist for the foreseeable future. So we find ourselves in a quandary: fundraising is an easy metric to use and may capture some traits that we value, but it is also a uniquely problematic attribute for political actors and observers to rally around. The widespread coordination around money as a focal point has a host of negative consequences for elections, representation, and American democracy.

Outline of Chapters

The book proceeds as follows. Chapter 2 first reviews other indicators of viability and support, namely prior political experience and endorsements. I then elaborate on the value of money and the idea of fundraising as a form of self-presentation. Candidate behavior certainly suggests that money matters. Fundraising data from 1980 to 2022 show that candidates raise more early money today, and they do so earlier in the cycle. Winners fare better, and usually dramatically so, in the money chase. Within-cycle dynamics illustrate that a candidate's track record of fundraising is a good indication of what follows, which underscores why candidates strive to make a strong first impression.

Chapters 3 and 4 further explore what candidates say and what they do. In chapter 3, I draw on an original survey of 2022 House candidates to uncover how candidates perceive fundraising and how it structures their time on the campaign trail. The survey offers additional insight into the value of money from the viewpoint of candidates. Almost all candidates say that fundraising is very or extremely important, and a majority point to the top fundraiser in their race as the most likely to win. The day-to-day experience of running for office is shaped dramatically by fundraising demands. Experienced candidates devote more time to fundraising than they do to any other campaign activity.

Chapter 4 adds to these findings by looking at what candidates do, focusing on those who are most sensitive to early indicators of viability. Analyzing more than two thousand dropout decisions reveals new patterns of strategic candidate exit. I find that experienced candidates who struggle to raise money are the most likely to drop out. Early money matters even more for candidate exit today: experienced candidates who fail to make fundraising inroads are more likely to drop out in the post-2000 era. The use of money as a signal of support does not appear to weed out flawed candidates, and it instead results in fewer experienced choices on the ballot.

Chapter 5 illustrates how donors and journalists use fundraising as a focal point. I return to the main fundraising data and show that donor support in the first quarter of a candidacy is a strong predictor of donor support in the second quarter. These results are supplemented by a conjoint experiment of donors who evaluated hypothetical candidates. Donors favor better fundraisers by large margins, which provides valuable causal evidence as well. I then draw on an original dataset of newspaper coverage of fundraising in nearly five hundred open-seat primaries from 1980 to 2020. Journalists see money as an increasingly newsworthy detail to include. Newspaper coverage reflects the frontloading noted in chapter 2, as journalists reference dollars earlier in the cycle.

Chapter 6 examines money and election outcomes. Money matters less in general elections today, and I focus on primaries where there is no partisan cue. Fundraising has the single largest impact on primary outcomes, and it matters more than prior political experience. The relationship is significant across decades, reinforcing the point that the salience of money can increase even if the effect does not. Data from the same conjoint survey demonstrate that primary voters are more supportive of hypothetical candidates who are better fundraisers. While voters are unlikely to follow fundraising like candidates, donors, and journalists do, money pays off at the ballot box at least indirectly.

In chapter 7, the spotlight turns to Congress. Money indeed talks in Washington, but there is little systematic evidence of how fundraising helps lawmakers or how party leaders reward better fundraisers. I find, first, that legislators who contribute more money to the party receive better committee assignments. Moreover, their policy priorities are privileged at stages where party leaders have significant control. Members of Congress who receive more money from certain sectors are also more effective lawmakers in that area. In short, fundraising continues to pay dividends after the election, starting when legislators enter the chamber and extending to their later policy successes.

Chapter 8 steps back and illustrates what else can be learned from the use of fundraising as a signal. I introduce new measures of competition based on preelection receipt shares and compare them with traditional measures of competition based on votes. When competition is measured with money, it looks markedly worse than vote shares suggest. The difference between vote share and fundraising measures is largest in open-seat primaries, or the best-case scenarios of competition. The disparity is driven largely by financial long shots who have little chance of winning. Money offers a new vantage point into the quality of competition and leads to worrisome conclusions.

Chapter 9 summarizes the main takeaways and insights of the book. I provide a brief overview of the history of campaign finance regulation and discuss leading proposals for reform. The current situation is both no one's fault and everyone's fault. Candidates, donors, journalists, and party leaders all operate within a money-driven ecosystem of politics. Yet the intense focus on dollars is troubling for American democracy, and the public overwhelmingly believes that campaign finance reform would be a step in the right direction.

CHAPTER TWO

Money as a Focal Point

In the 1960s, California lawmaker Jesse Unruh famously quipped that "money is the mother's milk of politics." Americans have long believed that money has an outsized influence, and the first movement for campaign finance reform dates back to the Progressive Era. The amount of money spent in elections today is staggering by historical standards. In 2022, candidates, political parties, and interest groups spent nearly $9 billion dollars in congressional elections alone (OpenSecrets 2023a). Contemporary critics of the corrosive impact of money come from the left, right, and center. As Harvard professor and activist Lawrence Lessig (2014) notes, "In a time of polarized politics, there's one thing that more than ninety percent of Americans agree on—that our government is broken. And broken because of the money in politics."

The notion that money matters in politics is central to how local and national journalists describe the horse race; it is directly incorporated into models of election forecasters; and it is at the core of discussions about how powerful party leaders are and which rank-and-file members are rising stars. Yet it runs counter to much of the academic research on the impact of money. Money is thought to play a more minor role because other variables are expected to drive both money and the outcome of interest. In other words, the outcome of interest—winning an election or voting for a piece of legislation—is shaped by something else that drives both donations and the outcome, like candidate competence, lawmaker ideology, or district partisanship.

The challenges of studying money are well known. Money is a complicated and messy variable. Some aspects of fundraising reveal attributes of candidate quality, like prior political experience, charisma, and grit. Receipts are additionally tied to access to elite and wealthy networks, and they reflect donor expectations around who is likely to win or may be influential or sympathetic in office. This book does not delve into the many attributes for which money serves as a proxy or tease out which attribute is most central in this bundle. Rather, the goal is to think about money differently and offer new insight into why fundraising continues to soar.

This chapter begins by reviewing other indicators of viability and support. I then elaborate on the argument introduced in chapter 1 on the value of money. Money provides access to material resources, but it also attracts attention and generates momentum. Fundraising is a form of self-presentation, and candidates strive to make a strong first impression. Their behavior certainly suggests that fundraising is important: fundraising data from 1980 to 2022 show that candidates raise more and more early money, and they do so earlier in the cycle, pointing toward a new timeline of congressional elections. While resource advantages and disadvantages tend to persist within the cycle, fundraising dynamics provide a window into changes in momentum as well.

The added value of starting with money is empirical and theoretical. For one, it allows us to understand how money matters in elections, why it is talked about so frequently, and why it is a top priority for those who want to win. Second, money provides far more variation than other indicators of strength. Even among lawmakers in office, campaign receipts differentiate members more than either prior political experience or vote shares, particularly as more officeholders are elected from safe districts. A third feature of fundraising is that it captures the preelection environment in a way that postelection vote totals do not. A fundraising lens allows us to explore how money matters in American politics long before the election and well after the votes have been cast.

Indicators of Viability and Support

Scholars often use the term "quality" as a stand-in for electability. Even Senate Republican leader Mitch McConnell famously lamented the lack of "quality" candidates in several key Senate races in 2022. Ample attention has been given to the measurement of candidate quality.[1] Political scientists care about quality because democratic government depends on competitive elections where outcomes are up for grabs. The most basic purpose that candidates serve is to provide an electoral threat. This perceived threat keeps officeholders in check and promotes a vibrant exchange of ideas among candidates. Viable competitors are the lynchpin in the electoral connection that Mayhew (1974a) highlighted as the building block of representation.

Of course, party leaders care about electability because it matters for who wins and thus which party gains majority control. Additionally, the emphasis on potential winners is apparent in media coverage of elections, where the most formidable contenders tend to receive more attention (e.g., Graber and Dunaway 2017). The most viable candidates are also the ones discussed by donors, party elites, and the candidates themselves. In the vast majority of congressional elections, very few candidates—and usually just one—are considered serious competitors. Even in the rare primaries with multiple candidates, one or two typically emerge as frontrunners. The remaining contenders are ignored or given only cursory attention.

The notion that money goes hand in hand with viability is not new. Scholars have examined this relationship since the FEC began collecting data in the 1970s. Several studies show that, in general elections, candidate quality is associated with fundraising success (Jacobson 1980; Green and Krasno 1988; Krasno and Green 1988; Squire 1989, 1991).[2] Money has been directly incorporated into measures of quality as well (Bond, Covington, and Fleisher 1985; Ragsdale and Cook 1987). However, the core difficulty of using expenditures to measure quality is that it mixes ability with the outcome of the election. As Jacobson (1990, 335) notes, "The amount of money raised by candidates depends, in part, on how well they are expected to do on election day. Campaign spending may affect the vote, but the (expected) vote affects campaign contributions."

As a result, the main way that "quality" has been measured is with prior political experience. Jacobson's (1989) measure—a binary indicator of those who held elected office previously—continues to be the most widely used in the study of congressional elections.[3] Hirano and Snyder (2014, 2019) use a measure of "relevant" experience to account for differences between legislative and executive offices. Others include distinctions based on the size and overlap of the constituency and level of office (Abramowitz 1988; Bond, Covington, and Fleisher 1985; Lublin 1994; Ragsdale and Cook 1987; Squire 1991; Stewart 1989). Green and Krasno (1988) created a seven-point scale to account for office experience, occupation, and celebrity status. Canon (1990, 1993) distinguished ambitious amateurs who want to win from experience-seeking amateurs who run for other reasons.

A number of scholars have also emphasized the importance of elite endorsements in establishing viability (Bawn et al. 2012; Cohen et al. 2008;

Dominguez 2011; Hassell 2018; Masket 2009). At the presidential level, most viable contenders have held office so a binary measure of experience is less useful. The analyses in Cohen et al.'s (2008) prominent book on presidential primaries define seventy-one presidential candidates who ran between 1980 and 2004 as viable because they had values on four different indicators: endorsements, media coverage, public opinion polls, and fundraising. The authors give particular attention to the impact of high-profile endorsements on viability and suggest that endorsements precede fundraising success. However, congressional elections are lower information contexts, and the salience of endorsements is less clear.

The candidates I interviewed provided a range of views on endorsements. One said she received over fifty endorsements from local officials and party leaders, while her opponent received zero endorsements and won the primary. At the other end, another said she dropped out of the race entirely because she did not receive the endorsement at the party convention.[4] However, the general sentiment was that endorsements provide some legitimacy but are not a clear path to victory. As one candidate put it, "[Endorsements] are good to have. They're like yard signs. You have to have enough yard signs to look legitimate. You have to have enough endorsements to be legitimate, but I don't feel like they're the key thing to make or break a race. [If I ran again,] I would just focus on getting the dollars, don't spend it too unwisely, and just try to get out and talk to more people." The interviews suggest that while party insiders do look at endorsements to some degree, they seem to weigh other measures more, especially fundraising. Moreover, political elites are often reluctant to endorse in the preprimary stage. For those who do step in, there is usually some evidence of fundraising success prior to when endorsements are made. With respect to prior political experience, previous work has found that experienced candidates raise more money and more early money than inexperienced candidates. Empirical patterns are often broken down by candidate experience throughout the book as a result. Here I am less interested in disentangling the bundle of attributes that are wrapped up in money than in rethinking the value of money.

The Value of Money

This book examines the use of fundraising as a signal and focal point. It is important to reiterate that the argument is not that candidates who raise more money are of higher quality. To the contrary, the chapters detail the myriad negative consequences of the emphasis on money for candidates, elections, and the makeup of institutions. In addition, money is tied to a range of attributes and characteristics that are not sorted through here. Yet failing to privilege fundraising risks downplaying a central organizing pillar in American politics. Campaign receipts are one of the main heuristics used to evaluate candidates and size up a race. The ability to raise money has become even more entrenched as a metric as fundraising demands continue to grow.

One reason that political actors and observers coordinate around money is because of what it can buy. Donations have direct implications for whether candidates can hire campaign support and purchase the goods and services that fuel campaigns. Candidates allocate considerable resources to direct mail and advertisements. An increasing amount of funds is spent on consultants who assist with messaging, fundraising, digital strategy, and social media (Dulio 2004; Medvic 2001; Sheingate 2016). Candidates need a steady stream of support to maintain their campaign apparatus, although a common strategy is to spend money late in the cycle. As one candidate explained, "In the last six weeks, the last two months, it's just hammering your opponent on TV and in the mail."

With respect to the material resources that campaign funds provide, one of the top fundraisers said, "I had a really top-notch team, one of the best in the country. You want to be able to hire the staff you need." Another who struggled to fundraise echoed this sentiment: "I would love to hire a campaign manager, a communications director, and other field directors to set up meetings and make contacts in the community. A great thing to spend money on is the logistics of a campaign."[5] Those running in large geographic areas highlighted mileage costs as well. The purpose of these expenses is to increase name recognition: "Having money allows you to send mailers, buy TV ads, and run a field program. That allows you to build name ID. And most of the time, primaries come down to name ID."

Yet material benefits are only part of the story. The previous chapter introduced the idea of fundraising as a form of presentation of self—"what is 'given' in words and 'given off' as a person" (Fenno 1977, 898). Unlike the interactions in Fenno's account, however, this presentation takes place well outside the district. There is no physical performance. Most observers do not meet with candidates and lawmakers directly. Fenno (1978) highlights how performances can convey a sense of qualification, a sense of identification, and a sense of empathy. Fundraising is most intricately tied to perceived qualifications. Most voters cannot identify with raising such large sums of money, nor does raising millions of dollars indicate that candidates and officeholders understand the needs or desires of others. Rather, it almost exclusively signifies support.

Fundraising numbers can shape and even change observers' perceptions of candidates. When asked what fundraising conveys, one journalist replied, "We see the total number as the power the candidate has." She also elaborated on how the reports filed by one candidate altered her view of the race: "I remember being surprised that [this candidate] had raised as much as [her top competitor]. Before I saw the FEC totals, I didn't consider her to be someone who could take on [the frontrunners]. Then when I looked at her numbers, I thought, 'Wow, I didn't know she could raise this much money.' I started being interested in her campaign." Candidates also reference the use of money as a signal in their fundraising appeals. A local newspaper article cited a candidate's email to donors that read, "Monday is my first FEC deadline of the campaign. . . . The media, the pundits, and our opponents will use our first reported totals as a measure of whether we can win" (Noble 2013).

Indeed, a strong fundraising haul gives off the correct impression to those who are watching. Several candidates spoke about the importance of early money and the need to "come out of the gate strong." A candidate's first report is their first performance. Early money is critical because it influences what comes next. One of the laws of fundraising is that money begets money (Biersack et al. 1993). As one candidate said, "If you can tell people, 'Look, we're starting with half a million dollars; I'm going to win this thing,' then you attract more money." Another echoed this idea: "If you don't have money, people with money are not going to be willing to donate to you, because it's a sign that your race is not winnable and that you're just not on the level where they're willing to invest money. It's a catch-22. If I had a bunch of money, people would donate a bunch of money, but getting a bunch of money, it's almost an impossible feat." Those who raise little to no early money are all but written off.

Again, the main argument is that money matters because influential political elites—candidates, donors, journalists, and party leaders—use fundraising as a signal and focal point. Most prior work examines the effect of money on votes in office or votes at the ballot box, but our main interest is in the mechanisms through which money matters well before and long after the election. The ability to raise money is rewarded in a variety of ways. Early money has a particularly potent feedback effect, whereby those who post formidable early totals are taken more seriously and seen as worthy of attention. Candidates understand these benefits, and this awareness shapes their incentives and strategies on the campaign trail.

To be sure, money is not an absolute determinant of electoral victory or office rewards. One candidate who significantly outraised her opponent and lost in the primary said, "It's a puzzle, and no one thing will do it. I think everybody thought I was going to win because I was doing so much better [in fundraising]." She said her opponent ultimately had a level of name recognition that she did not. We can similarly point to a handful of high-profile candidates who challenged heavily favored incumbents, raised a lot of money, and lost by large margins (Skelley 2021).[6] And there are certainly examples of top fundraisers not seeking higher office, not advancing to leadership, and not receiving their desired committee post. Representative Ocasio-Cortez was passed over to serve on the influential Energy Committee in the 117th Congress despite her clear fundraising success.

Yet candidates and elected officials are not slowing down in the money chase. To the contrary, fundraising ability only appears to be increasing in salience as political observers eagerly await the next quarterly report. While money does not guarantee victory, it makes it far more likely that a candidate "will catch fire." As one top fundraiser put it, "There's really not a good way to [build name recognition] without raising money. You hear, especially with the activist class, about running a really grassroots, organic social media campaign. That can happen, but it is rare. And for everyone who pulls off an AOC-style upset, there's a lot more people who think they're going to be able to do that and can't. Money is the only reliable way to get your name out there." Running for office comes with a lot of uncertainty, and one purpose of raising money is to decrease the uncertainty and improve the odds of winning.

Two changes in the broader political and technological context are relevant as well. First, as discussed in chapter 1, early money has become even more critical as the arena of competition has shifted to the primary stage and the action has moved earlier in the cycle. Second, detailed fundraising information can now be easily accessed on the FEC website. The FEC has collected this data since the 1970s, but it is far more accessible today, further contributing to the widespread use of money as a metric. The evolving modes of reporting across this period warrant additional discussion given the central role that transparency plays in this process.

An FEC staffer with more than twenty years of experience described how technological developments, namely the rise of the internet, have affected how fundraising information is obtained. He said that in the pre-

internet era, people called the press office for totals. If they wanted the reports, they came in to the public records office, or filings could be shipped
at a cost of five cents per page.[7] Those requesting mailed reports had to
pay up front and send a check, and it could take up to a month and a half,
depending on the mail and geographic location. The staff faxed summary
pages to those who requested them, and bike messengers would drop off
and pick up reports. The office was open for extra hours during reporting
periods, including on the weekends.

Candidates filed on paper forms, and each had their own folder, with
House candidates in manila folders and Senate candidates in green folders. Stacks of presidential candidate filings were placed on tables in the
public records office. Candidates came in to the office to drop off forms,
but the FEC staffer thought the main consumers of reports were journalists and, less so, researchers. He described the scene at the FEC: "People
checked in at the security desk, walked through a metal detector, and if
they passed, they'd say, 'I'm here to look at the reports of so and so.' They
would camp out, go outside to smoke, and wait all day until a report came
through. Reporters would bring coolers, laptops (in later years), and sit
there all day and go through reports."

Visitors to the office became less frequent as more people started using the internet. The FEC staffer said that "the meat of the reports really
hasn't changed," but today it is both faster and easier to access the data
than it was twenty or even ten years ago. The older reports were handwritten and hard to read. In the early days of the internet, the FEC had
forty-eight hours to put the reports online, whereas today reports are filed
electronically, and the data are available immediately. In short, transparency is now coupled with accessibility. These changes in the political and
technological landscape provide an important backdrop for why money,
and early money in particular, has become an increasingly salient metric.

Sources of Money

Raising early money is a top priority for candidates who want to win.
When asked where their early money came from, most candidates said
they started by reaching out to those in their personal and professional
networks. The first quarter is often referred to as the "friends and family"
quarter, and early support is a reflection of networks and relationships
(Gimpel, Lee, and Kaminski 2006). One candidate said, "You Rolodex

your contacts and you put down everyone you've ever met, from your elementary school friends to every school you went to, every job you had. You go through that immediately at the beginning. It was just one donation at a time, around-the-clock phone calls." Several accounts echoed Bonica's (2017) findings: "The reason [my opponent] raised so much money was simply other attorneys. If you analyze his donors, the majority of them are fellow attorneys. Attorneys give to attorneys." University networks came up as well, with one candidate noting "[the frontrunner] is a Stanford and Yale grad who has a huge network of alums."

Networks are also essential for building on their initial showing. One candidate said, "The thing that we were able to do pretty well was just growing the pie. We went through [our supporters] and saw that so and so is on a board with this other person, who's a big donor." They asked supporters to make introductions or host events. He said a lot of the time they said no, "but sometimes they said yes. And a warm introduction, that is just a night-and-day difference." Having access to wealthier personal and professional networks can continue to reap rewards throughout the cycle. Networks may be even more critical in an era where donors are increasingly inundated with requests for money.[8]

Because donations are public, different sources of money also have the potential to attract different kinds of attention. For example, those who raise more in their district may be better positioned to highlight local approval. Or self-funded candidates might either be lauded because they are not beholden to special interests or weakened because they do not have evidence of support. When asked whether anyone noticed where their money came from, one candidate who raised a lot of out-of-state money said, "There were ten to fifteen people who loudly complained about it on Twitter. But I'm very convinced it does not matter. I never heard it as a thing that came up from rank-and-file voters. And to the extent that it ever did come up, people understand that you're running against someone who is also raising a lot of money from out of state. To almost every voter, it's such a technical thing. Raising money out of state does not even begin to rise up to the level of something that [voters] pay attention to." A self-funded candidate who loaned her campaign more than $100,000 similarly said, "I kept expecting it to either help or hurt me. But people did not know where my money came from and did not ask. It just never came up."[9]

Candidates are a different story, however, and campaigns are very knowledgeable about who's getting money from whom. Candidates use FEC reports to learn who is supporting their competitors: "Was he getting money from outside the district? Was he getting a lot of veteran money? Was he getting a lot of lawyer money? Mostly he was getting family money. It was more of an eliminating thing to say, 'He's not getting money from members of Congress; he's not getting money from [so and so].'" The candidate quoted above similarly knew that her competitor had raised a lot of money from lawyers. Today candidates often look at FEC reports to draw inferences about their opponents and figure out where potential and actual donors stand.

Evidence of Money as a Focal Point

Candidate behavior suggests that they care about money. For one, successful candidates raise money earlier in the cycle. From 1980 to 2022, the share of nonincumbent primary winners who raised money before the primary rose from 66 to 85 percent. The share who fundraised by the end of the fourth and second quarters in the year before the election increased from 32 to 55 percent and from 9 to 26 percent, respectively. Among those with prior office experience, 70 percent raised money by the end of the year before the election in 2020 and 2022, compared to 36 percent in 1980. In 2020 and 2022, three-fourths of nonincumbent general election winners raised money by the end of the year before the election, versus half in 1980. Virtually all incumbents fundraise throughout their time in office across this period.

Some primary calendars have moved up, but the frontloading is not driven only by election dates. The top graph of figure 2.1 shows the first quarter that nonincumbent primary winners started fundraising when their primary was in the first quarter of the election year (January–March), the second quarter (April–June), or the third quarter (July–September).[10] The bottom graph presents fundraising patterns when the primary date did not change over time or also moved later, compared to when state primaries moved earlier. The y-axis values indicate the quarter of their first fundraising report. Each cycle has eight quarters, with one corresponding to January–March in the year before the election, and eight corresponding to October–December in the election year.

Winners in primaries held earlier do raise money earlier, as we would expect; however, there has been a clear shift to raising money earlier across contexts. More than 90 percent of primaries are in the second or third quarter of the election year. In the 1980s and 1990s, nonincumbent

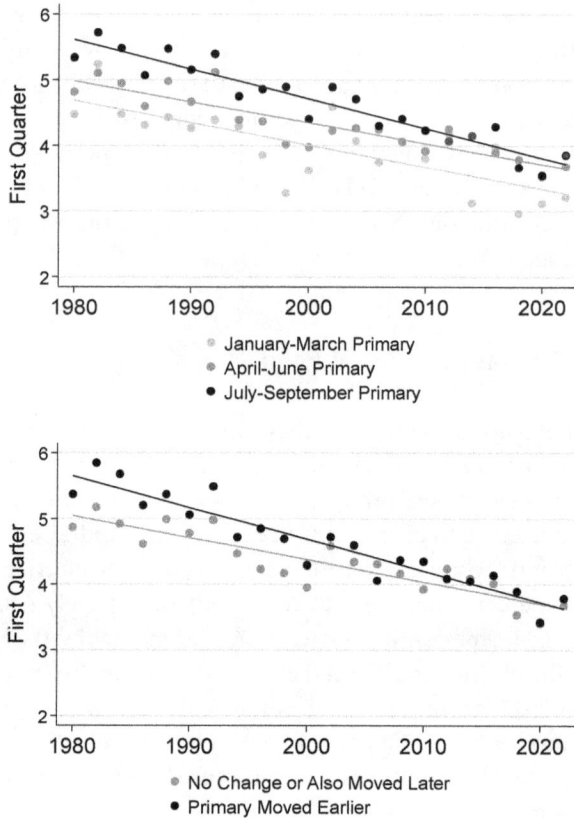

FIGURE 2.1. Primary Winners' First Fundraising Quarter
Average first fundraising quarter by nonincumbent primary winners and primary election date (*top*), average first fundraising quarter by nonincumbent primary winners in states where the primary election did and did not move earlier in the cycle (*bottom*)

primary winners in April–June primaries started raising money between the fourth quarter of the year before the election and the first quarter of the election year. However, in the late 2010s and 2020s, most report their first totals between the third and fourth quarter of the year before the election. The change is especially stark for those in July–September primaries: in the 1980s, nonincumbent winners started fundraising between the first and second quarters of the election year, whereas today they start between the third and fourth quarter of the year before the election as well.

Similar patterns emerge among nonincumbent primary winners in states where the primary date either did or did not move earlier in the election cycle (bottom graph). The black dots represent states where primaries moved earlier in the cycle over time. In the sample that did not move earlier (gray dots), there is either no change or no one-directional shift to an earlier date. For example, some calendars differ for midterm and presidential years. Winners in states where there was either no change over time or no one-directional shift toward an earlier primary date look similar to those where the primary moved earlier in the cycle over time. The difference between when winners first report fundraising numbers has diminished across subsets of races.

The shift in fundraising points toward a new timeline in congressional elections. As one candidate said, "The wrong assumption about politics is that you can take a hands-off [approach] in a primary, because everything is happening before the primary now." Candidacy decisions are also relative to their competitors, and the trend today is to enter earlier. One candidate remarked that he "probably got in too late." When asked to elaborate, he said his main competitor had entered a few months earlier and had already sewn up support from local donors. The rise in safe districts and the heightened relevance of primaries have contributed to the changing time horizon of congressional campaigns. Candidates must prove their viability well before November.

In addition to fundraising being frontloaded, the demands of early fundraising have skyrocketed. Figure 2.2 presents the median amount raised by candidates in their quarter of entry from 1980 to 2022. The top graph shows the values for the top two fundraisers in open-seat primaries in safe or competitive districts; the bottom graph shows the values for incumbents. All values are in 2021 dollars. Among open-seat candidates in competitive contexts, top fundraisers in the 1980s and 1990s raised around $100,000 in their first quarter in most years. The median amount increased to between $200,000 and $300,000 in the 2000s and 2010s and surpassed $300,000 in the 2020s. Even the second-highest fundraiser in open seats raised around $50,000 in their first report in the 1980s and 1990s, compared to $150,000 in the 2010s and $200,000 in the 2020s.

Incumbents have followed a clear upward trajectory in early fundraising as well, raising a median value of between $50,000 and $150,000 in their first reporting period in the 1980s and 1990s, compared to $300,000 in the 2010s and $400,000 in the 2020s.[11] These are huge sums of money to raise at the outset of a campaign. The demands of early fundraising keep ratcheting up for incumbents and nonincumbents alike. The stark increase in early fundraising is unlikely to just reflect campaign expenses or

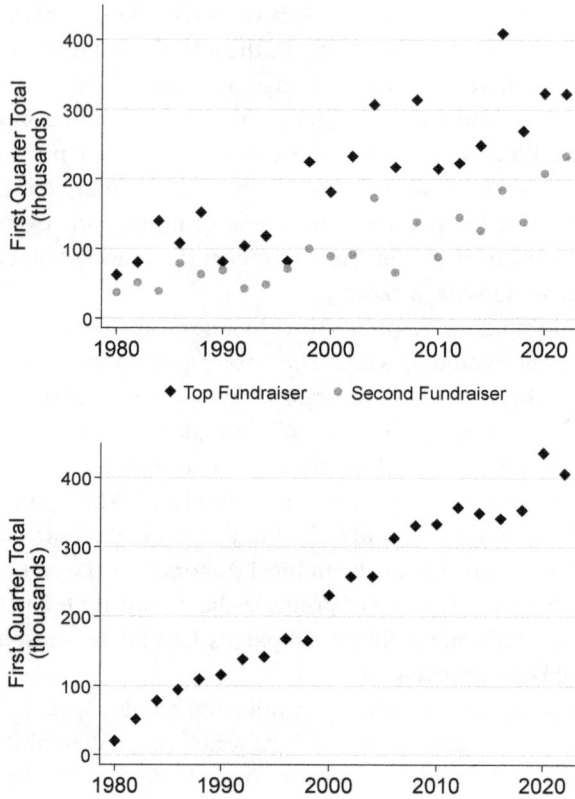

FIGURE 2.2. First-Quarter Receipts of Open-Seat Candidates and Incumbents
Median amount raised by the top two fundraisers in safe or competitive open seats in their
first fundraising report (*top*), median amount raised by incumbents in their first report (*bottom*). Values are in 2021 dollars.

changes in the primary calendar. Political observers turn to money in part
because there is limited information in most congressional races. Money
provides an objective indicator of how candidates stack up. Most of the
time, fundraising can be characterized as all or nothing.

All-or-Nothing Fundraising

When it comes to fundraising, the haves are easily distinguishable from
the have-nots. Money can be measured in many ways. Amounts provide
insight into the dramatic changes in fundraising, while receipt shares allow

for comparisons of advantage within races. The distributions of candidates' primary and general election receipt shares are presented in figure 2.3. Fundraising is bimodal. A total of twenty-five thousand primary candidates, or 73 percent, raised either more than 90 percent or less than 10 percent of all preprimary receipts in their race. Many of the top fundraisers were unopposed, either because they are incumbents who are almost certain to win or challengers who are almost certain to lose in November.[12] A sizable number raise little to nothing. One-fourth of all nonincumbents did not file a report with the FEC, indicating that they raised less than $5,000.

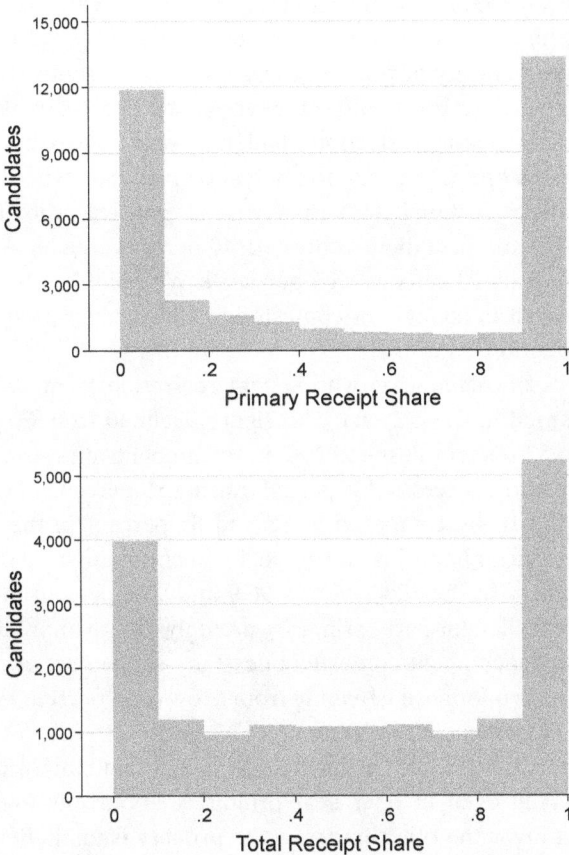

FIGURE 2.3. Receipt Shares of Primary and General Election Candidates
Number of primary candidates by their share of preprimary receipts (*top*), number of general election candidates by their share of general election receipts (*bottom*). Receipt share is calculated from quarterly and preelection FEC reports.

The share of all-or-nothing fundraisers is smaller in general elections, where 9,200 of the 17,900 general election candidates, or 52 percent, raised either more than 90 percent or less than 10 percent of the total funds raised by the two major party candidates. Almost all general election candidates who raise more than 90 percent of receipts—99.9 percent—are elected to office. The percentage of general election candidates who raise between 20 and 80 percent of total funds is 35 percent, compared to a mere 18 percent of primary candidates. Yet in both primary and general elections, most candidates are at the top or bottom of the pack. Disparities make the signal clearer. When candidates are so far ahead or behind, there is little ambiguity around who is most likely to win.

Despite the fact that serious competition *could* occur at the primary stage, the vast majority of primary races are in actuality uneventful. Primaries can be broken down into three types: incumbent-contested, where an incumbent is seeking reelection; challenger-party, where an incumbent is running in the opposite-party primary; and open seats, where no incumbent is seeking reelection in either party. Of all primaries with at least one candidate, half are incumbent-contested, 40 percent are challenger-party, and the remaining 10 percent are open seats. Winner-take-all fundraising is most apparent in incumbent-contested and challenger-party primaries where competition is lowest.

Two-thirds of incumbents who sought reelection from 1980 to 2022 were unopposed in the primary. This figure declined from 70 percent in the 1980s to 52 percent in the 2020s, but incumbents outraised challengers by large margins across this period, raising 89 percent of preprimary receipts in the 1980s, compared to 88 and 85 percent in the 2010s and 2020s. Nor do incumbents lose more: 96.4 percent of opposed incumbents won the primary in the 1980s versus 96.9 and 95.2 percent in the 2010s and 2020s.[13] Challenger-party primaries are only slightly more likely to be contested than incumbent-contested ones. Fifty-six percent of challenger-party races were unopposed, ranging from a low of 45 percent in the 2020s to a high of 64 percent in the 2000s.

Most of the action in the primary stage is in a small minority of races: open seats. And even in open-seat primaries, about one-fourth are in districts that favor the other party, so the primary is unlikely to be hard fought. In raw numbers, of the 18,300 primary winners, about 2,000 were in open-seat races; of those 2,000, 500 were in districts that favored the other party. The remaining 1,500, or 8 percent of all primary winners, ran in open-seat primaries in safe or competitive districts, where we would expect competition to be highest and thus the share of the winner's receipts to be lowest. It is important to reiterate that these races are a small fraction of House primaries.

Very few candidates win with little to nothing across primary types. In incumbent-contested races, only 3 percent of winners raised less than 10 percent of preprimary receipts. Alexandria Ocasio-Cortez (D-NY) and Dave Brat (R-VA), two high-profile underdog candidates who defeated powerful incumbents, fall into this rare category, raising 8 and 4 percent of receipts, respectively. In challenger-party and open-seat primaries, the values are only slightly higher, with just 6 percent of winners raising less than 10 percent of receipts. Even in open-seat primaries in safe or competitive districts—where primary competition is expected to be highest—only 5 percent of winners raised less than 10 percent of receipts.

The distribution of winners' war chests differs more across primaries, however. In incumbent-contested races, 89 percent of winners raised at least 80 percent of total receipts. Challenger-party primaries are slightly lower, with 72 percent of winners raising at least 80 percent of receipts. In the small number of open-seat primaries and the smaller number of open-seat primaries in safe or competitive districts, a much lower 31 percent and 24 percent, respectively, raised at least 80 percent of total receipts. Nonetheless, even in open-seat primaries in safe or competitive districts, winners raise an average of 52 percent of all receipts. In the full sample, primary winners raise a much higher average of 84 percent of receipts, but the disparity is still notable in the most competitive contexts.

Money as Indicator of Momentum

The patterns above highlight the clarity of the fundraising signal and the disparities in fundraising across candidates. Another reason why so many people follow the money is because it is dynamic. Candidates file reports every 90 days that detail their successes or woes. Reports are available to anyone and everyone, and their public release fits well into the horse-race coverage of elections. A sustained ability to raise money is crucial for the survival of a campaign. Momentum can be gained or lost depending on fundraising. Donations are a continual subject of discussion throughout the election cycle. Politicos eagerly await the next report, and they use this information to update expectations about likely winners and losers.

Previous studies have shown that seed money leads to future fundraising success in general elections (Biersack et al. 1993; Krasno et al. 1994), but we know little about how preprimary war chests evolve in the months before the election. Hassell (2018) finds that national party donors steer contributions to their preferred primary candidate, though it is less clear when these donors weigh in. This section explores whether the trajectory of fundraising changes and whether leading candidates solidify their advantage as the race continues on. If fundraising serves as a focal point, we would expect the advantage of the leading fundraiser to increase or remain constant across the cycle. We would not expect to see the top two candidates swap places.

The leading fundraiser in incumbent-contested races is nearly always the incumbent. Incumbents start raising money in the first quarter of the year prior to the election, and they raise more than 90 percent of receipts in the race throughout the preprimary period. The main exception to this pattern is incumbents who lose the primary. They start out strong, but their advantage declines across the cycle. The 113 incumbents who lost their primary from 1980 to 2022 raised 41 percent of receipts in the final reporting period before the primary, compared to an average of 94 percent of receipts raised by incumbents who won. Incumbent losses often come as a surprise, but fundraising trajectories can be used to differentiate between losses.

Some losses are upsets, and others are more expected. For example, Dave Brat's defeat of Eric Cantor (R-VA) and Alexandria Ocasio-Cortez's defeat of Joe Crowley (D-NY) are widely considered to be upsets. Ayanna Pressley's win over Michael Capuano (D-MA) in 2018 was also described as an upset in most coverage. By comparison, Andy Harris's victory over Wayne Gilchrest (R-MD) in 2008, David Trott's win in 2014 over Kerry Bentivolio (R-MI), Roger Marshall's defeat of Tim Huelskamp (R-KS) in 2016, and Marie Newman's victory in 2020 over Daniel Lipinski (D-IL) were more expected. In 2019, Steve King (R-IA) was removed from committees because of his comments on white supremacy, and Randy Feestra's win in 2020 was not especially surprising.

Fundraising disparities in these races map onto perceived vulnerability. Ocasio-Cortez had entered the race early and reported her first fundraising total of $18,126 in the second quarter of 2017, or four quarters before the primary in June 2018. Crowley raised more than 90 percent of receipts in each quarterly period and 75 percent of receipts in the final preprimary period. Brat posted his first fundraising total of $90,766 in the first quarter of 2014, or one quarter before the June primary. Cantor raised 92 percent of receipts in that quarter, 79 percent in the final preprimary period, and nearly $5.5 million in total before the primary. Capuano raised more

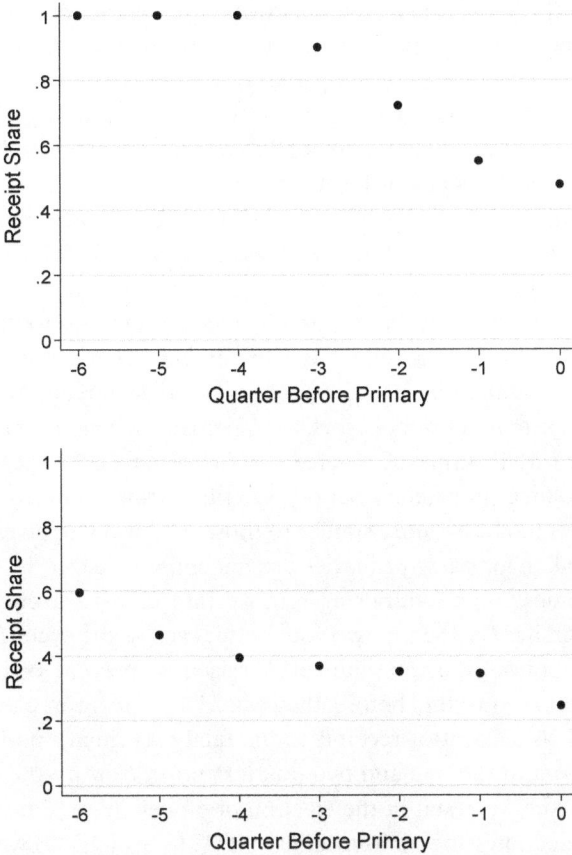

FIGURE 2.4. Incumbents Who Lost the Primary, Upsets versus Expected
Upset losses (*top*), expected losses (*bottom*)

Note: Median share of receipts raised by losing incumbents in each quarter before the primary. Zero corresponds to the final preprimary reporting period. The top graph includes top fundraisers in their primary and are considered to be upsets. The bottom graph includes incumbents who were not top fundraisers in their primary and are considered to be more expected losses.

than Pressley in each quarter, though the disparity was not quite as large. However, Gilchrest, Bentivolio, Huelskamp, Lipinksi, and King were all outraised by their opponents before the primary.

I examine how fundraising changed in races where incumbents lost in upsets versus expected defeats. I use a simple measure of an upset as whether the top primary fundraiser lost.[14] Figure 2.4 presents the median share of receipts raised by losing incumbents in each quarter. The top graph plots the fundraising trajectory of losing incumbents who raised the most in the preprimary period and whose losses are considered to be upsets. The bottom graph plots the fundraising trajectory of incumbents who were outraised before the primary and whose losses were more expected. The zero on the x-axis corresponds to the final reporting period before the primary, and the values correspond to the quarters before the primary.

The financial fortunes of losing incumbents decline across the cycle, but clear differences emerge. For one, incumbents who lost in upsets start out at a higher mark than those who were outraised. Perhaps more notable is where incumbents who were outraised end up. In the final preprimary period, the median share raised by incumbents who were outraised is a mere 25 percent of receipts. By comparison, top fundraisers showed fewer signs of vulnerability until later and raised 48 percent of receipts in the final preprimary period. In fact, the 5 percent of incumbents who won the primary with less than 57.5 percent of the vote raised 56 percent of receipts in the final preprimary period. The fundraising of incumbents who lose in upsets might be more similar to those who win narrowly.

Most challenger-party primaries are uncompetitive, but in those with close outcomes, later fundraising totals reinforce early trends. Receipt shares are similar for the top two vote-getters across the cycle. In the final preprimary period, the top vote-getter raised 46 percent of receipts; in the one and two quarters before, they raised 48 percent in each. The top loser raised 30 percent of receipts in the final preprimary period and 31 and 30 percent in the one and two quarters prior. Nor are these kinds of races very likely to result in the election of officeholders. Only 4 percent of general election winners from 1980 to 2022 (379 of 9,570) were elected from challenger-party primaries.

Competition is highest in open-seat primaries, and resources are more evenly distributed among the leading contenders. It is worth first discussing some features of the data that matter for comparing candidate war chests within the cycle. Virtually all incumbents start fundraising in the first quarter of the election year, but open-seat candidates start raising money later. Because some candidates enter earlier, they will have a larger advantage simply because other candidates have not yet entered. If they are a leading fundraiser, their early fundraising share will be less affected by the entry of other candidates; but if better fundraisers enter later, the receipt share of the weaker ones in the earlier period will not accurately reflect their standing.

Figure 2.5 shows the median fundraising share of the top two fundraisers across the election cycle after both of the top two fundraisers have

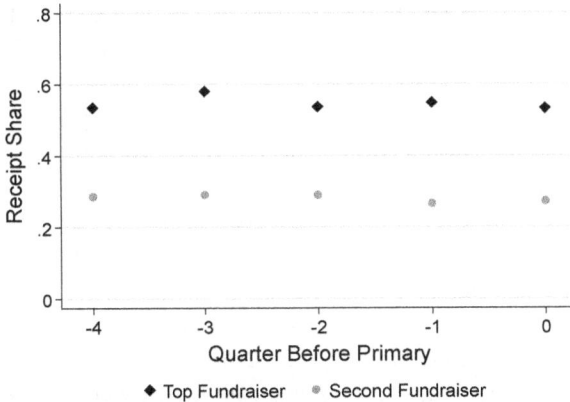

FIGURE 2.5. Receipts Raised by Top Two Fundraisers in Open Seats, across Election Cycle

Note: Median share of receipts raised by the top two fundraisers in each quarter before the primary. Zero corresponds to the final preprimary reporting period.

entered the race, working back from the quarter of the primary election. Fundraising shares are calculated with respect to all candidates in the race; zero corresponds to the final preprimary reporting period. The top two fundraisers follow similar trajectories. The top fundraiser raises 50 to 60 percent of receipts in each quarter before the primary, and the second-highest fundraiser raises between 25 and 30 percent of receipts. Sometimes financial fortunes do change, but receipt shares are often sticky across the cycle.

Today candidates raise hundreds of thousands of dollars in their first quarter, or what is often called the "friends and family" quarter. They reach out to their full personal and professional networks at the outset of the campaign. These dynamics provide additional insight into the payoffs that ensue: for the most part, candidates who start out with an impressive fundraising haul cement their early lead in later quarters, which reinforces why the first fundraising impression is so important.

What We Set Aside

Money and politics is a large terrain. This book sets aside other aspects of the fundraising landscape, including independent expenditures and party contributions. Outside money enters far later and is typically reserved for general elections. Independent expenditures play a much smaller role in the preprimary period. Only 3 percent of primary candidates who ran from 1982 to 2022 have nonzero values of independent expenditures made against them before the primary (1,084 of 33,865), and the median amount for these candidates is $2,700 (in 2021 dollars).[15] Ten percent have nonzero values of independent expenditures made for them before the primary (3,267 of 33,865), and the median amount is $130.

In addition, outside money is clustered in the small fraction of general elections that are viewed as potential partisan gains or losses.[16] Independent expenditures have skyrocketed in evenly split districts, but they nonetheless remain low in safe partisan districts. In 2022, $570 million was spent against general election candidates in competitive districts. Nearly fifteen times as much was spent against candidates in competitive districts than against those in uncompetitive ones (a total of $570 million versus a total of $39 million), even though the vast majority of general election candidates run in lopsided districts. Much of the outside money spent in congressional elections is directed toward around thirty to forty races that are expected to be close.

Contributions from political party committees are set aside for similar reasons. On average, 0.5 percent of candidates' preprimary receipts are party contributions, and the mean value is $1,000 (in 2021 dollars; the median values are 0 percent and $0). (These values are from 1988 to 2022 due to data availability.) Party contributions as a share of total receipts is also low, at 1.0 percent (1.2 percent for nonincumbents and 0.5 percent for incumbents), though it is higher when the sample is limited to those who received any party contributions (4.6 percent for nonincumbents and 0.8 percent for incumbents). The mean value of total party contributions is $3,900 (the median is $0), with incumbents and challengers receiving $7,100 and $2,900, respectively; for those who received any party contributions, the value is around $11,000 for both—higher, but not especially large.

Nor was there a significant change after the passage of the Bipartisan Campaign Reform Act of 2002, commonly known as the McCain-Feingold Act. Party contributions did decrease as a share of overall receipts, but the magnitude is quite small. From 1988 to 2002, party contributions made up 0.9 percent of preprimary receipts, compared to 0.3 percent from 2004 to 2022. With respect to total receipts, party contributions made up 1.8 percent and 0.6 percent of receipts in the pre- and post-McCain-Feingold eras, respectively. It is certainly possible that these data do not capture the full influence of party donors (see Hassell 2018), but party contributions have been a small fraction of early receipts and total receipts across this period.

While La Raja and Schaffner (2015) find that independent expenditures are much higher in states with limits on party spending, most early money at the congressional level is from individuals. The increase in outside money in competitive districts does support the argument that money is seen as essential for victories, but these contests are not the typical House race. A surge in outside money undoubtedly upends campaigns, though this happens in relatively few races and comes much later in the cycle. In addition, party committee contributions have never made up a large share of early money, and limits on party committees are unlikely to explain the surge in the amount of early money or the frontloading in fundraising discussed above.

Our main interest is how money serves as a focal point long before later players decide where to spend. The slow but steady changes in fundraising from election to election cast doubt on the idea that they are attributable to a single year, law, or court decision. Rather, the increased emphasis on money and early money is more likely a reflection of larger trends in American politics and the political and technological developments detailed above and in chapter 1. For one, the hardening of party loyalties and the rise in lawmakers from safe districts have shifted the timeline of congressional elections earlier. In addition, the fact that fundraising data are publicly available and easily accessible makes the money signal a particularly convenient heuristic to use.

Moving beyond the Ballot

One implication of starting with money is that our analytical lens moves beyond the ballot. A fundraising lens comes with a variety of benefits. First, it allows us to broaden our view of candidate behavior. Preprimary dynamics matter for the trajectory of campaigns, yet we have a pinched understanding of elections because of our reliance on the ballot.[17] The utility of running for office can evolve for many reasons, but a key wild card for candidates is whether they will be able to raise money. Changes in the financial horse race are important because they fuel perceptions about electability. Scholars have long grappled with the influence of money on election outcomes, but less attention has been given to how fundraising shapes the candidate pool before Election Day.

A second benefit of turning toward money is that it raises new questions about who counts as a candidate. One definition of a candidate is to be a choice on the ballot, but a candidacy is more than just a snapshot of votes received. Candidates engage in a variety of campaign activities months before the election. They canvass voters, meet with community leaders, participate in debates, and raise money. Perhaps the most vital role of candidates is to provide an electoral threat, which is why so much attention has been directed at measuring quality. The emphasis here is on fundraising because of its connection to perceived viability. A competitor who can raise a lot of money is far more of a threat than a long shot on the ballot.

A final feature of fundraising is that it can be aggregated at multiple levels. The ability to raise money can be assessed both within and beyond the boundaries of a race. The reference group can be primary competitors, general election competitors, or elected officials. Within races, fundraising totals can be used to measure which candidate has raised the most and the size of their advantage. The dynamic nature means that changes within the cycle can be captured as well. Among elected officials, receipts can be used to measure their stature in the party. Lawmakers spend a lot of time dialing for dollars, but they vary dramatically in how much money they bring in. A measure of fundraising advantage will differ depending on the reference group.

To be sure, there are limitations of fundraising data as well. First are the temporal constraints. While reformers sought to regulate political spending in the early twentieth century, the campaign finance provisions of these laws were largely ignored. The passage of the Federal Election Campaign Act in 1971 initiated fundamental changes in federal campaign finance law. The 1974 amendments established the FEC, an independent agency that administers the reporting system for disclosures. Congress adopted additional amendments in 1979 that simplified reporting requirements, and the 1980 cycle is the first election year when disclosures are readily available. As a result, the time frame of analyses based on fundraising are limited to the contemporary era.[18]

A second limitation is that the value of a fundraising lens is contingent on an association between money and various outcomes of interest, including perceived viability, candidate behavior, and election results. In places where fundraising is either not associated with electability or mandated to be more equitable across candidates, other measures would be more useful. However, in the American context, money is unquestionably an asset for those who want to win. There is dramatic variation in fundraising across candidates, and while top fundraisers do not win all the time, they usually do. Candidates who fail to raise money are all but certain to lose.

Summary

The starting point of this book is that money is a widely used indicator of viability and strength in American politics. This expectation orients the larger discussion about why money matters in elections. Money is important for both material and symbolic reasons, and it is the main metric that influential stakeholders use to compare candidates in low-information environments, in part because campaign dollars are both publicly available and readily accessible. The emphasis on money influences campaign strategy and candidate behavior. Today, candidates raise money earlier and earlier in the cycle, and they raise more early money today than in previous decades. Early money is crucial for those who want to be seen as viable contenders.

We could look at a number of places to examine how money is used as a focal point. The analyses focus on a handful of key players in American politics and detail several mechanisms through which money exerts its influence. Because candidates are the main actors, additional attention is given to what they say and what they do. Donors contribute to the momentum by echoing the decisions of prior donors. Journalists are mindful of the money signal and cover fundraising as an attribute worth noting. Party leaders reward better fundraisers with more desirable institutional positions. The cycle repeats in the subsequent election. The next chapter turns to how a variety of actors coordinate around money, starting with the performers themselves—candidates.

CHAPTER THREE

What Candidates Say: Perceptions and Priorities

The conventional wisdom is that spending in elections has diminishing returns. A recent *FiveThirtyEight* article notes, "Once you've established that you're real and that enough people are paying attention to you to give you a decent chunk of money, you reach a point of diminishing returns" (Koerth 2018). Opposed candidates never receive 100 percent of the vote no matter how much they spend. Yet candidates, for their part, strive to post higher and higher totals. Indeed, one of the top recommendations in a *Washington Post* article on "How to Run for Congress" is to "start raising money and don't stop (even when you'd like to)" (Berkowitz and Alcantara 2019). Candidates today run in a money-driven ecosystem where they are told—by consultants, party leaders, and how-to guides— that more money is better.

We know a lot about how much candidates raise, but far less about how candidates view fundraising and how it shapes their experiences on the campaign trail. Candidate perceptions lift the curtain on how candidates use money as a signal and help explain why they spend so much time raising money. As one 2022 House candidate who raised a few hundred thousand dollars before the primary said, "My finance team would give me lists, and I'd literally call through for eight to twelve hours a day most days and basically beg people for money." Even incumbents who do not have a sizable national following spend a lot of time raising money. This behavior makes more sense when money is conceptualized as an indicator of viability and strength.

To understand how money operates as a focal point, we begin with candidates. Candidates are the stars in the performance of fundraising, and the spotlight is on them. This chapter draws on an original survey of 2022 US House candidates to peer into how candidates perceive fundraising and how they allocate their time. Most respondents say that fundraising matters a lot, that the ability to raise money is a valuable attribute, and that top fundraisers are more formidable competitors. Experienced candidates, or those who have held prior elected office, spend more time raising money than they do on any other campaign activity. In addition, candidates who meet with national party leaders allocate a significant amount of time to fundraising.

Political scientists have long used surveys to study the perceptions and attitudes that underlie elite behavior (e.g., Carnes 2018; Maestas et al. 2006; Stone and Maisel 2003). The survey allows us to gain new insight into why money matters from the perspective of candidates themselves. Their responses illustrate that fundraising is a central part of the day-to-day activities of running for office. When the pressure to raise money reigns, candidates strive to post higher and higher totals, perpetuating the increase in fundraising demands and reinforcing the value of money. The consequence is that candidates invest their time—often a full day's work for those who are most viable—crafting messages and refining policy positions with donors, rather than voters, on the receiving end.

Survey Details

Publicly available fundraising records reveal a lot about fundraising behavior, but they tell us little about how candidates see the value of money and how fundraising demands mold their experiences as a candidate. To examine these questions, I (along with my collaborator, Ryan Mundy) conducted a survey of a subset of US House candidates who ran in 2022. We collected the email addresses of all candidates who were running in open seats, in seats rated by the Cook Political Report as toss-ups as of April 2022, in primaries where the leading fundraiser raised less than 57.5 percent of receipts, and/or in primaries where a nonincumbent raised over $500,000 in receipts.[1]

We collected the email addresses of a total of 1,130 candidates.[2] We emailed the survey to candidates at the end of April 2022 before the first primaries in May, and we sent reminders in mid-May and October after the primary season. The initial email stated that the purpose was to learn how fundraising shaped their experience running for Congress, and no deception was involved. We received 137 fully or partially completed surveys from nonincumbents. The 12 percent response rate is comparable to other surveys of elites and is higher than a typical public opinion survey (see Carnes 2018). The responses were merged with covariates including prior political experience, funds raised, and seat type, but no identifying information is included here.

The full sample was 61 percent Republican and 39 percent Democrat due to the electoral winds and expectations heading into 2022. Respondents matched the partisan makeup of the sample—62 percent of respondents were Republicans and 38 percent were Democrats—perhaps reflecting the shared distaste of fundraising across party lines. Experienced candidates comprised 23 percent of the full sample but only 17 percent of respondents, but those who responded are unlikely to differ from those who did not.[3] Women make up 28 percent of the full sample and 31 percent of respondents. Of the 137 respondents, 63 were in open seats, and 74 were in districts with an incumbent (47 percent of the full sample were in open seats, compared to 46 percent of respondents).

States and districts are not provided here for anonymity reasons, but respondents are geographically diverse and reflective of the full sample. Twelve percent of survey respondents are from the Northeast, 17 percent are from the Midwest, 33 percent are from the South, and 38 percent are from the West. (Regions are defined by the US Census Bureau.) In the full sample, 13 percent of candidates are from the Northeast, 19 percent are from the Midwest, 41 percent are from the South, and 27 percent are from the West. Thus, while the numbers are slightly different, they correspond to the geographical distribution in the full sample.

We should be mindful of the limitations of small samples, but the survey provides a valuable opportunity for further exploration of how candidates perceive the meaning and value of money. Their responses complement what can be gleaned from public fundraising records. The survey asked candidates how important fundraising is, why it is important, where most of their early money came from, and which sources of information they used to assess their chance of winning the primary or general election. Another question probed how candidates perceive the electoral benefits of being able to raise money alongside other attributes like prior political experience and strong community ties.

Candidates were asked about their strongest competitor in the primary election as well. Respondents rated the candidate who they thought was their top opponent on a host of metrics, including fundraising, endorsements, and support from voters and party leaders. They were additionally prompted to provide the name of their strongest primary competitor. This open-ended question demonstrates whether *they* point to top fundraisers as more formidable opponents. It is impossible to know whether respondents would have said the same individual(s) absent the fundraising cue, but top fundraisers should nonetheless be named as the strongest competitors if candidates use fundraising as an indicator of viability and support.

Finally, candidates reported the number of hours they spent on fundraising and a variety of other campaign activities. I examine how they allocate their most precious resource: their time. The analyses focus mostly on descriptive patterns, but the last section turns to the factors that predict hours spent fundraising. The survey asked candidates whether they were recruited to run and by whom, and I explore how fundraising behavior is influenced and bolstered by different actors. Demographic questions were included at the end of the survey, but responses are missing for between 15 and 25 percent of the sample depending on the question, so these factors are largely excluded from the analyses. The full text of the survey is provided in the appendix.

How Candidates View Money

The vast majority of candidates say that fundraising is important. Eighty-one percent of respondents said that fundraising is very or extremely important for congressional candidates today, with 59 percent saying that fundraising is extremely important. Among prior officeholders, the share who said that fundraising is very or extremely important increases to 91 percent; not one experienced candidate said that fundraising is not at all or slightly important (the remaining 9 percent said that fundraising was moderately important). For most candidates, fundraising was somewhat harder than they expected (mean of 4.0 on a 5-point scale). The median response for experienced candidates is that fundraising was much harder than they expected (mean of 4.2).

Respondents highlighted a variety of benefits associated with fundraising. Eighty percent said that fundraising allows candidates to pay for direct expenses like staff and campaign infrastructure, and 85 percent said that money allows them to buy advertisements for their campaigns. Yet a comparable 71 percent noted that money is valuable because it conveys support in media coverage; 66 percent pointed to the support it attracts from party leaders; and 58 percent said it helps with later fundraising. (Respondents were able to select multiple options.) These latter responses highlight the less tangible benefits associated with a strong fundraising haul and the implications for attracting attention and building momentum.

In open-ended responses, candidates indicated that money "scares off other candidates," "helps hone [the candidate's] message," and "keeps out negative news." The broader significance of fundraising is readily apparent to those running for office. Respondents said that fundraising is "part of 'the game' of viability," "an unfortunate measure of one's relevance as a candidate," and "a (poor) proxy and validator for support." Yet one respondent had a more positive take, saying that "fundraising is the vehicle through which the political industry finds talent." A common sentiment is that fundraising "is the only way to compete in today's society." As another candidate put it, "You need name ID to win, and that's literally impossible without money."

Candidates said they turn to their personal and professional networks to raise money. Similar to the interviews, most respondents said their early money—contributions in the first three months of their campaign—came from people they know: 72 percent said that friends, family, and acquaintances in the district donated their early money, followed by 40 percent who said their early donors were in their professional networks. About 20 percent raised early money from social media followers and local fundraising events, and 14 and 8 percent raised early money from local and national party donors, respectively. Eight percent said their early money came from themselves. (Respondents were able to select more than one source.)[4]

Respondents also evaluated whether a variety of attributes help candidates win elections. The attributes included the ability to raise money, the ability to self-fund their campaign, prior political experience, and strong community ties. This question allows for an examination of fundraising ability along with other characteristics that may be viewed as electorally beneficial. One might expect strong community ties to be seen as the most helpful for victories. The four-point scale ranges from hurts candidates a lot to helps candidates a lot, and a no effect option was provided.

Figure 3.1 shows the share of respondents who said that each attribute helps a lot. Access to dollars is seen as a clear boon: 88 percent said that the ability to raise money helps candidates a lot, and 73 percent said that the ability to self-fund helps a lot. Among those who have held lower-level office, these values are 94 and 82 percent, respectively. By comparison, a lower 78 percent of respondents (and 76 percent of experienced candi-

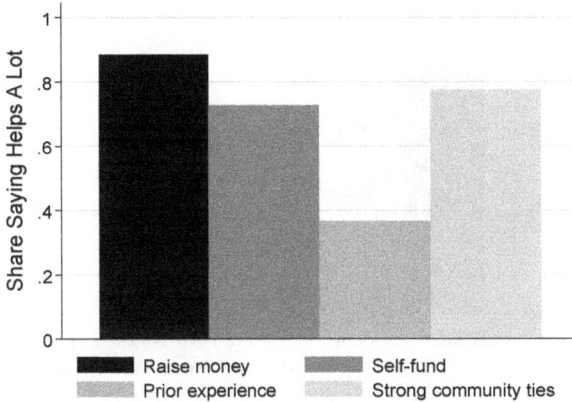

FIGURE 3.1. Perceived Electoral Value of Various Attributes

Note: Share of respondents who said the attribute helps candidates a lot.

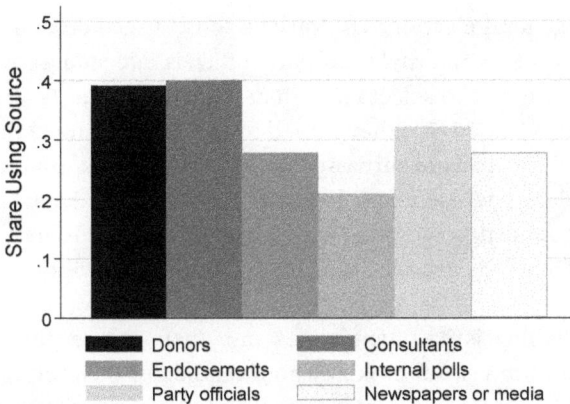

FIGURE 3.2. Sources Used to Assess Own Electoral Viability

Note: Share of respondents who said they used each source of information to assess their chance of winning the primary or general election. Respondents were able to select more than one source.

dates) said that having strong ties in the community helps a lot. While experienced candidates tend to raise more money, the value of experience is seen as much lower than the value of money: 37 percent said that having prior office experience helps a lot, though half of experienced candidates said so.

Additionally, many candidates turn to donors to draw inferences about their campaign. Figure 3.2 presents the share of respondents who used a particular source of information to assess their chance of winning the

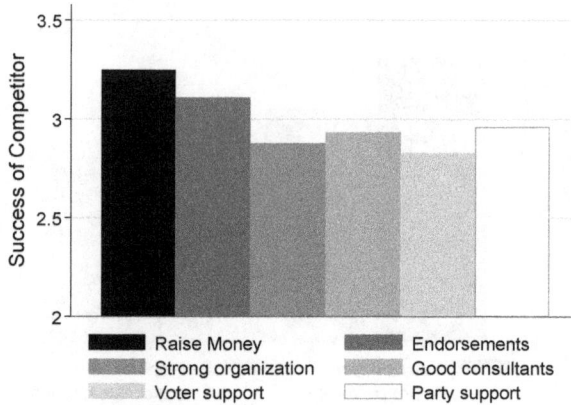

FIGURE 3.3. Success of Top Primary Opponent at Campaign Activities

Note: Average perceived success of their strongest primary competitor at a variety of campaign activities. The four-point scale ranges from very unsuccessful to very successful.

primary or general election. The various sources include donors, consul-tants, endorsements, internal polls, party officials, and media coverage. Re-spondents were able to select more than one source. Nearly 40 percent of respondents indicated that they turned to donors to evaluate their chance of winning.[5] Donors were surpassed only by consultants. Smaller percent-ages looked at endorsements, internal polls, party officials, and media coverage. It is unsurprising that candidates use donors to gauge their vi-ability in light of the awareness of fundraising totals by both donors and candidates.

Equally telling is how candidates rate their competitors. These re-sponses allow for a closer look at whom candidates themselves see as the most formidable. Respondents evaluated how successful they thought their strongest primary competitor was in six different campaign areas: raising money, receiving group endorsements, building a strong campaign organization, hiring good consultants, and attracting voter and party sup-port. The 4-point scale ranges from very unsuccessful to very successful. Average values are provided in figure 3.3. Across the six areas, respon-dents rated their strongest competitor the highest on fundraising. The av-erage rating of their top competitor is 3.25 in fundraising, followed by 3.11 in receiving endorsements.[6] Respondents rated their strongest competitor the lowest on attracting voter support (2.83).

As noted above, respondents were asked to provide the name of their strongest competitor. I use their responses to see whether they are more

likely to list the top fundraiser as their top competitor. Eighty-eight respondents filled in the name of at least one opponent. Among the eighty-
three respondents who had more than one primary opponent, 63 percent
listed the name of the top fundraiser in the primary (fifty-two); 17 percent
listed the name of the second-highest fundraiser (fourteen); and 12 percent listed the name of the third-highest fundraiser (ten). For the most part,
candidates themselves say that their opponents who raise more money are
also more formidable.

In addition, those who are seen as top opponents raise a lot of money.
Among those in primaries with more than two candidates, the median
amount of preprimary receipts raised by their stated top opponent is
$770,000. This sample includes those who listed incumbents as their top
opponent. In the subset of seventy-one respondents who did not list incumbents, the median preprimary amount raised by their top opponent is
still high at $650,000. Of these seventy-one respondents, two-thirds of the
top opponents they listed won the primary, and one-third of the top opponents they listed lost. Of the twenty-five perceived top opponents who
lost, a plurality—40 percent—was the top fundraiser in the primary. Only
six respondents listed candidates who raised less than $100,000 in prepri-
mary receipts as their top opponent.

To be sure, top fundraisers do not always win, nor are they always perceived as the most formidable. But candidates clearly think that money is a
valuable attribute; they leverage their personal and professional networks
to post a strong financial showing; and they rely on donors as a source of
information about the viability of their campaign. Most respondents say
their top opponent was especially successful at raising money, and leading
fundraisers are typically viewed as the top competitors. And unsurprisingly, the competitors who are generally seen as more formidable today
raise a lot of money in the preprimary period.

Online Fundraising Platforms

Recent changes in the infrastructure of fundraising have further transformed how candidates raise money. Many donations are now steered
through ActBlue and WinRed, the parties' centralized online fundraising
platforms. The platforms provide donors with an easy-to-use hub and aim
to simplify the giving process. ActBlue was founded much earlier, in 2004,
and it grew dramatically in the 2010s. More than $4 billion was raised

for Democratic candidates through ActBlue in 2020; WinRed entered the scene later in 2019, but it passed the $2 billion mark in 2020 (OpenSecrets 2023c). While ActBlue continues to outraise WinRed, WinRed has quickly become the dominant Republican fundraising platform (Holzberg 2021). Nearly all candidates who raise money use one of the two.

Respondents were asked how ActBlue and WinRed influenced their ability to raise money. Most candidates said the platforms made fundraising easier, though partisan differences do emerge. Half of Republicans stated that WinRed made fundraising much easier or somewhat easier, with 40 percent indicating it had no effect. Only 9 percent said that WinRed made fundraising harder. Democrats' evaluations of ActBlue were more positive, with 84 percent saying that ActBlue made fundraising much easier or somewhat easier. Only 12 percent said it had no effect, and a mere 4 percent said it made fundraising harder. These partisan differences may reflect the fact that ActBlue has been around for much longer than WinRed.

Candidates also evaluated how other factors influenced their ability to raise money, including social media like Facebook and Twitter, local campaign events, interest group endorsements, and endorsements from party leaders. Across the board, online fundraising platforms were rated most favorably with respect to making fundraising easier, followed by local campaign events. For candidates, the rise of fundraising platforms has particularly affected the setup of campaign websites and the process by which candidates receive and report donations. The survey responses indicate that they have largely eased the fundraising process as they were intended to do. Yet the next section demonstrates that candidates still spend a lot of time raising money, regardless of whether that money comes through an online platform.

How Candidates Spend Their Time

The allocation of candidates' time is important because of what it reveals about their priorities. Moreover, Miller (2016) finds that, at the state legislative level, candidates' time investment has meaningful effects on vote shares, particularly for nonincumbents. Respondents reported how much time they spend on fundraising and other campaign activities, including contacting voters individually, attending public events and meeting with groups, meeting privately with community leaders, and meeting privately

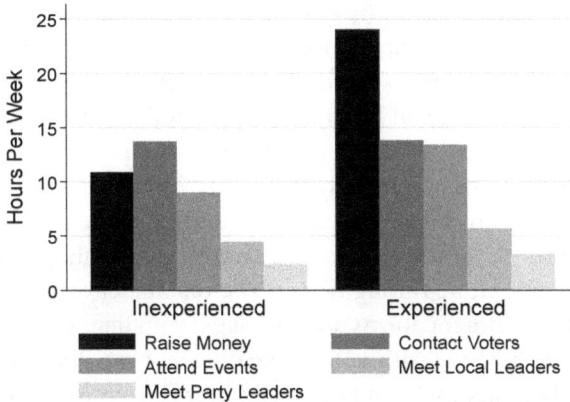

FIGURE 3.4. Number of Hours per Week on Various Campaign Activities

Note: Reported number of hours that experienced and inexperienced candidates spend on fundraising and other campaign activities.

with local and national party leaders.[7] As Carnes (2018) demonstrates, running for office is more than a full-time job: those with prior office experience spend an average of sixty hours per week on these various activities combined. Inexperienced candidates spend less time but still an average of thirty-nine hours per week running for Congress.

Figure 3.4 shows how many hours per week candidates spend on these activities, broken down by experienced and inexperienced candidates. Candidates vary in how much time they devote to raising money. Experienced candidates report spending an average of twenty-four hours per week on fundraising, more than double the average of eleven hours for inexperienced candidates ($p < 0.01$). Experienced candidates running in open seats devote even more time to raising money (twenty-seven hours, on average, compared to twenty-one in nonopen seats). Experienced candidates who raised over $100,000 in preprimary receipts report spending an average of twenty-nine hours on fundraising per week.[8] The upper range of time spent dialing for dollars is striking, with one-fourth of experienced candidates devoting at least forty hours per week to fundraising alone.

Candidates with prior office experience spend far more time fundraising than on any of these other campaign activities, which indicates how crucial they perceive money to be for their electoral prospects. Beyond fundraising, prior office experience matters less for how candidates allocate their time. The other main difference is that experienced candidates spend about four more hours per week, on average, attending public events ($p < 0.05$). Both inexperienced and experienced candidates allocate around fourteen hours per week contacting voters. Experienced and inexperienced candidates spend far more time fundraising than they do meeting with local community leaders or with local and national party leaders.

Candidates may be compelled to prioritize fundraising for several reasons. As discussed in chapter 2, the national party places a large premium on fundraising. Those who are encouraged to run by the national party might spend more time raising money. The remainder of this chapter examines how recruitment efforts are associated with time spent fundraising and time spent meeting with voters. The outcome variables are the number of weekly hours that candidates say they devote to each. The main independent variables are whether the candidate was encouraged to run by the national party, the state party, the local party, or local community leaders. I account for how important they think fundraising is, their prior political experience, and seat type. Other specifications include gender, education, and whether their annual household income is greater than $150,000, but the sample size diminishes as a result.

The results are provided in table 3.1. Models 2 and 4 include the demographic variables noted above. Candidates who were encouraged to run by national party officials spend significantly more time raising money than those who were not. The magnitude of the relationship is sizable as well. They spend about ten more hours per week, on average, on fundraising than those who were not encouraged by the national party. This finding echoes the qualitative accounts indicating that money is the primary metric that national party leaders use to evaluate viability.

Candidates who have held prior elected office are expected to spend at least five more hours per week on fundraising than inexperienced candidates, on average. Experienced candidates who were encouraged to run by national party officials are predicted to devote twenty-five hours per week to fundraising, on average, compared to fourteen hours for experienced candidates who were not encouraged by the national party. For inexperienced candidates, the predicted values are nineteen hours per week for those in touch with the national party, compared to nine hours for those who were not.

The results are similar when education, income, and gender are included as well (models 2 and 4). It is difficult to make specific claims about tradeoffs between time spent fundraising and time spent meeting with voters, but time is a finite resource, and it is plausible that one has negative

TABLE 3.1 **Sources of Recruitment and Allocation of Campaign Hours**

	(1)	(2)	(3)	(4)
	Time Fundraising	Time Fundraising	Time with Voters	Time with Voters
Encouraged by	10.41**	10.16**	−3.84	−3.21
National Party	(3.21)	(3.43)	(4.52)	(5.10)
Encouraged by	5.49	3.87	6.46	8.43
State Party	(3.59)	(3.82)	(5.06)	(5.68)
Encouraged by	−1.99	−0.92	−7.96*	−9.00*
Local Party	(2.59)	(2.92)	(3.65)	(4.35)
Encouraged by	4.11†	2.92	4.53	4.68
Local Leaders	(2.13)	(2.32)	(2.99)	(3.45)
Importance of	2.66*	2.76*	−3.37*	−2.88†
Fundraising	(1.02)	(1.07)	(1.44)	(1.59)
Experienced	5.06†	7.42*	−0.23	−2.78
	(2.89)	(3.17)	(4.07)	(4.71)
Open Seat	2.17	3.20	1.05	0.47
	(2.01)	(2.26)	(2.83)	(3.36)
Education		0.23		−0.63
		(0.96)		(1.42)
Over $150,000		−4.44†		2.73
HH Income		(2.48)		(3.68)
Woman	−1.39	−0.87	−0.97	−1.00
	(2.21)	(2.40)	(3.12)	(3.56)
Constant	−4.78	−5.29	28.12**	29.29**
	(4.69)	(6.51)	(6.60)	(9.68)
Observations	116	100	116	100
R^2	0.37	0.35	0.12	0.11

Note: Data are from a survey of 2022 US House candidates. Results are from OLS regressions, and standard errors are in parentheses. The dependent variable in models 1 and 2 is the number of hours candidates spend fundraising; the dependent variable in models 3 and 4 is the number of hours candidates spend meeting with voters. †$p < 0.10$, *$p < 0.05$, **$p < 0.01$.

consequences for the other. Candidates who say that fundraising is important predictably spend more time raising money. More troubling is that those who say that fundraising is important also report spending less time meeting with voters. Those encouraged by local party leaders report spending less time meeting with voters as well.

Again, we should be mindful of the small sample size, but the results provide valuable insights from the perspective of candidates and show that candidates see fundraising as essential for their campaigns. The findings reveal clear differences in which candidates prioritize fundraising. In particular, experienced candidates and those encouraged by the national party devote a significant time to raising money, which reflects not only a belief that fundraising matters but also the fact that candidates structure their time around this belief.

Summary

This chapter drew on an original survey of 2022 House candidates to explore how candidates perceive money and how it molds their experience on the campaign trail. The vast majority of respondents think that money is important, and they cite material and immaterial reasons alike for why money is an asset. Candidates look to donors to provide assessments of their viability, and they name leading fundraisers as their top competitors. Perhaps most striking is how candidates allocate their most valuable resource: their time. Experienced candidates and those encouraged to run by the national party spend a significant amount of time on fundraising. This finding highlights how fundraising activity is perpetuated and reinforced by a variety of actors.

The next chapter turns to another way in which the performance of fundraising affects candidate behavior: by influencing the decision to drop out before the election. Scholars have focused in large part on the factors that predict who runs for office, but we know much less about why some candidates call it quits in the critical preprimary period. Exit decisions showcase another mechanism through which money's influence operates. By looking beyond vote totals and wins and losses, we gain a better understanding of how money matters in elections. Donors shape the trajectory of campaigns months before the election by winnowing the choices long before voters have their say.

CHAPTER FOUR

What Candidates Do: Dropout Decisions

State representative Walt Rogers raised nearly $150,000 in his 2014 bid for Iowa's First Congressional District. He was widely thought to be the leading Republican candidate for the open House seat before he dropped out in February 2014. In his announcement, Rogers said, "It is no secret that running for Congress requires an enormous amount of money, and raising money takes a lot of time." His opponent, businessman Rod Blum, won the primary by nearly twenty points and was elected to Congress after a narrow two-point general election victory. Democratic county commissioner and former state legislator Priscilla Taylor raised more than $160,000 in her 2016 campaign for Florida's Eighteenth Congressional District before dropping out.[1] In a letter to supporters, Taylor similarly cited fundraising as a key factor: "Unfortunately, it has become increasingly clear to me that we will not be able to raise the funds necessary to run a successful congressional campaign." Her opponent won the primary by almost thirty points.

There are more and more candidates like Rogers and Taylor in congressional elections today. Figure 4.1 shows the number of candidates who raised money but dropped out from 1980 to 2022. The total has ranged from a low of 22 in 1990 to a high of 331 in 2022. Dropouts as a proportion of nonincumbents on the ballot have ranged from 2 percent in 1994 to 19 percent in 2022. Dropouts are not included in the vast majority of studies of elections because they were not on the ballot.[2] However, a ballot-centered view disguises the range of competitors, and we have a pinched understanding of how money matters for the trajectory of campaigns as a result. While candidates drop out for myriad reasons, many at least attribute their exit decisions to early fundraising woes.

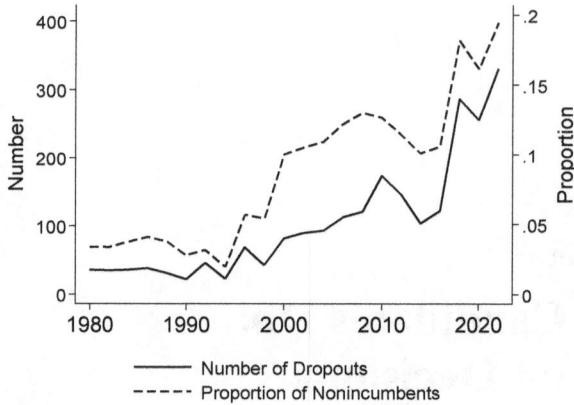

FIGURE 4.1. Number of Dropouts in House Races, 1980–2022

Note: Dropouts are those who filed with the FEC and raised money but were not on the ballot. On-ballot candidates were collected from the America Votes series and the FEC.

This chapter turns to another way in which money shapes elections: by influencing candidate exit. I analyze 2,300 dropout decisions from 1980 to 2022 and provide the most comprehensive study of dropouts to date. Moving beyond the ballot reveals new patterns of *strategic candidate exit* and illustrates how early money disparities influence the choices that voters have. While prior work has uncovered systematic differences in the entry of experienced candidates, I find that experienced candidates who fail to make early fundraising inroads are most likely to exit. What is more, the relationship has changed dramatically over time. Experienced candidates who struggle to raise early money are far more likely to drop out today than in previous decades.

In additional analyses, I show that candidate exit is not a reflection of changes in the primary calendar or filing deadlines. I also examine the exit decisions of sitting state legislators who are and are not up for reelection. State legislators who are up for reelection to the state legislature are more likely to drop out than those who are not, but the relationship is driven by those who raise little money. Reelection status is not associated with candidate exit among better fundraisers. I then draw on Bucchianeri, Volden, and Wiseman's (2025) state legislative effectiveness scores and find little evidence that dropouts are lower-quality lawmakers. Primary dates, career incentives, and legislative productivity appear to play a smaller role in exit decisions than early money.

Strategic Candidate Exit

A long line of research has examined candidate entry and the decision to run for office. Scholars have focused on factors like whether the national political environment is favorable, whether the partisan tilt of the district is favorable, and whether an incumbent is retiring or seeking reelection (e.g., Carson and Roberts 2005; Carson, Engstrom, and Roberts 2007; Cox and Katz 1996; Hirano and Snyder 2019; Jacobson 1989; Jacobson and Kernell 1983). But these variables rarely change after a candidate takes initial steps to run and are better able to explain whether a candidate runs at all rather than why they change their mind. What can evolve within an election cycle—and is hard to know in advance—is whether candidates will be seen as viable.

Studies of presidential elections have given more attention to early and evolving campaign dynamics, perhaps because of the higher visibility of presidential candidates. Some of this work has explored the "money primary" and its implications for success (e.g., Adkins and Dowdle 2002; Aldrich 1980; Goff 2005; Mayer 2003; Norrander 2006). Bawn et al. (2012) and Cohen et al. (2008) have generated new interest in how endorsements influence nominations, broadening our view of how prenomination activity matters for the choices on the ballot in presidential contests. Data hurdles have left the early action at other levels of office, including congressional office, far more opaque by comparison.[3]

Bonica (2017) and Hassell (2018) provide two important exceptions to the focus on the ballot and the only studies of candidate exit at the congressional level. Both highlight the role of money, with Bonica pointing to early money and Hassell focusing on party-connected donors. Bonica finds that, from 2010 to 2014, an early fundraising deficit is associated with candidate exit. Hassell analyzes elections from 2004 to 2014 and shows that candidates who receive more money from national party donors are less likely to drop out. Yet many questions remain because there is no roadmap for studying or even defining dropouts. For example, Hassell includes candidates who raise money in two quarters, whereas Bonica includes those who raise money in the first ninety days of their candidacy.[4]

The analyses here build on their work in two ways. First, the main focus is on how different kinds of candidates use early fundraising disparities as a signal. Lower-level officeholders have played a central role in the study of candidate entry because they are in the pipeline to higher office, they enter races strategically, and they are most likely to be elected.[5] Again, experienced candidates are often called "quality" candidates because they have run successful campaigns and served in office before. The exit of experienced candidates is particularly relevant for our understanding of the calculus of candidacy. Second, I leverage the long time horizon of the data to show how the salience of early money as a signal has changed over time.

Candidates drop out for many reasons, but those who want to win are mindful of what early totals mean. Many candidates talk about how they used money to gauge their chance of victory. One former state legislator who dropped out said, "I was having a hard time raising money. I was spending more [personal] money on the race than I wanted, and I could just tell that I wasn't getting the traction I needed." Candidates certainly behave as if early money is important, and fundraising patterns have clearly changed in recent decades. As noted in chapter 2, primary winners now raise money earlier in the cycle, and the amount of early money raised continues to reach record highs.

Experienced candidates have long been known to make different entry decisions. The question here is instead how their exit decisions differ. Two main hypotheses are examined in the sections below. The first is that experienced candidates who fail to make fundraising inroads are more likely to drop out because of what a weaker haul conveys. The second hypothesis concerns the relationship between early money and candidate exit over time. The marginal effect of early fundraising disparities is expected to be larger in the current money-driven era than in previous decades. The political and technological changes detailed in the previous chapters provide a backdrop for why early money is an increasingly salient metric.

It is not at all obvious that experienced candidates will make different exit decisions. Experienced candidates do not enter races lightly. The foundation of the strategic candidate entry framework is that experienced candidates are more knowledgeable about their electoral prospects prior to their entry, which explains why they select the races they do. They might similarly have a better sense of how much money they can raise or decide that the electoral opportunity is too good to pass up. Nor is dropping out costless. As one former state lawmaker said in hindsight, "I should have stayed in. It really was damaging to get out. At the time I thought coming in third or fourth was the worst possible thing that could happen to my political career. It turns out that probably quitting the race hurt my career much more than sticking it out would have. It hurts your credibility when you run for almost eighteen months in a race and raise a hundred thousand in small donations. You let thousands of people down that you didn't even stick it out."

When asked if they were offered anything in exchange for dropping out, most candidates said they were not, particularly those in office at the time. However, one former state legislator said he was: "I ended up negotiating a deal [with the eventual primary winner] where I would step out, and he would endorse me [in a future campaign]. My wife and his wife and I all met, the four of us. We had something in writing that said he would help me with my next major race."

I asked about the arrangements of the deal and how it was enforced. In his case, it was not: "He ended up getting beat pretty badly in the general [election], and he never lifted a finger for me. I ran four years later, and he wouldn't even return my call, much less write a check or do anything. I tried to reach him in the current race that I'm running, and he won't return my calls. There's no way to ensure that an agreement's going to be upheld. The only currency is trust really." Nor is it always obvious how much a future endorsement will be worth: "The other problem is when the person who promises to help loses the race, they have no power base. If you've got a sitting congressman who owes you a huge favor, and you can get an endorsement from a sitting congressman in a competitive primary, that's a big deal because most incumbents won't endorse in a competitive primary." This candidate dropped out to clear the way for someone who was never elected. While some deals may come through, they are laden with uncertainty due to a lack of enforcement mechanisms. Candidates factor in a lot of considerations, but experienced candidates who think they can win likely prefer a congressional seat to most offers. It is simply hard to know in advance how the race will unfold. Even for experienced candidates who have a leg up in the money race, a well-funded competitor can thwart their ambitions in an era where early money is seen as a primary indicator of viability.

I mostly set aside the question of why some candidates struggle to raise money. Early money reflects a combination of experience and ability, access to rich donors, personal wealth, and other characteristics. Nor is there a one-size-fits-all metric of what a strong fundraising haul is, as some candidates stay in at thresholds where others drop out. Another part is luck insofar as fundraising is relative to their competitors. If an opponent is very rich, even those who post a respectable showing may throw in the towel. And to be sure, the winnowing process is not entirely bad. But as the final section demonstrates, these efforts do not appear to be weeding out flawed or weak candidates who somehow got elected to lower-level office.

Dropouts: An Overview

The main obstacle to studying dropouts is data collection, as it is difficult to find those who initiated a campaign but withdrew before the election. Here dropouts include those who filed to run with the FEC and raised money but did not appear on the primary ballot. One advantage of this measure is that these individuals have taken a costly first step of running for office. Raising money attracts attention from political observers, and it conveys to the public and other competitors that the individual intends to be viable. This measure thus captures the more serious contenders in the preprimary period. It excludes those who initiated a candidacy in another way and also did not appear on the ballot, but the importance of money makes fundraising an appropriate starting point.

I draw on the dataset introduced in chapter 1 to examine dropout decisions across this period. The dataset includes all reports filed within the election cycle and whether the individual held prior elected office, the most commonly used measure of "quality." Between 1980 and 2022, there were 2,283 candidates who raised money but were not on the primary ballot.[6] Dropouts are also more likely to have served in lower-level office: 28 percent of dropouts are experienced candidates, compared to 22 percent of nonincumbents on the ballot ($p < 0.01$). Of the 648 experienced dropouts, 253 were in open seats, compared to 226 and 169 in challenger-party and incumbent-contested primaries, respectively.

The next section examines early money and strategic candidate exit from 1980 to 2022. The dependent variable is coded one if the individual raised money but dropped out before the primary and zero if they were on the primary ballot. The main independent variables are the candidate's share of early money raised and whether the individual held prior elected office. I use the amount in the candidate's first fundraising report as a share of the leading early fundraiser's total. The candidate in the race with the highest value in their first report thus has a value of one. This measure captures the candidate's first fundraising impression and their relative strength in the race. I include interactions between early money, experience, and decade to test the expectations outlined above.[7]

I control for several electoral and institutional factors that affect competition and entry decisions, including seat type, district partisanship, and the state party rules governing preprimary endorsements. I use Jacobson's (2015) data to measure district partisanship. District partisanship is coded as safe when the party received more than 57.5 percent of the presidential vote, competitive when the party received between 42.5 and 57.5 percent, and hopeless when the party received less than 42.5 percent (Hirano and Snyder 2019). Each model includes a binary variable for open-seat and challenger-party races, with incumbent-contested races as the baseline. I also control for the month of the primary election, the number of state legislators in a state, the number of on-ballot candidates in the race, gender, and party. State and year fixed effects are included to account for differences in the electoral environment.[8]

The Decision to Drop Out

The results are presented in table 4.1. In models 2 and 3, the sample is divided into earlier and later time periods (1980–98 and 2000–22); model 4 includes an interaction between early money and decade. Across models, candidates who raise more early money are less likely to drop out, which conforms to Bonica's (2017) and Hassell's (2018) findings. Yet prior work on dropouts draws exclusively on recent data, and the longer time horizon offers insight into temporal changes in exit patterns. Consistent with figure 4.1, model 4 illustrates that dropouts have become more prevalent in recent years. Another pattern to emerge is that experienced candidates are more likely to drop out, on average, than inexperienced candidates.

The main question here is how candidates respond differently to early fundraising disparities and in different ways over time. Experienced candidates are expected to be acutely aware of the financial horse race, and the increased salience of early money may mean that it matters more for candidate exit today. The results provide clear support for these expectations. Across models, the likelihood of dropping out decreases for experienced candidates who raise more early money relative to their competitors. Moreover, the magnitude of the coefficient on early money differs in models 2 and 3. In model 4, the interaction between early money and decade is also negative, indicating that the association is even starker in recent elections.

Figure 4.2 plots the marginal effect of early money on the likelihood of candidate exit by decade and experience. Predicted values are calculated from model 4 in table 4.1, with indicator variables for each decade (1980s, 1990s, 2000s, 2010s, and 2020s). For experienced candidates, a shift from raising 0 percent of the top fundraiser's receipts to leading the race decreases the probability of dropping out by seven percentage points in the 1980s but by thirty-six points in the 2020s. For inexperienced candidates, a similar shift decreases the likelihood of exit by a mere two percentage points in the 1980s but by fifteen points in the 2020s.

TABLE 4.1 **Early Money, Experience, and Candidate Exit**

	(1)	(2)	(3)	(4)
	All	1980–1998	2000–2022	Interaction
Early Fundraising Share	−0.92**	−0.49*	−1.03**	−0.68**
	(0.08)	(0.19)	(0.09)	(0.13)
Experienced	0.83**	0.60**	0.87**	0.81**
	(0.08)	(0.20)	(0.09)	(0.08)
Experienced × Early Fundraising Share	−1.01**	−1.00**	−1.00**	−1.02**
	(0.13)	(0.27)	(0.15)	(0.13)
Decade				0.54**
				(0.03)
Decade × Early Fundraising Share				−0.10*
				(0.04)
Open Seat	0.54**	0.32	0.63**	0.55**
	(0.10)	(0.23)	(0.12)	(0.11)
Challenger Party	0.33**	−0.07	0.46**	0.35**
	(0.09)	(0.20)	(0.11)	(0.09)
Competitive District	0.54**	0.21	0.61**	0.51**
	(0.06)	(0.14)	(0.07)	(0.06)
Safe District	0.49**	0.42*	0.55**	0.46**
	(0.10)	(0.17)	(0.12)	(0.10)
Open Seat × Safe District	0.15	0.28	0.07	0.16
	(0.14)	(0.25)	(0.16)	(0.14)
Preprimary Endorsements	0.13	−0.28	0.08	0.08
	(0.16)	(0.40)	(0.20)	(0.16)
Primary Election Month	0.03	−0.06	0.03	0.04
	(0.03)	(0.08)	(0.03)	(0.03)
Number of State Legislators	0.11	0.12	0.16	0.12
	(0.24)	(0.46)	(0.27)	(0.24)
Number of Candidates	−0.25**	−0.25**	−0.25**	−0.25**
	(0.02)	(0.06)	(0.03)	(0.02)
Woman	−0.13*	0.15	−0.17**	−0.12*
	(0.06)	(0.15)	(0.07)	(0.06)
Republican	−0.08	−0.09	−0.08	−0.13*
	(0.05)	(0.11)	(0.06)	(0.05)
Constant	−4.75*	−3.01	−4.36†	−5.08**
	(1.95)	(3.58)	(2.30)	(1.95)
Observations	25,687	9,859	15,591	25,687
Log-likelihood	−6,586.18	−1,424.54	−5,092.61	−6,654.95

Note: Results are from logistic regressions from 1980 to 2022. Standard errors are clustered at the race level. The dependent variable is whether the candidate dropped out of the race. The models include state and year fixed effects. $†p < 0.10$, $*p < 0.05$, $**p < 0.01$.

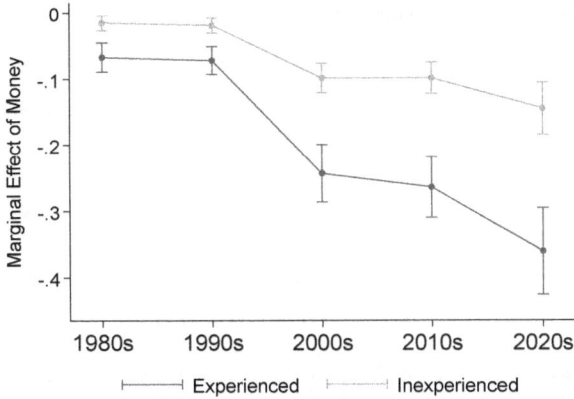

FIGURE 4.2. Marginal Effect of Early Money on Candidate Exit

Note: Values are calculated from model 4 in table 4.1, with indicator variables for each decade.

Put differently, for experienced candidates who raise 35 percent of the top fundraiser's receipts (the mean for dropouts), their likelihood of exit increases from 6 percent in the 1980s to 27 percent in the 2020s. For inexperienced candidates who raise 35 percent of the top fundraiser's receipts, their likelihood of exit is 4 percent in the 1980s versus 19 percent in the 2020s. By comparison, the probability of dropping out for both experienced and inexperienced top fundraisers is much lower, at 9 and 11 percent, respectively, in the 2020s. In short, while early fundraising disparities are associated with the exit decisions of all candidates, the patterns are starker among experienced candidates and even more so in recent decades.

It is possible that the results instead reflect changes in primary election calendars or in primary election filing deadlines. Indeed, some states have moved their primary dates and filing deadlines earlier in the cycle. I draw on Boatright's (2013) primary elections data to examine this possibility further. In table 4.2, the sample is split by candidates in states where the primary election month did and did not change over time (models 1 and 2) and in states where the primary ballot filing deadline did and did not move earlier in the cycle (models 3 and 4).[9]

The patterns are consistent with those above. Experienced candidates who struggle to raise money are more likely to drop out in states where the primary calendar both did and did not change over time (models 1 and 2). In addition, they are more likely to drop out in states where the primary ballot filing deadline did and did not move earlier in the cycle (models 3

TABLE 4.2 **Changes in Primary Election Dates and Filing Deadlines**

	(1)	(2)	(3)	(4)
	No Change, Month	Change, Month	No Change, Filing	Change, Filing
Early Fundraising Share	−0.35	−0.56**	−0.61**	−0.49*
	(0.28)	(0.14)	(0.19)	(0.20)
Experienced	0.49**	0.84**	0.86**	0.75**
	(0.18)	(0.08)	(0.12)	(0.10)
Experienced × Early Fundraising Share	−0.79**	−1.03**	−1.03**	−0.99**
	(0.29)	(0.14)	(0.20)	(0.18)
Post-2000	1.59**	1.65**	1.33**	1.85**
	(0.21)	(0.09)	(0.13)	(0.14)
Post-2000 × Early Fundraising Share	−0.70*	−0.48**	−0.37†	−0.60**
	(0.28)	(0.14)	(0.20)	(0.20)
Open Seat	0.60*	0.48**	0.25†	0.79**
	(0.28)	(0.11)	(0.15)	(0.14)
Challenger Party	0.34	0.28**	0.09	0.52**
	(0.26)	(0.09)	(0.13)	(0.12)
Competitive District	0.43**	0.55**	0.47**	0.58**
	(0.13)	(0.07)	(0.10)	(0.08)
Safe District	−0.24	0.49**	0.15	0.64**
	(0.28)	(0.10)	(0.15)	(0.13)
Open Seat × Safe District	1.11**	−0.01	0.25	−0.00
	(0.33)	(0.15)	(0.21)	(0.18)
Preprimary Endorsements	0.60**	0.32**	0.47**	0.38**
	(0.09)	(0.04)	(0.06)	(0.05)
Primary Election Month	−0.08	0.12**	−0.01	0.17**
	(0.06)	(0.01)	(0.02)	(0.02)
Number of State Legislators	0.03**	0.02**	0.01	0.03**
	(0.01)	(0.01)	(0.01)	(0.01)
Number of Candidates	−0.26**	−0.23**	−0.22**	−0.25**
	(0.05)	(0.03)	(0.03)	(0.04)
Woman	−0.11	0.03	−0.02	0.00
	(0.14)	(0.07)	(0.09)	(0.08)
Republican	−0.23†	−0.03	−0.04	−0.05
	(0.12)	(0.06)	(0.08)	(0.07)
Constant	−3.04**	−4.33**	−3.10**	−5.08**
	(0.50)	(0.20)	(0.23)	(0.27)
Observations	4,812	20,875	10,214	13,453
Log-likelihood	−1,227.41	−5,557.74	−2,781.69	−3,699.34

Note: Results are from logistic regressions from 1980 to 2022. For models 3 and 4, the data are from 1984 to 2022. Standard errors are clustered at the race level. The dependent variable is whether the candidate dropped out of the race. The models include state and year fixed effects. †$p < 0.10$, *$p < 0.05$, **$p < 0.01$.

and 4). The interaction between early fundraising and the post-2000 era is negative across models as well. The findings are indicative of a new temporality of congressional elections where candidacies are benchmarked to FEC reporting timelines and quarterly deadlines rather than to state primary election dates or state filing deadlines, likely due in part to the emphasis on early money.

With respect to the control variables, the probability of exit is higher in open seats, challenger-party primaries, and safe and competitive districts where primary competition is greater (Hirano and Snyder 2019; Stone and Maisel 2003). The likelihood of dropping out decreases as the number of primary candidates increases. Women candidates are less likely to exit the race as well, though the relationship is driven by Democratic women. This result differs from Niven's (2006) analysis of Florida state legislators in 2000 and 2002, which may reflect changes over time in the entry, support, and success of women candidates, particularly on the Democratic side (e.g., Crowder-Meyer and Cooperman 2018; Teele et al. 2018; Thomsen and Swers 2017; Thomsen 2021).

In sum, the exit of candidates who struggle to raise money suggests that the early money signal is important and has become increasingly so over time. What is more, the soaring fundraising demands in recent years mean that leading fundraisers need to raise far more money to take the top spot. Experienced candidates are most sensitive to an early fundraising deficit, and they are even more sensitive to resource disparities in the current money-driven era. A long line of work has tracked the entry patterns of experienced candidates, but exit decisions also have consequences for the trajectory of races and the choices on the ballot.

Opportunity Costs and Candidate Exit

Of course, a variety of factors matter for dropout decisions. Lower-level officeholders have different opportunity costs that influence progressive ambition, like whether they are up for reelection. One sitting state legislator who dropped out explained that he had to decide between two career options in March of the election year due to filing deadlines: "I either had to stay in the primary and give up my [state] House seat or get out of the primary and go back to my [state] House seat." He said he would have had to give up leadership opportunities in the state legislature for what "looked like a pretty good chance I could lose the primary." His assessment was based in large part on the behavior of donors and a commitment by his wealthy opponent to self-fund.

This candidate raised over $125,000 in his first quarter, but "blew through" the money too quickly and struggled in his second quarter. He had already received money from the more frequent donors in the district and thought his fundraising path was narrowing. When asked whether he was pressured to drop out and support the other leading candidate, he said no; it was about "our fundraising numbers and the timing of me hav-ing to get back into my [state] House race." He pointed to one lackluster event in particular: "We just had a fundraiser a few days before we made a decision, and that fundraiser wasn't as effective as we had hoped. We thought we could get a certain level of dollars at that event, and [it] would be a good boost to get us into the next quarter, but that didn't happen. That was one of the factors that led to us getting out." The candidate of course knew that he would have had to give up his state House seat before he launched his campaign; what he did not know was whether he would gain frontrunner status in the months before the election.

This section further explores the dropout decisions of nearly eight hun-dred sitting state legislators who ran for the US House from 2000 to 2016.[10] I use Klarner's (2018) dataset of state legislative elections and Fouirnaies and Hall's (2022) data on term-limited legislators to categorize those who were and were not up for reelection. Unsurprisingly, more dropouts were up for reelection and risked losing their state legislative seat: 66 percent of dropouts were up for reelection, compared to 53 percent of nondrop-outs ($p < 0.01$). Nondropouts were also more likely to be term limited and thus did not risk losing their seat because they were ineligible to run again (20 versus 10 percent; $p < 0.05$). Contrary to what we might expect, a simi-lar percentage of dropouts and nondropouts were in the middle of their state legislative term and did not risk losing their seat (23 versus 27 per-cent; not significant).

State legislators who are up for reelection face different incentives than those who are not, but I examine how reelection status is associated with dropping out across fundraising levels. While those who raise less money might be sensitive to losing their state legislative seat, reelection status might have a limited impact on exit decisions when candidates fare better in early fundraising. I ran the same models as the previous section and in-cluded a binary variable for whether state legislators were up for reelection. The results are provided in table 4.3. Model 1 includes all sitting state leg-islators, and I split the sample into those who raised less than the median of $110,000 in their first report and those who raised more in models 2 and 3, respectively.

Similar to the bivariate patterns, the results for the full sample in model 1 indicate that those who are up for reelection are more likely to drop out than those who are not. However, splitting the sample into higher and lower fundraisers shows that the relationship between reelection status and exit decisions is driven by those who struggle to raise money. Among

TABLE 4.3 **Dropout Decisions among Sitting State Legislators, by Reelection Status**

	(1)	(2)	(3)
	All Sitting State Legislators	First Qtr, Under $110,000	First Qtr, Over $110,000
Up for Reelection to State Legislature	0.45†	0.53†	−0.05
	(0.25)	(0.29)	(0.57)
Early Fundraising Share	−2.89**	−2.26**	−3.08**
	(0.36)	(0.50)	(0.91)
Open Seat	−0.01	0.08	−0.80
	(0.43)	(0.52)	(0.87)
Challenger Party	−0.11	−0.09	−1.05
	(0.43)	(0.52)	(0.82)
Competitive District	0.24	0.50	0.17
	(0.42)	(0.47)	(1.15)
Safe District	−0.10	−0.20	0.81
	(0.56)	(0.65)	(1.30)
Open Seat × Safe District	−0.01	0.37	−0.67
	(0.54)	(0.65)	(1.08)
Preprimary Endorsements	0.27†	0.40*	0.14
	(0.16)	(0.19)	(0.34)
Primary Election Month	0.15*	0.15*	0.21
	(0.06)	(0.08)	(0.14)
Number of State Legislators	0.01	−0.03	0.13**
	(0.02)	(0.02)	(0.04)
Number of Candidates	−0.34**	−0.32**	−0.51**
	(0.06)	(0.07)	(0.18)
Woman	−0.64*	−0.66*	−1.92†
	(0.30)	(0.33)	(1.00)
Republican	−0.36	−0.29	−0.83†
	(0.24)	(0.28)	(0.50)
Constant	−0.46	−0.25	−1.43
	(0.73)	(0.87)	(1.82)
Observations	762	381	381
Log-likelihood	−249.53	−172.45	−62.97

Note: Results are from logistic regressions from 2000 to 2016. Standard errors are clustered at the race level. The dependent variable is whether the candidate dropped out before the primary. †$p < 0.10$, *$p < 0.05$, **$p < 0.01$.

state legislators who raise less money, the predicted probability of dropping out is 29 percent for those who are up for reelection, compared to 19 percent for those who are not. Among those who fare better in fundraising, the relationship is not significant. The predicted probability of dropping out in this sample is 2 percent for both those who are and are not up for reelection.

We might wonder if experienced dropouts are just lower quality than experienced candidates who remain in the race. Most measures of quality are binary indicators of whether the candidate has held *any* elected office; other measures of relevant office experience include those who have held state legislative office (Hirano and Snyder 2019). While measuring quality *within* state legislators is difficult, I use Bucchianeri et al.'s (2025) state legislative effectiveness scores (SLES) to examine the effectiveness of dropouts and nondropouts. State legislative effectiveness scores follow Volden and Wiseman's (2014) measures of effectiveness (LES) at the congressional level. The LES is a comprehensive measure combining fifteen metrics of the bills each member sponsors, how far they move through the lawmaking process, and their substantive significance.

Among sitting state legislators who run for Congress, dropouts are no less effective than those who stayed in the race. The median SLES score for dropouts is 1.03, compared to 0.99 for nondropouts (not significant). Dropouts are similar to nondropouts on a host of SLES metrics, including their current SLES and lagged SLES values. Dropouts even have slightly higher scores "relative to expectations" (2.12 versus 1.96; $p < 0.05$), but this may reflect the fact that nondropouts are campaigning for Congress during the session. Overall, effectiveness scores do not differ for dropouts and nondropouts, and there is little evidence that dropouts are less effective lawmakers.

Nor do a host of other metrics suggest that sitting state legislators who drop out are lower quality. Ten percent of dropouts are party leaders, compared to 14 percent of nondropouts; 33 percent of both dropouts and nondropouts are committee chairs; and 45 percent of dropouts are on power committees, compared to 52 percent of nondropouts. Dropouts and nondropouts have been in office for an average of 3.6 and 3.7 terms, respectively. In terms of electoral security, 20 percent of dropouts and 26 percent of nondropouts were unopposed in their prior general election. None of these differences are significant. At least among sitting state legislators, reelection incentives and legislator quality appear to play a smaller role in exit decisions than early money.

Even in the full sample of experienced candidates, it is not the case that experienced dropouts raise paltry sums of money. From 2000 to 2022, experienced dropouts raised an average of $73,000 in their first report, less than the $149,000 raised by experienced nondropouts but still reflective of support (the median values are $36,000 and $74,000, respectively; in 2021 dollars). Another point is that, for experienced dropouts, the distance to their top competitor's early haul is huge: experienced dropouts trailed the top early fundraiser by $303,000, on average, compared to $184,000 for experienced nondropouts (the median values are $171,000 and $46,000, respectively). They were probably not destined to lose from the start as much as they underperformed in the early money chase for a variety of reasons that are not sorted through here.

Scholars of American politics care about different candidate attributes. Some care about gender and race; others care about ideology; and others care about experience. The exit of candidates with these attributes will be more or less troublesome to different political observers. The focus here is on experienced candidates because they are more sensitive to early money disparities, but the experience benefit in primaries is much larger than that for either gender or ideology. The breadth of studies on quality are rooted in the fact that voters tend to prefer experienced candidates. While we are unable to say why these experienced dropouts did not raise as much money, their exit is worrisome because of what it means for the choices on the ballot.

Why Dropouts Matter for Voters

The final section turns to the choices on the ballot in races where an experienced candidate dropped out. The exit of experienced candidates may be more or less concerning depending on the other options that voters have to choose from. Figure 4.3 shows the number of experienced candidates on the ballot in primaries with at least one experienced dropout. The sample is limited to safe or competitive districts where candidates have a shot at winning the general election. The top graph includes primaries with no same-party incumbent (challenger-party primaries and open seats), and the bottom graph is further limited to only open seats.

In primaries with an experienced dropout, there was either zero or one experienced candidate on the ballot in nearly two-thirds of primaries with no same-party incumbent (top graph). Even in the best-case scenarios of electoral competition—open-seat races in safe or competitive districts—46 percent of primaries with an experienced dropout had either zero or one experienced candidate on the ballot (bottom graph).[11]

The number of experienced candidates on the ballot also has implications for whether primaries are likely to be hard fought. Figure 4.4 depicts the likelihood that an open-seat primary is competitive when more experienced candidates are on the ballot. I draw on both vote share and fundraising measures of competition, where primaries are coded as competitive if the top vote-getter and top fundraiser received less than 57.5 percent of votes and receipts, respectively (Hirano and Snyder 2019; Thomsen

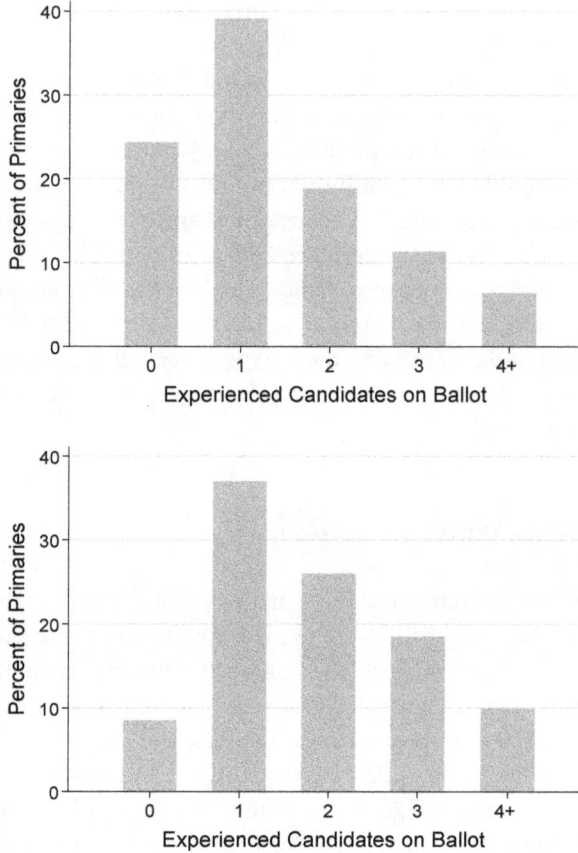

FIGURE 4.3. Number of Experienced Candidates on the Ballot in Primaries with an Experienced Dropout

No same-party incumbent (*top*), open seats (*bottom*)

Note: The *y*-axis is the percent of primaries that fall in each category and thus total 100 percent. The top graph includes all primaries with no incumbent, and the bottom graph is further limited to open seats. The sample is limited to safe and competitive districts.

2023). (These measures are detailed in chapter 8.) The sample is again limited to primaries without an incumbent in safe or competitive districts.

With both vote share and fundraising measures, each additional experienced candidate is associated with an increase in the likelihood of a competitive race. The largest jump between values is from one to two experienced candidates on the ballot. With the vote share measure (top graph), the likelihood the primary is competitive increases from 38 percent when there is one experienced candidate on the ballot to 80 percent when there are two. With the receipt share measure (bottom graph), the likelihood the primary is competitive increases from 27 percent when there is one experienced candidate on the ballot to 61 percent when there are two. Two experienced candidates on the ballot are better than one, at least from the perspective of competition.

It is impossible to know whether outcomes would have been different had experienced candidates stayed in the race, but exit decisions may

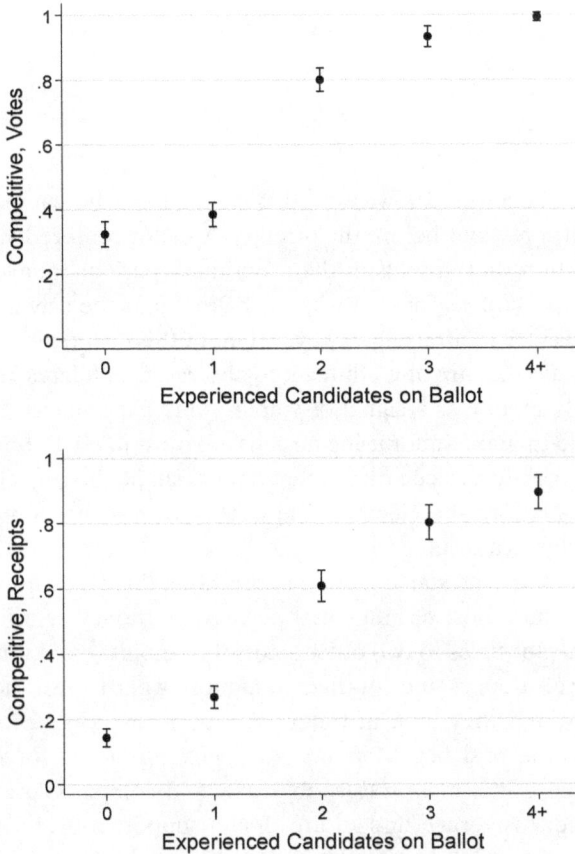

FIGURE 4.4. Likelihood of Competitive Primary by Number of Experienced On-Ballot Candidates
Vote share (*top*) and fundraising measures of competition (*bottom*) are shown, where primaries are coded as competitive if the top vote-getter and top fundraiser received less than 57.5 percent of votes and receipts.

affect a party's chance of winning in November. The party of the experienced dropout won the general election in 20 percent of safe or competitive districts where there was no experienced candidate on the primary ballot, but the party of the experienced on-ballot candidate won in 44 percent of those with at least one experienced candidate on the primary ballot. In open seats, the party of the experienced dropout won the general election in 53 percent of races where there was no experienced candidate on the primary ballot, but the party of the experienced on-ballot candidate won in 71 percent of races with at least one experienced primary candidate. Parties could potentially improve their odds of winning in November by convincing experienced candidates to remain in the race.

Summary

This chapter began by showcasing two candidates who campaigned for office but dropped out before the primary. A ballot-centered view misses the early action that unfolds in the preprimary period. Today we would overlook important reasons for why the ballot looks the way it does if we failed to consider fundraising. A key insight of this chapter is that money matters in ways that are often difficult to observe. Candidates increasingly look to early money as a signal of viability, and experienced candidates who struggle to make fundraising inroads are most likely to bow out. The reliance on money as a cue means that donors shape the trajectory of the race months before the election. The quality of primary competition is likely to suffer as a result.

Candidates are the starting point in this book due to their central role in elections, but a host of influential players use money as a focal point. The next chapter turns to two other actors who monitor and reinforce the money chase — donors and journalists. Donors want to use their money efficaciously, and they look at fundraising performances to infer which candidate is the best bet. Money is an appealing metric for journalists as well because it is measurable, objective, and comparable across candidates. Media coverage and future donor support are two additional mechanisms through which early money shapes elections. Early donors thus lay the groundwork for which candidates are able to attract attention and later financial support.

CHAPTER FIVE

Donors and Journalists

In April 2023, nearly a year before the March 2024 primary, the *Orange County Register* ran an article titled "Who Has Raised, and Spent, the Most for Katie Porter's Congressional Seat?" The article described the state of the open-seat race in California's Forty-Seventh Congressional District. For content, the piece detailed the FEC reports filed in the first quarter of 2023, referencing candidate fundraising totals and cash on hand just weeks into the race. The article indicated that Republican Scott Baugh, who narrowly lost to Representative Porter in 2022, had raised $530,000 in the first quarter. On the Democratic side, state senator David Min had raised $520,000 in the first quarter, closely followed by the $420,000 raised by lawyer and community organizer Joanna Weiss (Kang 2023).[1] Baugh and Min are fixtures in Orange County politics. Both have served in the California state legislature and run for Congress before. Weiss likely exceeded expectations the most with her early totals. In March 2023, TheLiberalOC ran a blog post titled, "Joanna Weiss for Congress Raises More Than a Quarter of a Million Dollars in Three Weeks." The post then weighs in on what these numbers illustrate: "The impressive fundraising effort is a testament to Weiss's strong grassroots support and the enthusiasm surrounding her campaign." Weiss is then quoted, saying, "Thanks to this strong fundraising support, I am confident we can continue to build the momentum we need to hold the seat in November 2024." EMILYs List endorsed Weiss in June 2023, notably after she had demonstrated an ability to raise money.

In a recent interview, former Ohio representative Anthony Gonzalez elaborated on the messages that early totals send. He explained, "There is something that happens in politics, where people want to back the winner and they want momentum. Part of the goal with the advice on you need to raise a lot of money quickly is you're sending a signal to the market" (*Acquired* 2022). Along with other candidates, the "market" includes donors who are attentive to early totals and journalists who bolster their coverage with data. In a low-information environment, early donors provide a signal to later donors who seek to support the frontrunner, and they provide journalists with numbers and metrics to convey the dynamics of the race.

This chapter builds on the argument that money serves as a key focal point in politics by detailing how donors and journalists coordinate around dollars. Starting with donors, I first draw on fundraising totals across the cycle. I find that first-quarter fundraising is a strong predictor of second-quarter fundraising. Candidates who start out with more money continue to benefit in the next quarter, which reinforces why the first fundraising impression is important. In addition, I conducted a conjoint experiment among a sample of politically active Americans who donate money to candidates. The preference for better fundraisers is similarly apparent in the conjoint study of donors. These results provide valuable causal evidence of how donors favor candidates who raise more money.

The focus then turns to journalists. Headlines like "Who's Winning the Money Race" and "What We Learned in the Latest Campaign Cash Reports" abound, but there is little systematic data on the media coverage of fundraising. I look at fundraising coverage in more than three thousand newspaper articles in nearly five hundred open-seat primaries from 1980 to 2020. I show that newspaper articles often reference campaign receipts, indicating that journalists view money as newsworthy and relevant to the public. Articles that mention money appear earlier in the cycle today, reflecting the frontloading outlined in chapter 2. The triangulation of data highlights the mechanisms through which money permeates elections and showcases how a host of political actors prop up money as a signal.

Donor Support in the First and Second Quarters

Candidates try to post strong early totals in part because it is believed to matter for future donor support. I leverage the dynamic nature of fundraising to explore this question further. The sample includes those who raised money and did so in at least two reporting periods before the primary. The main independent variable is the total amount in the candidate's first FEC report. The dependent variable is the amount raised by

TABLE 5.1 **Relationship between First- and Second-Quarter Fundraising**

	(1)	(2)	(3)
	Nonincumbents	Primary Winners	Incumbents
Q1 Receipts	0.46**	0.47**	0.61**
	(0.02)	(0.03)	(0.04)
Q1 Receipts × Q1 Receipts	−0.00**	−0.00**	0.00
	(0.00)	(0.00)	(0.00)
Experienced	6.94**	26.56**	
	(2.33)	(3.74)	
Open Seat	18.83**	7.27	
	(3.27)	(8.18)	
Challenger Party	9.05**	−14.88†	
	(2.53)	(7.60)	
Competitive District	16.83**	28.52**	4.02
	(1.94)	(3.07)	(5.78)
Safe District	14.58**	35.39**	−22.37**
	(2.99)	(6.25)	(5.74)
Open Seat × Safe District	13.59**	18.16†	
	(4.51)	(9.30)	
Preprimary Endorsements	−12.00*	−17.10†	4.29
	(4.91)	(8.90)	(10.15)
Primary Election Month	−0.06	1.54	0.44
	(0.96)	(1.71)	(1.78)
Number of State Legislators	−3.56	−4.67	9.39
	(5.77)	(9.39)	(16.54)
Number of Candidates	−3.25**	−2.03†	0.33
	(0.49)	(1.09)	(1.80)
Woman	13.59**	14.07**	8.75
	(2.08)	(3.52)	(5.48)
Republican	−14.19**	−18.58**	14.96**
	(1.80)	(3.24)	(3.53)
Constant	39.75	45.76	−32.69
	(43.86)	(72.08)	(119.15)
Observations	12,630	5,934	8,672
R^2	0.36	0.39	0.54

Note: Results are from OLS regressions from 1980 to 2022. Standard errors are clustered at the race level. The dependent variable is the amount raised in the candidate's second quarterly report. The models include state and year fixed effects. †$p < 0.10$, *$p < 0.05$, **$p < 0.01$.

the candidate in the quarter after they filed their first FEC report. For example, if the candidate's first report is the third quarter of the year before the election, the independent variable is the amount in that report, and the dependent variable is the amount in the fourth quarter. I include first-quarter fundraising squared, along with the same political and electoral variables in chapter 4.[2]

The results are presented in table 5.1. Model 1 includes all nonincumbents who fit the criteria noted above; model 2 is limited to nonincumbent

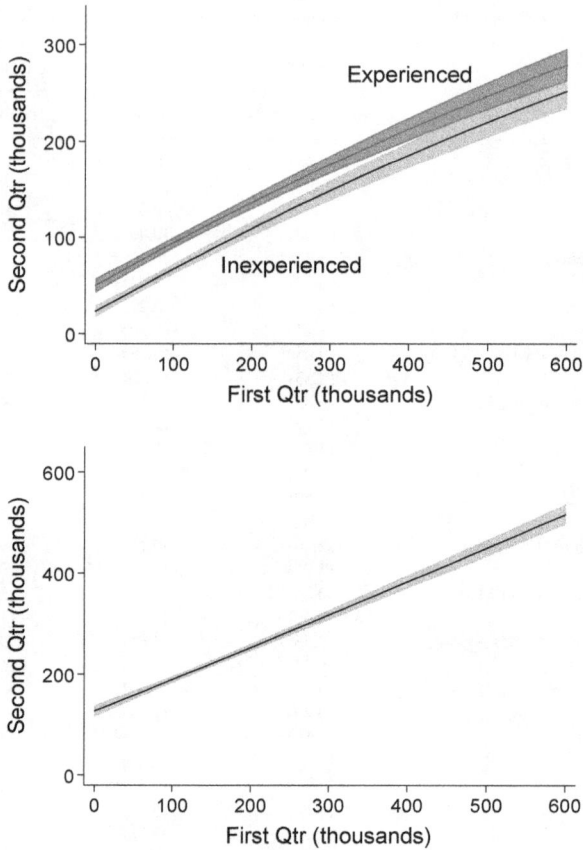

FIGURE 5.1. Relationship between First- and Second-Quarter Fundraising
All nonincumbents who raised money (*top*), incumbents (*bottom*)

Note: Values are calculated from models 1 and 3 in table 5.1. Amounts are in 2021 dollars.

primary winners; and model 3 is limited to incumbents. The independent and dependent variables are in 2021 dollars and measured in thousands. As expected, across models, the top line in the candidate's first FEC report is positively associated with donor support in the next reporting period. Among nonincumbents and incumbents alike, those who raise more in their first performance continue to raise more in the subsequent one.

Predicted values from models 1 and 3 are plotted in figure 5.1. The top graph is broken down by experience since experienced candidates tend to raise more early money. In the sample of nonincumbents, experienced candidates who raise $100,000 in first-quarter receipts are expected to raise $94,000 in their second quarter; for inexperienced candidates, this value is $67,000 (top graph). Experienced and inexperienced nonincumbents with a weak first-quarter performance post less than stellar numbers in the next period as well. The magnitude of the increase declines at higher values of first-quarter fundraising, which is indicated by the negative squared term. The coefficient is similar for primary winners (model 2), but they unsurprisingly raise more first- and second-quarter money.

Most candidates consistently have higher or lower numbers across the cycle, but nonincumbents often raise less in their second quarter than in their first, in part because they reach out to their full networks at the outset of the campaign. One said the middle period—what he called the "dog days" of fundraising—can be especially hard: "It's all a slog, but by the time you get to the second quarter, and until you get pretty close to the election, you end up in this weird spot where most people aren't paying attention, and most institutional donors don't want to play in a primary because they see it as a waste of money. The universe of people who are excited about you as a candidate, think the district is in play, are paying attention, and are willing to get involved in a primary gets to be pretty small." The results illustrate why the first quarter is critical even if the top line in their second quarter may not be quite as high as that in their first.

The patterns for incumbents are similar, but the coefficient on first-quarter receipts is larger than for nonincumbents. Incumbents do not appear to experience a "dog days" period like nonincumbents do, and most tend to have similar totals in their second quarter as they do in their first (bottom graph). Incumbents also post higher second-quarter totals, as we would expect. Those who raise $200,000 in their first quarter are predicted to raise $250,000 in their second. Unlike the nonincumbent models, the squared term on first-quarter fundraising is not statistically significant for incumbents.

The coefficients on the political and electoral variables are consistent with prior work. Experienced candidates raise more money in their second fundraising report than inexperienced candidates, on average. Second-quarter fundraising is higher in open seats and safe and competitive districts, but it declines for incumbents in safe districts. Second-quarter fundraising is lower for candidates running in states with preprimary endorsements. Among nonincumbents, women raise more second-quarter money than their male counterparts. Republican nonincumbents raise less money in their second quarter than Democrats, but Republican incumbents raise more, on average.

In short, first-quarter fundraising is a clear predictor of second-quarter fundraising. Empirical patterns need not be surprising to be important. The relationships conform to the conventional wisdom that it is crucial to "come out of the gate strong," because it matters for whether their campaign will gain momentum and attract attention from donors in subsequent quarters. While many successful candidates are unable to match their first-quarter totals in the second quarter, they strive to make a strong first impression because of its implications for the trajectory of the race. The behavior of donors at least suggests they are attentive to the signal of fundraising and that they look to a candidate's track record when deciding how to spend their money.

Effect of Money on Support among Donors

The previous section examined fundraising dynamics with data from real-world elections. Because of the well-known challenges of studying money, I draw on a conjoint survey to gain additional causal leverage. The sample is limited to very informed and politically active Americans: validated primary voters who have donated to political campaigns. Most conjoint studies use nationally representative samples or samples of all voters. This sample is unique because it homes in on a highly engaged subset of the public that is particularly likely to use money to draw inferences about viability. Moreover, they themselves donate money to candidates and make choices about how to allocate their money in actual elections.

The full sample includes one thousand validated primary voters, with five hundred Democrats and five hundred Republicans. The survey was conducted by YouGov in February 2019; the sample was validated with primary voting records.[3] The next chapter looks at all of these primary voters; here the focus is just on the donors. Fifty percent of respondents had donated to a candidate or party, and 50 percent had not. This figure is similar to the 42 percent of primary voters in the Cooperative Election Study who reported that they had donated money to a candidate, campaign, or political organization (Schaffner, Ansolabehere, and Luks 2022).[4] Republicans are less likely to have donated than Democrats, but not by much: 45 percent of Republicans donated, compared to 54 percent of Democrats.

Respondents evaluated pairs of hypothetical candidates who share their party affiliation. One feature of conjoint experiments is that they allow for several characteristics to be varied, and fundraising is randomly assigned along with a host of other attributes. I use a paired conjoint survey design where two candidate profiles are presented next to each other (e.g., Hainmueller, Hopkins, and Yamamoto 2014; Hainmueller, Hangartner, and Yamamoto 2015). Respondents were asked to choose which candidate they would support in a primary election and rate the favorability of each. Each respondent evaluated seven pairs of candidates.

The characteristics in the profile were informed by prior research on voter preferences and behavior. I randomized the candidate's financial and local support (raised virtually no money, raised a lot of money, received few local endorsements, received many local endorsements), ideology (more liberal or conservative than most same-party members of Congress [for Democratic and Republican voters, respectively], more moderate than most same-party members, rarely works across the aisle with the other party, often works across the aisle), type of experience (city councilor, mayor, state legislator), gender (male, female), and age (35, 45, 55, 65).[5] The text of the survey is in the appendix.

The main question is how fundraising ability affects support among donors. Like previous studies, I estimate the average marginal component effect (AMCE) (e.g., Doherty, Dowling, and Miller 2019; Hainmueller, Hopkins, and Yamamoto 2014; Kirkland and Coppock 2018; Teele, Kalla, and Rosenbluth 2018). The AMCE represents the average difference in the probability that a candidate is selected if, for example, they raise a lot of money compared to if they raise virtually no money, where the average is computed given all combinations of the other attributes. An indicator for whether the respondent selects the candidate is regressed on the above characteristics. I use cluster-robust standard errors to correct for within-respondent clustering.

Figure 5.2 shows the effect of each candidate attribute on the donor's likelihood of selecting the candidate. The full model is provided in the appendix. As expected, candidates who raise a lot of money are favored significantly—by thirteen percentage points—over those who raise virtually no money. Indeed, a lack of campaign funds is a clear red flag to donors.

Candidates who receive many endorsements from local leaders benefit the most. They receive an eighteen-point increase in the likelihood of being selected, and those described as having few endorsements from local leaders receive a four-point increase. In the real world of elections, however, it is unclear how much even donors are aware of endorsements,

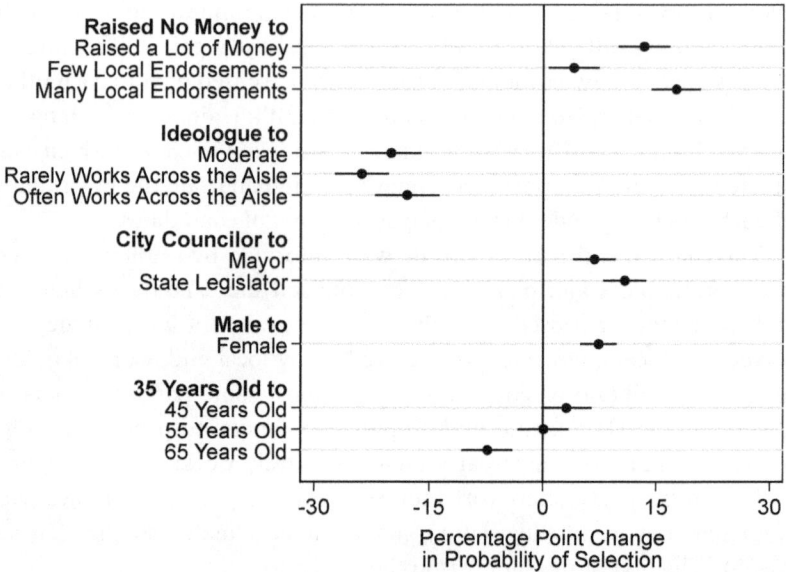

FIGURE 5.2. Effect of Candidate Fundraising on Support among Donors

Note: Effects of candidate characteristics on support among donors. Data are from a 2019 YouGov survey of validated primary voters. This sample is limited to those who donate money.

particularly in the preprimary stage before many actors are willing to endorse. Campaign dollars are, by comparison, easier to access, easier to measure, and easier to rank across candidates. Moreover, donors may be reluctant to declare as large a preference for strong fundraisers as they do in real life, simply because it is a more unseemly shortcut to admit to using.

In addition to supporting better fundraisers, donors strongly prefer more liberal Democrats and conservative Republicans to candidates who often work across the aisle and ideological moderates. They also favor those with mayoral and state legislative experience, women, and younger candidates. I include interactions between donor status and each attribute to test whether donors differ from nondonors. The interactions between donor and candidate ideology are the only ones that are significant. Donors favor ideologues over moderates by twenty percentage points, whereas nondonors do so by eleven points. This finding echoes previous work showing that donors hold more extreme policy views than nondonors and contribute to ideologically proximate candidates (e.g., Bafumi and Herron 2010; Barber 2016; Barber, Canes-Wrone, and Thrower 2017; Bonica 2014; Hill and Huber 2017; Magleby, Goodliffe, and Olsen 2018).

One implication is that moderate candidates can offset some of the ideology penalty by raising money. For example, a moderate woman state legislator with financial backing stands a better chance of gaining primary support (her likelihood of being selected is 0.60 among donors). Yet like endorsements, it is not always easy to tell which candidate is more or less extreme. In a study of top-two primaries in California, Ahler, Citrin, and Lenz (2016) find that primary voters fail to distinguish moderate from extreme candidates. Moderates who raise money may be able to leverage the clarity of money as a signal to rally support. Those who seek to elect moderates to office need to not only recruit more to run but finance their campaigns as well (Thomsen 2014, 2017).

Partisan differences may also emerge in light of Grossmann and Hopkins's (2015) finding that Republicans prize ideological purity whereas Democrats are a coalition of social groups. The black dots in figure 5.3 correspond to Democratic donors, and the gray squares correspond to Republican donors. The effect of fundraising is apparent among Republicans and Democrats, but the magnitude is smaller for Republicans (eleven versus sixteen points). Republican donors favor conservatives over

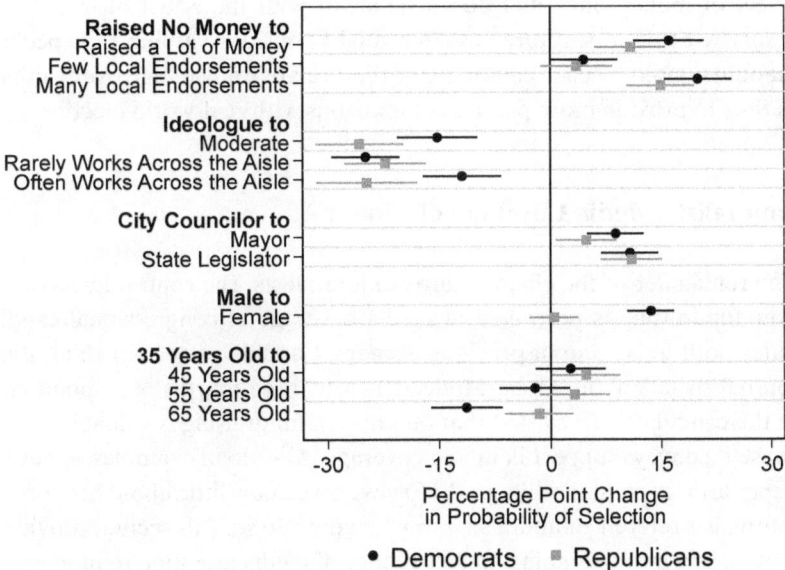

FIGURE 5.3. Effect of Candidate Fundraising on Support among Donors, by Party

Note: Effects of candidate characteristics on support among donors. Data are from a 2019 YouGov survey of validated primary voters. This sample is limited to those who donate money.

moderates to a greater degree than Democratic donors favor liberals over moderates. Finally, the preference for women candidates is limited to Democratic donors, which is consistent with prior research (Schwarz and Coppock 2022; Scott et al. 2019; Teele et al. 2018; Thomsen 2021).

Unsurprisingly, the same patterns are apparent with candidate favorability evaluations. Respondents rated each candidate on a 7-point scale ranging from very unfavorable to very favorable. Candidates who raised a lot of money were evaluated 0.32 points higher than those who raised virtually no money, or about half of the size of the (negative) effect of being ideologically moderate. Those who received few local endorsements and many local endorsements were rated 0.12 and 0.38 points higher, respectively, than those who raised virtually no money.

In sum, the conjoint survey allows us to further examine the causal effect of fundraising on donor support. The experiment is an especially valuable supplement given the endogeneity concerns that have long plagued the study of money and politics. The findings provide additional evidence for the argument that better fundraisers are rewarded in many ways. When asked to evaluate pairs of hypothetical candidates, donors are more likely to support those who raise money. Although it is difficult to compare the effect of money on actual donor behavior with the effect of money in a survey of donors, future research might consider varying the specific amounts raised by each candidate or their relative advantage over a competitor to provide more precise comparisons with real-world elections.

Journalists: Media Coverage of Money

The remainder of the chapter turns to journalists. The central question is how fundraising is portrayed in media coverage of congressional candidates both today and in previous decades. Candidates at least think that journalists talk about money. Indeed, nearly three-fourths of respondents in the candidate survey said that one reason fundraising is valuable is because it conveys support in media coverage. Anecdotal examples of newspaper articles on money abound. However, we know little about how often journalists reference fundraising or when they do so. This section provides new insight into the timing and frequency of media attention to money.

I focus on the most competitive primaries to see how fundraising is covered in races where the outcome is least certain. The sample is limited to open-seat primaries in safe or competitive districts where the top vote-getter received less than 57.5 percent of votes, and the top fundraiser raised less than 57.5 percent of receipts (Hirano and Snyder 2019; Thomsen 2023; see chapter 8 on measuring competition). There are five hundred primary races from 1980 to 2020 that fit these criteria. To be sure, candidates in uncompetitive races are also expected to be portrayed as long shots or frontrunners by their fundraising totals, but we lack the data to answer that question here.

A research assistant collected data on all newspaper articles that mentioned the name of the top fundraiser or top vote-getter in the primary (both if they were different) during the two-year election cycle (from January of the year before the election to December of the election year). The data were collected from Newspapers.com, the most comprehensive database of newspapers across this four-decade period. Of the full sample of 500 primary races, 485, or 97 percent, had newspaper coverage of the top two fundraisers or vote-getters before the primary election.[6]

The dataset includes 6,592 unique articles, with 3,167 articles before the primary and 3,425 after; this chapter only looks at the preprimary articles. Each article was coded for whether it referenced money or fundraising in the race, whether it referenced fundraising by the top vote-getter or top fundraiser, and whether it referenced fundraising by the other candidates (all are zero or one). The articles were additionally coded for whether they noted the occupation or experience of the top vote-getter or top fundraiser, whether they noted the occupation or experience of the other candidates, whether they indicated that the primary was competitive, whether a scandal was mentioned, and whether polling was mentioned (all are zero or one). Binary values were used for simplicity.

Virtually all articles provide biographical information for the leading candidate(s). Ninety-four percent of articles (2,979 of 3,167) note the occupation or experience of the top fundraiser or top vote-getter. Sixty-six percent note the occupation or experience of any of the other primary candidates. By comparison, one-third of articles mention money or fundraising; however, when the primary is described as competitive, 54 percent of articles mention money. Thirty percent of articles mention fundraising by the top vote-getter or top fundraiser, and 18 percent mention fundraising by any of the other candidates. At the primary race level, at least one article mentions fundraising in 80 percent of races; in races described as competitive, this value increases to 89 percent. Thus, a nontrivial share of articles mention money, and most of these races have some preprimary coverage of fundraising.

Additionally relevant is whether newspaper coverage has changed over time. At the primary race level, each race has 6.5 unique articles, on average (median of 6). While local news coverage has clearly declined in recent decades (Hayes and Lawless 2015, 2021; Peterson 2021), this trend does not seem to extend to the most competitive contests. The average number of articles ranges from 4.8 in 2008 to 7.5 in 1998, but there is no decrease over time (see the appendix). However, the number of races with attention to early fundraising has increased: 75 percent of races had at least one article about fundraising in the pre-2000 period, compared to 84 percent of races post-2000 ($p < 0.05$). The fact that fundraising has soared in close contests where overall coverage has not declined suggests there is more to this story than changes in the media environment.

At the article level, more coverage mentions fundraising today, but the magnitude is not especially large: 36 percent of post-2000 articles mention fundraising, compared to 30 percent of pre-2000 articles ($p < 0.01$). Thirty-two percent of post-2000 articles mention fundraising by the top vote-getter or top fundraiser, compared to 27 percent of pre-2000 articles ($p < 0.01$). Ninety-four percent of both pre- and post-2000 articles listed the leading candidate(s)' occupation or experience so the norm of including biographical attributes in newspaper coverage is long-standing and has remained in place over time. But fundraising is often and increasingly among the factors that journalists highlight.

When journalists discuss money is also important because it conveys information about the state of the race and how candidates stack up. Newspaper coverage increases when the primary is closer, likely because voters are paying attention, and the pool of competitors has solidified. Across this period, 44 percent of preprimary articles appear either in the month before or the same month as the primary. Yet coverage has become more frontloaded in recent cycles: half of the articles were in the month before or the same month as the primary in the pre-2000 period, compared to 39 percent post-2000 ($p < 0.01$). Similarly, 12 percent of the articles appeared at least six months before the primary in the pre-2000 period, compared to 22 percent post-2000 ($p < 0.01$).

Figure 5.4 shows the average number of months before the primary that articles appear, broken down by decade and whether they mentioned money. A few patterns emerge. As noted above, both fundraising and nonfundraising coverage in the post-2000 period is earlier in the cycle. In addition, coverage that mentions fundraising is closer to the primary than nonfundraising coverage. Articles that make no mention of money

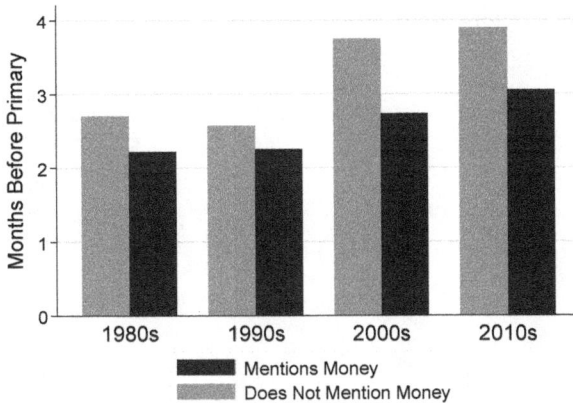

FIGURE 5.4. Timing of Newspaper Coverage of Fundraising

Note: Average number of months before the primary for newspaper articles that do and do not mention money, broken down by decade.

appear, on average, 3.8 months before the primary in the post-2000 period and 2.6 months before the primary in the pre-2000 period. Coverage that mentions fundraising appears, on average, 3.1 months before the primary in the 2010s, 2.7 months before the primary in the 2000s, and 2.2 months before the primary in the pre-2000 period.

In the 80 percent of primary contests with any fundraising coverage, the very first coverage of money similarly appears earlier in the cycle today. In the 1980s and 1990s, the first article that mentioned money appeared 3.4 months before the primary, on average. In the 2000s, the first coverage appeared 4.0 months before the primary. In the 2010s, the first coverage of money jumped to 5.1 months before the primary, on average.

I also examine the predictors of fundraising coverage while accounting for other factors. The dependent variables are whether fundraising is mentioned at all and whether fundraising is mentioned for the leading candidate(s) in the race. I include indicator variables for each decade to explore change over time. To measure proximity to the primary, the article is coded one if it is in the month before or the same month as the primary and zero if it is more than one month before the primary. I include an interaction between proximity to the primary and decade to examine temporal patterns. I control for whether the primary is described as competitive in the article and whether the seat is in a safe district (versus competitive) to capture the electoral context.

TABLE 5.2 **Preprimary Newspaper Coverage of Fundraising**

	(1)	(2)
	Any Mention of Fundraising	Fundraising of Leading Candidate(s)
1990s	0.15	0.10
	(0.19)	(0.20)
2000s	0.33†	0.38†
	(0.19)	(0.20)
2010s	0.30†	0.30
	(0.18)	(0.18)
Close to Primary	0.61**	0.64**
	(0.21)	(0.21)
Close to Primary × 1990s	−0.29	−0.29
	(0.25)	(0.26)
Close to Primary × 2000s	−0.23	−0.36
	(0.27)	(0.28)
Close to Primary × 2010s	−0.01	−0.03
	(0.24)	(0.25)
Indicates Competitive Primary	0.81**	0.85**
	(0.13)	(0.13)
Safe District	0.17*	0.13†
	(0.08)	(0.08)
Constant	−1.29**	−1.42**
	(0.16)	(0.17)
Observations	3,167	3,167
Log-likelihood	−1,962.12	−1,885.61

Note: Results are from logistic regressions, with standard errors in parentheses. The sample includes preprimary newspaper articles in competitive open-seat primaries in safe or competitive districts. †$p < 0.10$, *$p < 0.05$, **$p < 0.01$.

The results are shown in table 5.2. Consistent with the patterns above, preprimary articles in the 2000s and 2010s are more likely to mention fundraising in general and fundraising by the leading candidates than those in the 1980s. While fundraising coverage is now more frequent and appears earlier, journalists still tend to discuss money closer to the election. Articles in either the month before or the same month as the primary are more likely to mention fundraising than articles further out from the election. The interactions between primary proximity and decade are not significant, suggesting that articles closer to the primary are not more likely to cite money today. Coverage in competitive contests and safe districts also highlights money more, perhaps because the primary is often the most central in selecting officeholders.

Predicted values are plotted by decade in figure 5.5. Across this period, newspaper coverage in either the month before or the same month as the primary (black line) is more likely to mention money than earlier coverage (gray line). The probability that articles right before the primary mention fundraising is 39 percent, compared to 29 percent for those that are two or more months out from the primary. This value increases slightly over time for both earlier and later coverage. The probability that earlier coverage mentions money increases from 24 and 27 percent in the 1980s and 1990s, respectively, to 31 and 30 percent in the 2000s and 2010s. For coverage that is right before the primary, this value increases from 37 and 34 percent in the 1980s and 1990s, respectively, to 40 and 44 percent in the 2000s and 2010s.

These data provide a new look into newspaper coverage of fundraising in a subset of primaries where the outcome is least certain. Taken together, the results demonstrate that fundraising is one aspect of elections that journalists choose to highlight. The fact that fundraising coverage is more likely as the election nears is consistent with the expectation that journalists view money as relevant in elections and see it as valuable information for the public to know. Furthermore, while fundraising has never been as widely cited as candidate backgrounds, coverage of money has increased in recent decades. Fundraising is mentioned earlier in the cycle today than in the pre-2000 period, again reflecting broader shifts in the arena of competition.

Changes in fundraising behavior and media coverage of course go hand in hand. Candidates start raising money earlier today, and journalists cover fundraising totals earlier as a result. Journalists, like candidates and donors, face informational constraints. Indeed, as the journalist quoted

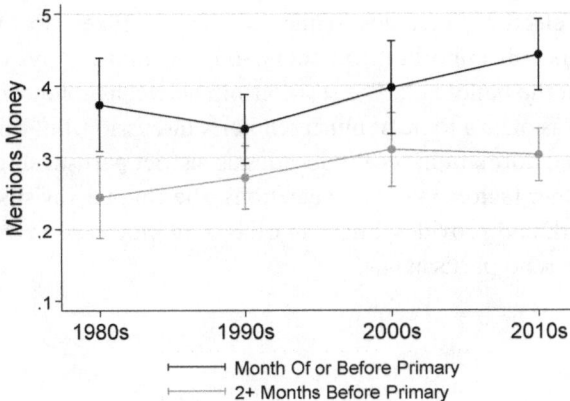

FIGURE 5.5. Probability that Preprimary Newspaper Article Mentions Money

Note: Values are calculated from model 1 in table 5.2.

in chapter 1 asked, "What other way is there to separate the serious candidates from the ones who aren't?" Journalists operate in a broader social environment where "big data" is increasingly valued. Articles about how much candidates raise are easy stories to write. Money is one of the few pieces of hard data that journalists can use. Receipts are publicly available and readily accessible, and they can be quickly compared across contenders in the race.

Summary

This chapter demonstrated that donors and journalists also use money as a focal point. Dynamic fundraising data showed that first-quarter fundraising is a clear predictor of second-quarter fundraising. The conjoint survey provided causal evidence of the impact of fundraising ability on support among donors, which is particularly valuable in light of the challenges of studying money. With respect to journalists, an analysis of more than three thousand newspaper articles from 1980 to 2020 illustrated that fundraising is used as a noteworthy detail and an increasingly salient piece of information across this period. Coverage is more likely to mention money closer to the primary, indicating that journalists think that fundraising offers a valuable window into the race.

The results collectively illustrate that actors beyond candidates view money as a signal of viability. Donors and journalists are additional players in the money-driven ecosystem of politics. The next chapter turns to voters and election outcomes. While voters are unlikely to follow campaign dollars, it is important to understand how money pays off, at least indirectly, at the ballot box. The relationship between money and election outcomes was once a topic of much scholarly discussion, but this question has remained dormant in recent decades as district partisanship has overwhelmed other factors in general elections. The chapter revisits this older body of work and provides a new analysis of money in primary elections where there is no partisan cue.

CHAPTER SIX

Voters at the Ballot Box

In June 2018, Alexandria Ocasio-Cortez sent shockwaves through New York and Washington. At twenty-eight years old, she upset Representative Joe Crowley, a ten-term incumbent and the fourth-ranking House Democrat, in the primary. Ocasio-Cortez, then employed as a bartender and waitress, received 57 percent of the primary vote and defeated Crowley by nearly fifteen points. Crowley reported $3.4 million in preprimary fundraising, nearly eleven times Ocasio-Cortez's preprimary haul of $313,000. Four years earlier, in June 2014, Republican House Majority Leader Eric Cantor faced a similarly stunning primary defeat by Dave Brat. Cantor reported $5.5 million in preprimary receipts, twenty-six times the $209,000 that Brat had raised. Brat, an economics professor with no prior political experience, won the Republican primary by eleven points.

These races stand out because they are exceptions to the rule. Underdogs prevailed over powerful incumbents, and inexperienced political outsiders triumphed over decades of Washington experience. They were also surprising because of the margin by which the losers outraised the winners. Yet in another way, both contests resemble the overwhelming majority of House races in the United States. Most of the time, fundraising is tilted toward one candidate, and competitors have vastly unequal resources in their bids for office. The outcomes, precisely because they defied conventions, made the races memorable, but the fundraising dynamics were rather typical. In contemporary congressional elections, the bulk of candidates raise either all or nothing.

Most candidates who are heavily outraised and outspent do not experience the fates of Ocasio-Cortez or Brat. Instead, they fail to gain traction and ultimately lose by large margins. The entrenchment of the multimillion-dollar campaign has not deterred candidates from running, and the number of candidates has increased as fundraising demands continue to soar. But the rising price tag matters for whether candidates can mount a credible campaign. As political scientist Thomas Mann notes, "Those who are trying to break through for the first time face an increasingly daunting challenge in raising enough money to get themselves known" (qtd. in Jones 2012). The amount of money needed to clear this bar is much higher today than it was four decades ago.

The association between money and victory patterns has long been evident. In general elections, top spenders win over 90 percent of the time (OpenSecrets 2020). Even in wave elections, the candidate who raises and spends the most usually wins. Scholars have been more skeptical, however, about the causal effect of money, because donors tend to bet on candidates who are most likely to win. Several studies in the 1980s and 1990s sought to untangle the influence of spending, but the question has remained dormant since. Here I revisit the relationship between money and election outcomes and explore changes over time. Recent work has suggested that money indeed plays a leading role in primaries where there is no partisan cue (Bonica 2017; Hassell 2018).

This chapter provides a new look into fundraising patterns in primary and general elections from 1980 to 2022. I first review the most prominent studies of how campaign spending is associated with general election votes, and I replicate previous analyses with current data. The effect of money on election outcomes has been a subject of much debate, and the analyses indicate that money has even *less* of an impact on general election vote shares in the 2000s than it did at the height of these studies in the 1980s and 1990s. District partisanship has become an increasingly important determinant of general election outcomes, providing further motivation to turn our attention to the primary arena.

I then delve into the relationship between fundraising and primary outcomes across this four-decade period. Fundraising has the single largest impact on primary victory patterns, and it matters more than prior political experience. I also extend Bonica's (2017) study of primaries and find that the effect of money on primary vote shares is positive and significant across decades, reinforcing the point that the salience of fundraising can increase even if the effect does not. I again draw on the conjoint survey used in chapter 5 and show that primary voters, too, are more likely to support hypothetical candidates who are better fundraisers. In short, while voters do not follow the dollars like candidates, donors, and journalists do, money is clearly valuable for those who want to win.

Impact of Spending on Vote Shares

Data challenges have long hindered our understanding of the effect of money on vote totals. A series of influential articles emerged after receipts and expenditures became publicly available in the 1970s. The main debate centered around how campaign spending influences general election vote shares.[1] While most agreed that challengers who spend more fare considerably better at the ballot box, the main point of contention was whether incumbents benefit as well. Jacobson (1978, 1980) was the first to show that incumbent spending has little to no effect on challenger vote share. Jacobson's explanation was that incumbents are well known before the campaign begins, and further campaigning provides only modest gains in support. Challengers, by contrast, are unknown at the outset of the campaign and benefit substantially from additional exposure.

This finding spurred various exchanges and extensions. Several studies used lagged variables, instrumental variables, and subsamples of close elections and uncovered larger effects of incumbent spending (Gerber 1998; Erikson and Palfrey 2000; Green and Krasno 1988, 1990). Others identified different patterns. Levitt (1994) examined repeat candidates and suggested that spending has little impact on election outcomes for either challengers or incumbents. Gerber (2004) presented experimental evidence that echoed Jacobson's initial results and concluded that "the possibility that incumbent spending fails to boost incumbent vote share needs to be taken more seriously." In a study of Senate elections, Abramowitz (1988) similarly demonstrated that challengers gain far more from spending than incumbents.

The methodological hurdles and inconsistent findings hindered a clear consensus on the relative and absolute magnitude of incumbent and challenger spending effects. The discussion has subsided in recent years, likely because general election outcomes are now primarily a reflection of district partisanship. In the contemporary context, the partisan tilt of the district is the best predictor of general election vote totals. A strong fundraising haul may help at the margins but is rarely decisive. At the same time, fundraising totals have skyrocketed among incumbents, challengers, and open-seat candidates alike. Prior research was skeptical of the limited effects of incumbent spending precisely because these results are difficult to reconcile with incumbent behavior.

Bonica (2017, 2020) instead suggests that scholars have found limited spending effects because they have looked in the wrong places. The focus on general elections obscures other ways that money matters. He shifts the attention to the primary stage and finds that early fundraising is positively associated with primary outcomes. Bonica analyzes primaries without an incumbent so the findings are not directly applicable to the debate on incumbent spending effects. Yet they offer new insights into when and where money matters for the selection of officeholders today. The increase in members from safe districts means that spending may have a limited impact in general elections but is likely to play a role in primaries.

Impact of Spending in a Partisan Era

The central question in prior work was whether and how much incumbent and challenger spending affected general election vote shares. I replicate the models in the exchange between Jacobson (1990) and Green and Krasno (1988) with data from 1980 to 2022 to explore over-time trends. The dependent variable is the challenger's vote share. Three independent variables—incumbent spending, challenger spending, and district partisanship—are most relevant here. I use the same instrumental variable approach. I include interactions between decade and incumbent spending, challenger spending, and district partisanship to examine how these relationships have changed. A full discussion of the data, variables, and models is provided in the appendix.[2]

Predicted values are plotted in figure 6.1. The marginal effect of incumbent spending on challenger vote share over time is shown in the top graph, and the marginal effect of challenger spending over time is shown in the middle graph. Incumbent spending is negatively associated with challenger vote share, but the confidence intervals are large, the magnitude of the effect is small, and like prior work, the results differ across specifications (tables are provided in the appendix).[3] The marginal effect of challenger spending on challenger vote share is positive and significant across this period, though the magnitude has clearly declined since the 1980s and 1990s.

The most dramatic change is the increase in the marginal effect of challenger-party strength on general election vote share (bottom graph). These patterns are reflective of the nationalization of congressional elections and the heightened role of partisanship in voting behavior. As previ-

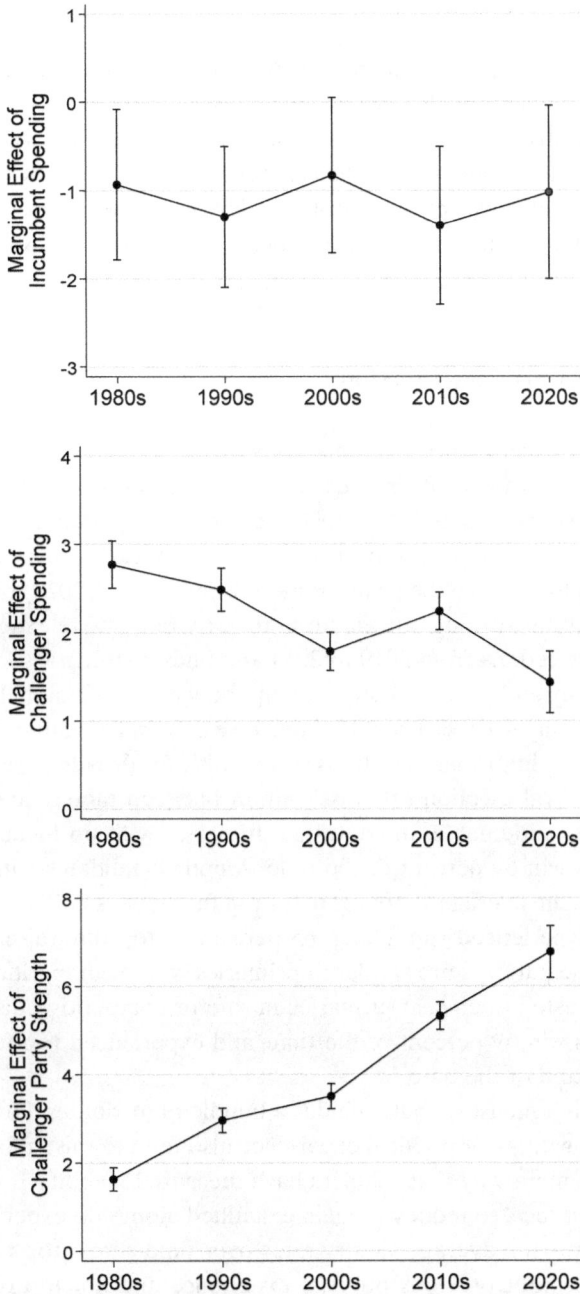

FIGURE 6.1. Marginal Effect of Candidate Spending and District Partisanship on Challenger Vote Share

Note: The top and middle graphs show the marginal effect of incumbent and challenger expenditures, respectively, on challenger vote share in US House general elections from 1982 to 2022. The bottom graph shows the marginal effect of challenger party strength on challenger vote share in general elections.

ous studies have detailed, the incumbency advantage has declined, partisan defections to incumbents have fallen, and very few members of Congress represent districts that lean toward the other party (Hopkins 2018; Jacobson 2015). Incumbent and challenger spending are likely to matter less in an era where district partisanship is highly predictive of the general election winner. The results set the stage for a deeper dive into partisan primaries.

Money and Primary Elections

Much of the recent work on primaries is driven by a recognition that primaries play a critical role in the selection of officeholders. Whereas earlier scholarship examined the effect of campaign expenditures in general elections, changes in the political and electoral context provide additional motivation to move to the primary stage. Bonica (2017, 2020) has laid the groundwork for turning our attention to early money. He examines congressional elections from 2010 to 2014 and finds a strong association between money and primary outcomes and between professional networks and fundraising success. I build on this research and examine the impact of fundraising in primary elections across this four-decade period.

Like general elections, the association between money and primary outcomes is undeniable. In contested primaries with no incumbent, top fundraisers win 69 percent of the time. Among candidates with political experience, the average victory rate for top fundraisers is 78 percent. And among inexperienced candidates, 65 percent of top fundraisers win the primary. The patterns are similar in primaries where competition is highest: in contested open-seat primaries in safe or competitive districts, top fundraisers win 69 percent of the time, and experienced top fundraisers win 75 percent of the time.

Money is a measure that includes a bundle of attributes. For example, candidates with prior political experience also tend to raise more money. In fact, the main way that scholars have measured viability is with prior office experience, so money is again examined alongside experience. Figure 6.2 shows the average victory rates over time across top fundraisers with and without previous political experience and not top fundraisers with and without experience. The sample includes all contested primaries without an incumbent. Across this period, experienced top fundraisers have the highest victory rates, followed by inexperienced top fundrais-

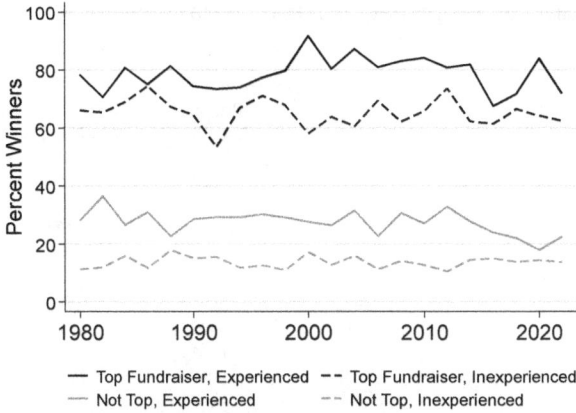

FIGURE 6.2. Primary Victory Rates by Money and Experience

Note: Primary victory rate for top and not top fundraisers with and without experience from 1980 to 2022. The sample includes contested primaries with no incumbent.

ers. Experienced and inexperienced candidates who are not top fundraisers rank third and fourth, respectively.

I use OLS regressions to further investigate the influence of money and experience. The dependent variables are whether the candidate won the primary and their primary vote share. The main independent variable is a binary indicator of whether the candidate was the top fundraiser in the primary. I include an interaction between top fundraiser and prior experience as well. I control for seat type (open-seat or challenger-party primary), district partisanship (safe, competitive, or hopeless), the share of the candidate's receipts that were loans, the number of candidates in the race, gender, and party. These variables are similar to those used in other studies of primary outcomes (e.g., Bonica 2017; Hall and Snyder 2015; Thomsen 2020).

The results are presented in table 6.1. Several patterns emerge. First, top fundraisers and experienced candidates are more likely to win the primary and receive higher vote shares, on average, than not top fundraisers and inexperienced candidates. The relationships are significant in all primaries without an incumbent (models 1 and 2) and in open-seat primaries in safe or competitive districts (models 3 and 4). While the additive benefit of being an experienced top fundraiser is clear, the interaction between the two is negative or insignificant, and the magnitude is small.

In addition, the coefficient is much larger for top fundraisers than for experienced candidates. The predicted probability that experienced top

TABLE 6.1 **Relationship between Money, Experience, and Primary Outcomes**

	(1)	(2)	(3)	(4)
	Win Primary	Primary Vote Share	Win Primary	Primary Vote Share
Top Fundraiser	0.47**	0.22**	0.53**	0.23**
	(0.01)	(0.00)	(0.02)	(0.01)
Experienced	0.17**	0.09**	0.18**	0.11**
	(0.01)	(0.00)	(0.01)	(0.00)
Top Fundraiser × Experienced	−0.00	−0.02**	−0.04	−0.03**
	(0.02)	(0.01)	(0.03)	(0.01)
Open Seat	−0.03**	−0.04**		
	(0.01)	(0.00)		
Competitive District	−0.02	−0.01*		
	(0.01)	(0.00)		
Safe District	−0.03**	−0.02**	−0.01	−0.03**
	(0.01)	(0.00)	(0.02)	(0.01)
Loan Ratio	−0.00	−0.00	−0.14**	−0.05**
	(0.00)	(0.00)	(0.02)	(0.01)
Number of Candidates	−0.02**	−0.03**	−0.01**	−0.02**
	(0.00)	(0.00)	(0.00)	(0.00)
Woman	0.08**	0.04**	0.02	0.02**
	(0.01)	(0.00)	(0.01)	(0.00)
Republican	0.01	0.01*	0.00	0.01*
	(0.01)	(0.00)	(0.01)	(0.00)
Constant	0.23**	0.37**	0.28**	0.30**
	(0.06)	(0.02)	(0.11)	(0.04)
Observations	13,924	13,924	5,135	5,135
R^2	0.31	0.58	0.35	0.62

Note: Results are from OLS regressions from 1980 to 2022. Standard errors are in parentheses. The dependent variable in models 1 and 3 is whether the candidate won the primary, and the dependent variable in models 2 and 4 is the candidate's primary vote share. The sample is limited to contested primaries. Models 3 and 4 are limited to open-seat primaries in safe or competitive districts. All models include district and year fixed effects. $\dagger p < 0.10$, $*p < 0.05$, $**p < 0.01$.

fundraisers win the primary is 0.78 in all primaries and nearly as high— 0.74—in safe or competitive open seats. Inexperienced top fundraisers are less likely to win than their experienced counterparts (these values are 0.61 in all primaries and 0.60 in safe or competitive open seats), but the bigger divide is between top and not top fundraisers. For experienced not top fundraisers, the likelihood of victory is 0.31 in all primaries and 0.25 in safe or competitive open seats. Predicted values are unsurprisingly the lowest for inexperienced not top fundraisers, at 0.14 in all primaries and 0.08 in safe or competitive open seats.

I also examine how much of the variance in primary vote shares is explained by the inclusion of different independent variables. Table 6.2 notes how the *R*-squared changes when experience and money are not included in the models to when they are. The R-squared is 0.36 in the full sample and 0.33 in safe or competitive open seats. This value increases to 0.40 and 0.42, respectively, when experience is included. When top fundraiser is added, the R-squared increases to 0.58 in the full sample and 0.61 in safe or competitive open seats.[4] These models included a binary measure of top fundraiser, but if primary receipt share is used instead, the R-squared is even higher, at 0.65 in the full sample and 0.75 in safe or competitive open seats. The inclusion of money clearly explains more of the variance in vote shares.

The final question in this section is whether the electoral benefits of money and experience have changed as fundraising demands have grown. I include interactions between top fundraiser and year and between experience and year to examine the association over time. The marginal effect of money and experience on primary outcomes is plotted by year in the top and bottom graphs of figure 6.3, respectively. The marginal effect of being the top fundraiser does not differ much for experienced and inexperienced candidates, nor does the marginal effect of experience differ for top and not top fundraisers. The marginal effect of being the top fundraiser is 0.51 and 0.47, on average, for experienced and inexperienced candidates, respectively. The marginal effect of experience is 0.22 for top fundraisers and 0.17 for not top fundraisers, on average.

The values are higher in some years and lower in others, but the larger difference is between the marginal effect of money versus experience across this period. Experience helps, but money helps more (and again, experienced candidates tend to raise more money). The argument is not that money yields more votes today than it used to. As shown in chapter 1, top fundraisers do not fare any better than their counterparts in the 1980s even though the amount of money that is needed to be the top fundraiser has soared. Rather, the stakes of early fundraising have increased because primaries now play a greater role in the selection of lawmakers and fundraising data are publicly available and easily accessible online.

TABLE 6.2 **Variance Explained with Money and Experience**

	Full Sample	Safe or Competitive Open Seats
Baseline	0.36	0.33
+ Experience	0.40	0.42
+ Top Fundraiser *or*	0.58	0.61
+ Primary Receipt Share	0.65	0.75

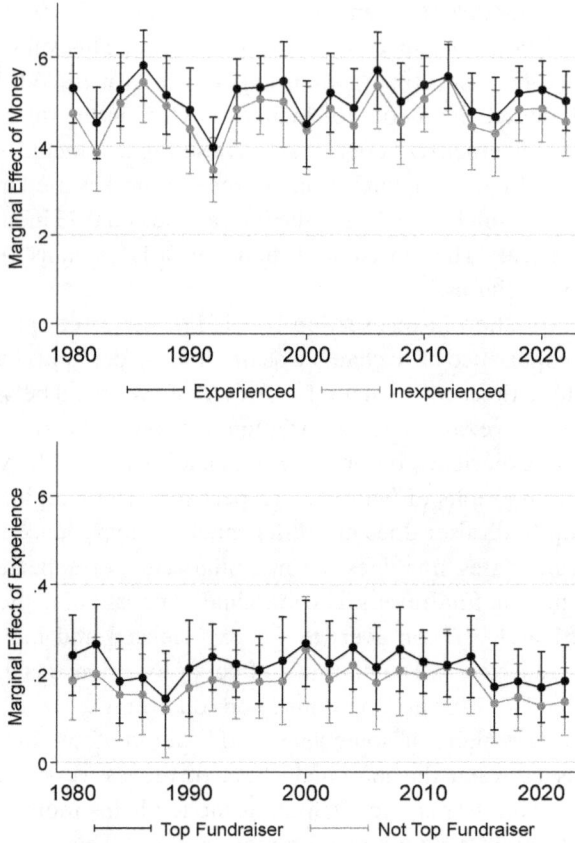

FIGURE 6.3. Marginal Effect of Money and Experience on Primary Victory

Note: Marginal effect of being the top fundraiser on primary victory for experienced and inexperienced candidates (*top*) Marginal effect of experience on primary victory for top and not top fundraisers (*bottom*). The sample includes contested primaries with no incumbent.

Estimating the Effect of Fundraising

The above analyses examined the association between money and primary outcomes, but scholars have long recognized the difficulty of estimating this relationship. Again, the main challenge is that fundraising is endogenous to the probability of winning, so the causal arrow could be reversed. Previous studies of general elections have used instrumental variable designs to address this concern (Green and Krasno 1988; Gerber 1998; Jacobson 1990). More recently, Bonica (2017) uses an IV design to estimate fundraising in primary elections. He uses the average income of the candidate's zip code to instrument for fundraising, and finds that fundraising has a positive effect on primary vote shares. I replicate this approach to buttress the results above.

Bonica (2017) leverages geographic variation in incomes within congressional districts. I similarly merge the zip code in the candidate's statement of candidacy with the IRS Statistics of Income (SOI) zip-code-level data to obtain the average income. If a different zip code is listed for their campaign committee, I use the average. The variable in the analyses is a relative measure of income compared to the other candidates in the race. Values greater than one indicate that the candidate's address is in a richer zip code relative to their competitors. The SOI data are only available from 1998 to 2022, so I create similar measures with per capita income data by zip code from US Census data for the full time period. The SOI zip-code-level averages are correlated with the Census zip-code-level averages at 0.83, and the relative measures are correlated at 0.80.

An additional challenge is related to modeling primary outcomes. Only two candidates compete in general elections, whereas in primaries the number varies. The models above controlled for the number of candidates, but here I follow Bonica's (2017, 166) measures of adjusted vote and receipt shares that are relative to contest-level averages. They are calculated as follows:

$$\widehat{\text{VoteShare}} = v_{ij} / \left(\frac{\Sigma(v_j)}{n_j}\right) \text{ and}$$
$$\widehat{\text{FundraisingShare}} = f_{ij} / \left(\frac{\Sigma(f_j)}{n_j}\right),$$

where v_{ij} is candidate i's total number of votes in primary contest j, f_{ij} is candidate i's fundraising total in the primary, and n_j is the total number of primary candidates. This normalizes the values relative to a baseline in which each candidate receives equal shares. The regression coefficient on fundraising can be interpreted as the relationship between outraising other candidates and outperforming them at the polls.[5]

The results are presented in table 6.3. Model 1 displays the OLS estimates of the association between receipt shares and vote shares. The first- and second-stage estimates of the two-stage least squares models with the SOI data are shown in models 2 and 3, respectively. Models 4 and 5 show the first- and second-stage estimates with the census data. The number of observations nearly doubles with the census data, but the coefficient on fundraising is virtually identical. The OLS estimate suggests that doubling the average fundraising total for candidates in the race translates into a 41 percent increase in vote share relative to the contest-level average. The magnitude decreases to a 31 and 30 percent increase with the IV estimates. The coefficients on fundraising share are very similar to the values reported in Bonica's (2017, 167) analysis of primaries.

Predicted vote shares are plotted across receipt share values in figure 6.4. The median adjusted receipt share of the top fundraiser in the race is twice the contest-level average, and the not top fundraiser's median receipt share is 19 percent of the contest-level average (the means are 2.1 and 0.5, respectively). Adjusted vote shares are predicted to be highest for experienced top fundraisers (161 percent of the contest-level average, compared to 124 percent for inexperienced top fundraisers). One distin-

TABLE 6.3 **IV Estimates of the Effect of Fundraising on Primary Vote Shares**

	(1)	(2)	(3)	(4)	(5)
	Vote Share	Receipt Share	Vote Share	Receipt Share	Vote Share
Fundraising Share	0.41**		0.31**		0.30**
	(0.01)		(0.04)		(0.05)
Experienced	0.31**	0.51**	0.37**	0.53**	0.37**
	(0.01)	(0.03)	(0.03)	(0.02)	(0.03)
Open Seat	−0.05**	−0.09**	−0.05**	−0.10**	−0.06**
	(0.00)	(0.01)	(0.01)	(0.01)	(0.01)
Competitive District	−0.04**	−0.07**	−0.06**	−0.06**	−0.05**
	(0.00)	(0.01)	(0.01)	(0.01)	(0.01)
Safe District	−0.05**	−0.07**	−0.08**	−0.06**	−0.06**
	(0.01)	(0.02)	(0.01)	(0.01)	(0.01)
Loan Ratio	−0.00	0.03	−0.01	0.00	−0.00*
	(0.00)	(0.03)	(0.01)	(0.00)	(0.00)
Woman	0.12**	0.20**	0.15**	0.16**	0.13**
	(0.01)	(0.03)	(0.02)	(0.03)	(0.02)
Republican	0.02**	0.01	0.02**	0.02**	0.03**
	(0.00)	(0.01)	(0.01)	(0.01)	(0.00)
Income (Zip Code, SOI)		0.49**			
		(0.04)			
Income (Zip Code, Census)				0.47**	
				(0.05)	
Constant	0.52**	0.40**	0.61**	0.42**	0.64**
	(0.01)	(0.05)	(0.04)	(0.05)	(0.04)
Observations	13,896	7,648	7,648	13,302	13,302
R^2	0.52	0.07	0.49	0.05	0.49

Note: The models follow the same format as Bonica (2017). The dependent variables are adjusted vote shares and receipt shares. The sample includes contested primaries with no incumbent from 1980 to 2022. Standard errors are clustered at the race level. All models include district and year fixed effects. †$p < 0.10$, *$p < 0.05$, **$p < 0.01$.

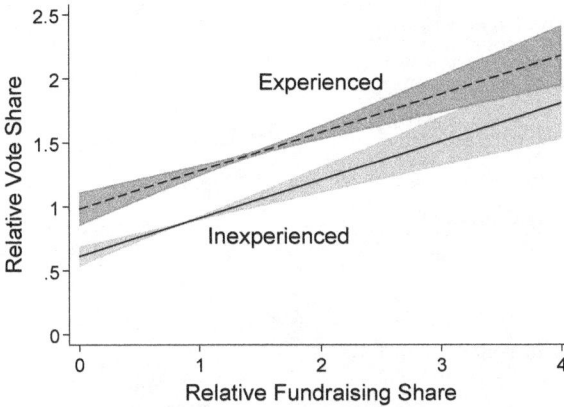

FIGURE 6.4. Predicted Effect of Relative Fundraising on Primary Vote Share

Note: Values are calculated from model 5 in table 6.3. Values are relative to contest-level averages. The sample includes contested primaries with no incumbent.

guishing feature of experience compared to money is that it is fixed before the election: a candidate either has it or they don't. Fundraising status, however, can change during the course of the campaign. To be sure, inexperienced candidates have to raise more to fare the same as experienced candidates, but they fare better with more money.

The control variables are consistent with previous research and the relationships above. Experienced candidates receive more votes, on average, than inexperienced candidates (e.g., Bonica 2017; Fowler et al. 2023; Hirano and Snyder 2019). Candidates running in open seats and in safe or competitive districts receive fewer votes than those running in less favorable electoral contexts. Women receive more votes than men, on average, though the relationship is driven by recent elections. In other work, I demonstrate that the electoral advantage of women is only apparent in Democratic primaries; Republican women fare the same in the primary as their male counterparts (Thomsen 2021). These relationships are statistically significant across models.

Effect of Money on Primary Voter Support

The analyses above drew on data from real-world elections to examine the relationship between money and victory patterns. The remainder of

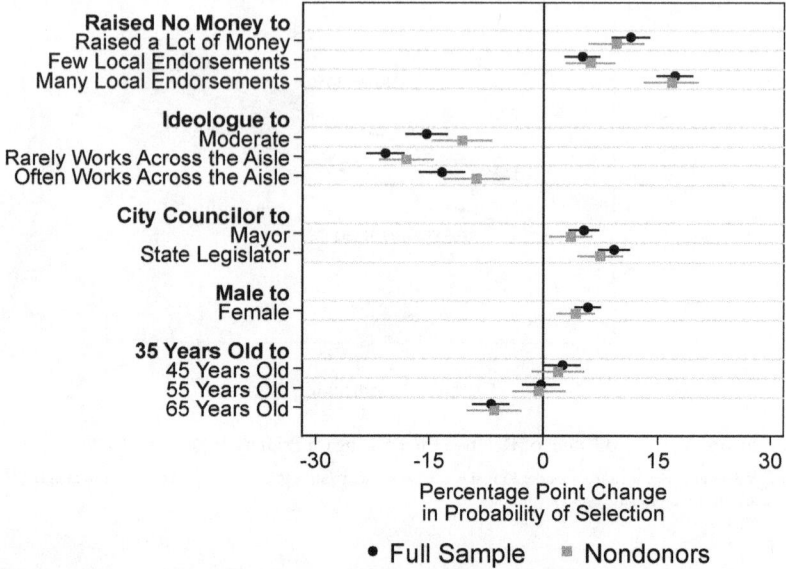

FIGURE 6.5. Effect of Candidate Fundraising on Support among Primary Voters

Note: Effects of candidate characteristics on primary voter support. Data are from a 2019 YouGov survey of validated primary voters.

the chapter provides a different vantage point by instead asking primary voters which candidates they would support. I draw on the same conjoint survey discussed in chapter 5, in which validated primary voters evaluated pairs of hypothetical candidates who share their party affiliation but vary on a number of attributes. Primary voters are of particular interest due to their increased relevance in the selection of officeholders. The sample includes one thousand validated primary voters (five hundred Democrats and five hundred Republicans).

The main question is whether primary voters are more supportive of candidates who raise a lot of money. Figure 6.5 shows the effect of each attribute on primary voter support. The results are presented for the full sample and for nondonors, indicated by the black dots and gray squares, respectively. (The results for just donors are provided in chapter 5.) In the full sample, candidates who raised a lot of money are favored by eleven percentage points over those who raised virtually no money. Among nondonors, the magnitude is slightly lower at nine points. With respect to party differences, the effect of fundraising on support among primary voters is apparent among both Republicans and Democrats, but the magnitude is smaller for Republicans (eight versus fifteen points).

Primary voters also favor candidates who receive few endorsements from local leaders and those who receive many endorsements from local leaders to those who raise no money by five and seventeen percentage points, respectively. These values are the same for nondonors as well. The relationships on the other candidate attributes reflect those in chapter 5.

Similar patterns are apparent with candidate favorability evaluations. In the full sample of primary voters, candidates who raised a lot of money are evaluated 0.25 points higher on the 7-point favorability scale than those who raised virtually no money. Among just nondonors, candidates who raised a lot a money are evaluated 0.19 points higher than financial long shots. Those who received many local endorsements are rated 0.32 and 0.26 points higher on the 7-point scale by all primary voters and nondonors, respectively, than those who raised virtually no money. Candidates who received few local endorsements are rated 0.13 points higher than those who raised no money in the full sample and 0.14 points higher among nondonors.

The size of the effect of money is in the same ballpark as endorsements and ideology, but these pieces of information differ in other ways that matter in real-world elections. As noted throughout, fundraising metrics are less subjective, and candidates are far easier to rank on campaign receipts than they are with respect to endorsements or issue positions. The data are also overseen by a government agency, rather than touted by the candidate themselves like endorsements and ideology. In addition, stated support for better fundraisers might be less popular to admit to than stated support for either locally endorsed candidates or ideologically extreme candidates, but we are unable to test this directly with the data here.

In sum, the conjoint survey allowed us to further examine the causal effect of fundraising on support among primary voters. The experimental results are a valuable supplement given the endogeneity concerns that have long plagued the study of money and election outcomes. The findings offer additional evidence that better fundraisers receive more support at the ballot box. Even though primary voters almost certainly do not monitor fundraising reports, a lack of money is nonetheless seen as a clear signal to them as well. Comparing the effect of money in real-world elections with the effect of money in a survey is difficult, but the patterns tell a consistent story across analyses.

Summary

This chapter replicated previous studies of the impact of spending in general elections with data from 1980 to 2022. The growing influence of district partisanship set the stage for an analysis of fundraising in primaries. Across analyses, there is a positive and significant relationship between fundraising and primary victory patterns. The conjoint survey gave more direct causal evidence from the perspective of primary voters. Taken together, the findings provide overwhelming support that money is an asset for candidates who want to win. Voters are unlikely to follow the money like candidates, donors, and journalists do, but the fact that top fundraisers reap rewards at the ballot box informs the use of money as a focal point.

The attention now turns to the institution of Congress, and I examine the implications of fundraising beyond the electoral environment. Party leaders are another key observer of campaign dollars. They set high fundraising benchmarks for prospective and actual candidates, and they monitor who is better and worse at raising money. Party leaders are keenly aware of which officeholders donate the most and least to the party team. Rank-and-file members readily acknowledge—and lament—that fundraising ability is associated with the allocation of institutional and party rewards. Fundraising is likely to be intertwined with policymaking in a variety of ways. The next chapter takes a closer look at this question.

CHAPTER SEVEN

Party Leaders and Office Rewards

In 2017, the nonpartisan organization Issue One released a report on how fundraising matters in Congress. The report draws on interviews with former lawmakers and looks behind the scenes at how party leaders reinforce the emphasis on fundraising. For one, both parties publicly showcase which members are at the top and bottom of the ladder. As former representative Trey Radel (R-FL) explained, "Every year members are expected to raise and pay dues to the committee. And you're reminded of it often. . . . Every time you walk into an NRCC meeting, a giant tally sheet is on prominent display that lists your name and how much you've given—or haven't. It's a huge wall of shame" (Beckel 2017). The Democrats also distribute spreadsheets at their conference meetings that lay out how much members have given to the party (Zeleny 2006).

The report further revealed that fundraising is at least perceived to be rewarded in office. Former lawmakers explained how the selection of members to various positions is based on their ability to raise money. As former representative Cliff Stearns (R-FL) notes, "Committee leadership is decided by who can raise and give the most money—not the most competitive or competent or best speaker or most politically astute, but who is able to raise the mega bucks." Former representative Sue Myrick (R-NC) put it simply: "The people who raised a lot of money got better committee assignments than those who did not" (Beckel 2017). Representative Radel echoed, "When you donate big to the congressional committee, you land on a better committee."

While better fundraisers are seen to be privileged in Congress, there is little systematic evidence of the extent to which fundraising either helps members within the chamber or matters for legislative activity. I draw on Stewart and Woon's (2017) data on committee assignments and Volden and Wiseman's (2014) data on lawmaker effectiveness to uncover how party leaders reward better fundraisers in office. I find that, among newly elected members and incumbents who transfer committees, legislators who contribute more money to the party indeed receive more prestigious committee assignments. I then demonstrate that the policy priorities of top party donors are privileged at various stages of the legislative process where party leaders have significant control.

In the last section of the chapter, I turn to interest groups that direct contributions to lawmakers. I use receipt patterns across six different sectors and Volden and Wiseman's (2014) issue-by-issue effectiveness scores to examine whether lawmakers who receive more money from a particular sector are more effective in that policy area. There is a strong relationship between sector receipts and member effectiveness, which is consistent with prior work highlighting the legislative subsidy that lobbyists provide (Hall and Deardorff 2006). In short, fundraising has clear connections to lawmaking, starting when members enter the chamber and extending to their later policy successes. The results provide ample evidence that fundraising continues to pay dividends after the election.

Fundraising for the Party Team

A variety of factors shape why some members are better fundraisers than others. Previous research has shown that leadership positions, committee assignments, and majority-party status are associated with fundraising totals (e.g., Ansolabehere and Snyder 1998; Berry and Fowler 2018; Cox and Magar 1999; Heberlig et al. 2006; Heberlig and Larson 2012; Kistner 2022; Romer and Snyder 1994). Several recent studies at both the state and federal level find that political action committees (PACs) strategically allocate contributions to members who sit on relevant committees or have influence over the legislative agenda (Berry and Fowler 2018; Fouirnaies 2018; Fouirnaies and Hall 2018; Powell and Grimmer 2016). Here I examine money as an independent variable and ask how party contributions are associated with office rewards and legislative activity.

Party leaders and committee chairs contribute the most to the party's coffers, but even rank-and-file members face increasing demands to support the party team (Powell 2012). Figure 7.1 presents the average contribution to party committees among rank-and-file members over time, broken down by party (in 2021 dollars). Party committees include the national party committees (DNC, RNC) and the congressional campaign committees (DCCC, NRCC). The black line corresponds to Republicans, and the

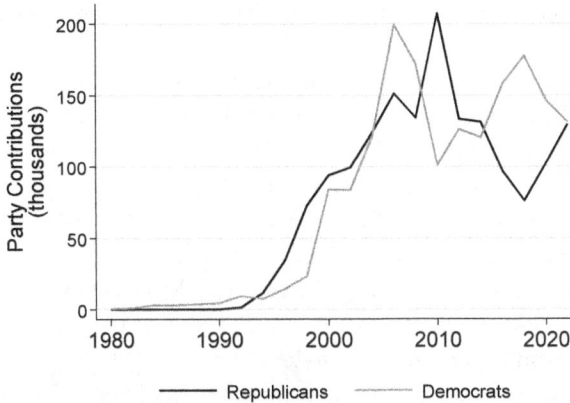

FIGURE 7.1. Party Committee Contributions by Rank-and-File Members

Note: Average amount of contributions to national party committees (DNC, RNC, DCCC, NRCC) by rank-and-file members from 1980 to 2022. The sample excludes party leaders and committee chairs.

gray line corresponds to Democrats. Contributions to party committees were uncommon until the mid-1990s and have increased significantly over time. The amounts also reflect expected party fortunes in different cycles, with Republicans contributing more in 2010 and Democrats doing so in 2006 and 2018.

Party leaders and committee chairs are not included in these totals, and the numbers are still striking. Since 2000, rank-and-file members of Congress have contributed, on average, between $100,000 and $200,000 to the party committees most cycles. Among Democrats, the average is around $150,000 in recent elections, though some contribute more than others. For example, in the cohort of newly elected Democrats in 2018, Representatives Madeleine Dean (PA), Veronica Escobar (TX), Sylvia Garcia (TX), Debra Haaland (NM), and Jennifer Wexton (VA) were at the top of the class, with each contributing more than $200,000 to the party in the 2019–20 cycle.

Among Republicans, average party donations by rank-and-file members have been above $100,000 in most years since 2000, but the amount decreased in a couple of recent cycles, and most notably in the 2017–18 cycle. Similar variation is apparent on the Republican side, with some members contributing hundreds of thousands of dollars and others far less. Among Republicans newly elected in 2018, Kelly Armstrong (ND) and Greg Pence (IN) led the pack, donating $300,000 and $200,000, respectively, to the NRCC in the 2019–20 cycle. It is common for both Republicans and Democrats to give to their state and even local party committees as well, but the main concern here is the allocation of institutional rewards in Congress.

To be sure, both parties have a contingent of members who do not contribute to the national party committees. For some, it is more an act of protest. Alexandria Ocasio-Cortez's (NY) high-profile decision not to pay party dues during her first two terms in office is a good example. Nor did the other members of "The Squad" steer funds to the national party. On the Republican side, several party rabble-rousers, including Louie Gohmert (TX), Paul Gosar (AZ), Jim Jordan (OH), Mo Brooks (AL), and Tom Massie (KY), did not contribute to the party in recent cycles. Unsurprisingly, incumbents who lose are also less likely to contribute — around half did so — but their strategic considerations are likely perceived differently by party leaders.

Yet most members now direct some money from their campaign committees to the national party. Republicans started contributing to the party committees in 1994. In the 1993–94 cycle, 72 percent of Republican members contributed to the national party, a dramatic surge from the 10 percent in the 1991–92 cycle. By comparison, rates of party giving have been above 80 percent for Democrats since the 1990s. In the post-2000 era, 83 percent of both Republicans and Democrats donated some money to their national party committee. Since 2010, Republican rates of giving declined to 76 percent and reached a low of 58 percent in 2018, but the majority of rank-and-file Democrats and Republicans contribute to the party committees.

The party committees play a far greater role in the dissemination and redistribution of campaign funds today. Whereas individual members of Congress used to steer money to their colleagues' committees (and some still do), most members now route funds to the party. Both parties have a formal dues structure, with mechanisms in place to shame those who fail to pay up. These trends are consistent with the centralization of power and the increased control that party leaders have in Congress (Curry 2015). The analyses below leverage variation in party contributions to examine the institutional returns to officeholders, starting with whether those who donate more to the party team receive better positions in the chamber.

Allocation of Committee Assignments

Former and current members have lamented that fundraising is the pathway to better positions in office. As those quoted above explain, the central concern is that other attributes should decide who advances in the party and chamber, such as issue expertise and competence. One challenge of studying the allocation of institutional rewards is that much of the action is unobservable, and we lack data on member preferences and their requests. As a result, instead of using the full sample of elected lawmakers, I instead focus on two subsamples: newly elected members and incumbents who transfer committees. Both analyses use Stewart and Woon's (2017) data on committee assignments that extend from the 103rd to the 115th Congress (1993–2019).[1] Party contributions are measured in relation to similarly situated same-party colleagues, and party leaders and committee chairs are excluded from the analyses.[2]

I first examine whether newly elected members who contributed more money to the party prior to their election receive better committee assignments in their first term. The dependent variable is whether they received a position on one of the high prestige or power committees. Power committees include Appropriations, Budget, Energy and Commerce, and Ways and Means (e.g., Grimmer and Powell 2013).[3] I also constructed a measure of the member's committee portfolio value by summing their Grosewart committee scores (Groseclose and Stewart 1998).

The main independent variable is party contributions. I use binary measures of whether the candidate transferred money to the party prior to their election and whether the candidate was in the top 20 percent of party contributors among same-party newly elected members. I include a variable for whether the member held elected office previously to capture prior experience. Interestingly, the bivariate relationship is not significant: 21 percent of experienced candidates received a prestigious committee assignment versus 17 percent of inexperienced candidates. In addition, I account for whether they won in a safe district or open seat, ideology, gender, and party. Congress fixed effects are included in all models.

The second sample is limited to reelected incumbents who transferred to a new committee. Transfers are a more challenging subset of lawmakers. For one, not all members want to transfer, particularly more senior members, and we unfortunately do not have data on transfer preferences. It is also possible that not all first-term members want to sit on a power committee, but the assumption is that power committees are, in general, more highly coveted positions. The analysis nonetheless examines whether, at least among members who transfer, those who gave more money to the party in the previous election cycle are transferred to more prestigious committees. The sample is limited to transferring incumbents who were

TABLE 7.1 **Party Contributions and Committee Assignments, Newly Elected Members**

	(1)	(2)	(3)	(4)
	Power Committee	Power Committee	Portfolio Score	Portfolio Score
Transferred Money to Party	0.07†		0.13*	
	(0.04)		(0.06)	
Top 20 Percent of Party Donors		0.07†		0.14*
		(0.04)		(0.06)
Experienced Candidate	0.06*	0.06*	0.05	0.06
	(0.03)	(0.03)	(0.05)	(0.05)
Open Seat	−0.03	−0.03	−0.13*	−0.13*
	(0.03)	(0.03)	(0.05)	(0.05)
Safe District	0.03	0.03	−0.05	−0.05
	(0.03)	(0.03)	(0.05)	(0.05)
Moderate	−0.06	−0.06	0.14†	0.14†
	(0.05)	(0.05)	(0.08)	(0.08)
Woman	−0.04	−0.03	0.05	0.05
	(0.04)	(0.04)	(0.06)	(0.06)
Republican	0.08*	0.08*	0.08	0.07
	(0.03)	(0.03)	(0.05)	(0.05)
Constant	0.06	0.06	−0.07	−0.07
	(0.06)	(0.06)	(0.09)	(0.09)
Observations	835	835	835	835
R^2	0.04	0.04	0.07	0.07

Note: Results are from OLS regressions from 1993 to 2019, with Congress fixed effects. The dependent variable in models 1 and 2 is whether the MC received a prestigious committee assignment (Appropriations, Budget, Energy and Commerce, Ways and Means). The dependent variable in models 3 and 4 is the member's committee portfolio score. †$p < 0.10$, *$p < 0.05$, **$p < 0.01$.

not party leaders or committee or subcommittee chairs in the prior session, as the goal is to compare similarly situated members.

For the transferring incumbents, party contributions are calculated by year relative to their same-party colleagues who are not party leaders or committee chairs. I include a binary variable of whether the member was in the top 20 percent of party donors. Another continuous variable captures relative contribution size, with positive values indicating that the member gave more than the average rank-and-file member, and negative values indicating that they gave less. I account for seniority because more senior members who transfer committees may have different objectives and because party leaders may consider future career prospects in the allocation of committee assignments.

The results for the newly elected members are shown in table 7.1. The relationships are positive and significant across models. The patterns provide support for the expectation that leaders reward members who contribute to the party team. Incoming members who gave money to the party prior to their election are more likely to be appointed to a power committee in their first term in office. The probability of receiving a prestigious committee assignment is 33 percent for newly elected members in the top 20 percent of party donors, compared to 26 percent for other incoming members. Models 3 and 4 also indicate that newly elected members who donated to the party before they were elected have higher committee portfolio values.

Similar patterns are apparent among transferring members (table 7.2). Among members who transferred to a different committee, those who contributed more money to the party in the previous legislative session relative to their colleagues are more likely to be transferred to a power committee than those who gave less (models 1 and 2). Among transferring members, the probability that those in the top 20 percent of party donors transferred to a prestigious committee is 55 percent, compared to 41 percent of not top party donors. Models 3 and 4 show that those who

TABLE 7.2 **Party Contributions and Committee Assignments, Transferring Incumbents**

	(1)	(2)	(3)	(4)
	Power Committee	Power Committee	Portfolio Score	Portfolio Score
Top 20 Percent of Party Donors	0.14*		0.47**	
	(0.06)		(0.12)	
Relative Party Contribution		0.01*		0.01**
		(0.00)		(0.01)
Safe District	−0.04	−0.05	−0.07	−0.08
	(0.04)	(0.04)	(0.08)	(0.08)
Seniority	−0.02*	−0.02*	−0.04*	−0.04*
	(0.01)	(0.01)	(0.02)	(0.02)
Moderate	−0.11	−0.11†	−0.04	−0.05
	(0.07)	(0.07)	(0.14)	(0.14)
Woman	−0.04	−0.06	−0.09	−0.12
	(0.05)	(0.05)	(0.11)	(0.11)
Republican	−0.01	−0.00	0.13	0.14
	(0.05)	(0.05)	(0.09)	(0.09)
Constant	0.72**	0.74**	0.74**	0.82**
	(0.08)	(0.08)	(0.16)	(0.16)
Observations	653	653	653	653
R^2	0.07	0.07	0.07	0.06

Note: Results are from OLS regressions from 1993 to 2019, with Congress fixed effects. The dependent variable in models 1 and 2 is whether the MC received a prestigious committee assignment (Appropriations, Budget, Energy and Commerce, Ways and Means). The dependent variable in models 3 and 4 is the member's committee portfolio score. †$p < 0.10$, *$p < 0.05$, **$p < 0.01$.

steer more contributions to the party have higher committee portfolio values as well.

The results for newly elected members and transferring incumbents are broken down by party in the appendix. Among newly elected members, the relationships are much stronger for Republicans, and in fact, Republicans are driving the results. Some of the partisan difference among new members may be related to the committee term limits on the Republican side. Among transferring incumbents, the relationships are instead stronger in the Democratic sample. Even so, the fact that most rank-and-file members direct some campaign funds to the national party committees reflects a belief that party contributions matter on both sides of the aisle.

Giving heaps of money to the party does not always lead to better committee assignments, but it is one strategy members pursue. And for some, it pays off. In the 112th Congress (2011–12), Representative Lynn Jenkins (R-KS) received a coveted position on the Ways and Means Committee in her second term in office. In the prior election cycle (2009–10), she transferred $230,000 to the Republican Party, significantly more than the $170,000 average from her rank-and-file colleagues. Similarly, Representatives Terri Sewell (D-AL) and Suzan DelBene (D-WA) were assigned to Ways and Means in the 115th Congress (2017–18). Sewell transferred $260,000 to the Democratic Party in the prior cycle, and DelBene transferred nearly $250,000, far surpassing the $140,000 rank-and-file average (dollar amounts not adjusted here).

The trajectories of several newly elected members are notable too. For example, in 2010, Republican candidates Steve Womack (AL) and Tom Reed (NY) each transferred $50,000 to the NRCC prior to their election. Womack and Reed received spots on the prestigious Appropriations and Ways and Means Committees, respectively, in their first terms. Current Democratic leader Hakeem Jeffries (NY) transferred $100,000 to the DCCC in his first run for Congress in 2012, and he received a desirable position on the Budget Committee in his first term in office. Others wait a little longer. Debbie Wasserman Schultz (D-NY) first ran in 2004 and donated $100,000 to the DCCC in that cycle. She then contributed $200,000 to the party in her first term and was transferred to Appropriations in her second term.

It is impossible to know if these members would have received these positions anyway. The effect of party contributions on the allocation of committee assignments is hard to nail down, and a variety of factors certainly play a role in the selection of lawmakers to different positions. But at least among first-term members and transferring incumbents, those who contribute more to the party team are more likely to reap rewards in Congress. Better party fundraisers receive better committee assignments, on average. The results are consistent with the argument that party leaders who allocate committee assignments are mindful of donations, and they echo the views in the report detailed at the outset of the chapter. The next section turns to policy and delves into the association between fundraising and legislative activity.

Fundraising and Legislative Activity

There is a widespread belief that fundraising takes time and energy away from policy activities that lawmakers should instead devote their attention to. It is certainly plausible that members who spend more time dialing for dollars have less time to spend on legislating. However, the reliance on dollars as a focal point may instead mean that fundraising aids in legislative productivity. Party leaders, members, and interest groups know who raises a lot of money and who contributes to the party team. Better fundraisers may have more political capital and be better situated to advance their policies as a result. Indeed, a core implication of access-oriented theories is that contributions influence members' involvement in the legislative process (Hall and Wayman 1990).

Party leaders have immense control over the agenda and determine the trajectory of lawmakers' bills (e.g., Cox and McCubbins 2005; Curry 2015). As the interviews detailed, leaders place a large premium on fundraising and are likely to reward those who provide resources to the party team. Additionally, members can use their funds to help the reelection bids of copartisans and build stronger relationships with their colleagues. There are a variety of pathways through which fundraising could result in not only better committee assignments but also greater legislative productivity. If fundraising is rewarded by influential political players, dollars might be expected to yield certain policy benefits as well. I explore only a couple of observable implications here.

I draw on Volden and Wiseman's (2014) legislative effectiveness scores (LES) to examine how and where high party contributors may be aided in the legislative process. As noted previously, the scores are a comprehensive measure combining fifteen metrics of the bills each member sponsors, how far they move through the lawmaking process, and their substantive significance. The LES data are helpful for uncovering whether party leaders might exert their influence. The dataset includes measures of how lawmakers' bills fare at five stages in the legislative process: total bills sponsored, total bills that received action in committee, total bills that received action beyond committee, total bills that passed the House, and total bills that became law.

The main independent variable is a binary variable of whether the member was in the top 20 percent of party contributors relative to their rank-and-file colleagues. All models account for the member's effectiveness score in the previous session and their total receipts raised in the previous election due to the likely relationship with later fundraising patterns. I use the same control variables as Volden and Wiseman (2014, 44), including seniority, state legislative experience, experience in a professionalized state legislature, majority-party status, power committee, distance from the chamber median, race, gender, congressional delegation size, previous vote share, and vote share squared. The sample excludes party leaders and committee and subcommittee chairs.

The relationships are not statistically significant across this four-decade period, which is consistent with the argument that money has become more salient over time. However, different patterns emerge in more recent years. This subset of results is shown in table 7.3. The models are limited to the 112th to the 117th Congresses (2011–2023), when fundraising has reached record highs and become an increasingly relevant metric. Separate models are provided for the five stages of the legislative process discussed above, ranging from bill sponsorship activity to bill passage.

Rank-and-file members who are top party contributors do not sponsor more bills on average (model 1). But the results in models 2 and 3 indicate that top party contributors have more bills that receive action in committee and beyond. Perhaps most importantly, top party contributors also have a greater number of bills that pass the House chamber and even become law (models 4 and 5). At least with these metrics, there is little evidence that fundraising hurts members' legislative efforts. To the contrary, they seem to fare better in some aspects of lawmaking, particularly those overseen by House leadership. Party leaders have a direct hand in which legislation is able to advance in the policymaking process.

Additional analyses of first-term members (not shown) demonstrate that party contributions are not associated with the advancement of legislation among newly elected members like they are in the full sample of lawmakers. None of the relationships reach conventional levels of significance.

TABLE 7.3 **Party Contributions and Legislative Activity (2011–2023)**

	(1)	(2)	(3)	(4)	(5)
	Bills Sponsored	Action In Committee	Beyond Committee	Passed House	Became Law
Top 20 Percent of Party Donors	−0.26	0.24*	0.18†	0.21*	0.08*
	(0.72)	(0.10)	(0.10)	(0.09)	(0.04)
Lagged Effectiveness Score	3.72**	0.67**	0.72**	0.56**	0.16**
	(0.66)	(0.10)	(0.11)	(0.08)	(0.03)
Lagged Receipts	0.22	−0.04	−0.01	−0.02	−0.02†
	(0.25)	(0.03)	(0.03)	(0.02)	(0.01)
Seniority	−0.04	−0.00	−0.00	−0.00	0.01
	(0.14)	(0.02)	(0.01)	(0.01)	(0.01)
State Legislative Experience	1.00	0.13	0.11	0.01	0.07
	(1.26)	(0.17)	(0.16)	(0.13)	(0.07)
Experience × Legislative Prof.	−1.95	−0.10	−0.15	−0.07	−0.04
	(3.60)	(0.45)	(0.42)	(0.34)	(0.18)
Majority Party	5.18**	0.70**	0.75**	0.34*	0.00
	(1.66)	(0.21)	(0.20)	(0.17)	(0.09)
Power Committee	−1.71†	−0.57**	−0.50**	−0.36**	−0.11*
	(0.89)	(0.12)	(0.10)	(0.08)	(0.04)
Distance from Median	4.09	−1.58**	−1.39**	−1.20**	−0.42**
	(3.80)	(0.40)	(0.36)	(0.31)	(0.16)
Female	0.87	−0.06	0.10	0.09	0.01
	(1.06)	(0.11)	(0.11)	(0.09)	(0.05)
African American	−1.14	0.10	0.17	0.23	0.04
	(1.50)	(0.17)	(0.17)	(0.15)	(0.06)
Latino	−2.68†	0.21	0.04	0.01	0.03
	(1.56)	(0.18)	(0.17)	(0.14)	(0.09)
Size of Congressional Delegation	0.04	0.00	0.00	0.00	0.00
	(0.03)	(0.00)	(0.00)	(0.00)	(0.00)
Vote Share	−0.16	−0.12**	−0.11**	−0.08*	−0.04**
	(0.28)	(0.04)	(0.04)	(0.03)	(0.01)
Vote Share Squared	0.00	0.00**	0.00**	0.00*	0.00**
	(0.00)	(0.00)	(0.00)	(0.00)	(0.00)
Constant	15.06	5.58**	4.92**	3.95**	1.73**
	(10.50)	(1.48)	(1.33)	(1.09)	(0.53)
Observations	1,409	1,409	1,409	1,409	1,409
R^2	0.20	0.32	0.35	0.29	0.10

Note: Results are from OLS regressions from 2011 to 2023, with Congress fixed effects. Standard errors are clustered by member. The sample excludes party leaders and committee chairs. $†p < 0.10$, $*p < 0.05$, $**p < 0.01$.

It takes time and experience to develop a legislative reputation, and first-term members who demonstrated an ability to fundraise perhaps do not yet have the institutional knowledge needed to move their bills through the chamber. For whatever reason, it appears that these particular legislative benefits of contributing to the party team crystallize later in the member's tenure.

Fundraising and Effectiveness by Sector

Party leaders who set the agenda are not the only actors who have a hand in whether members can achieve their policy goals. Interest groups are also mindful of the needs and incentives of lawmakers. Lobbyists provide lawmakers with policy information, legislative labor, and, of course, money. Contributions influence members' involvement in the legislative process (Hall and Wayman 1990), with lawmakers more active in areas where they receive a legislative subsidy (Hall and Deardorff 2006). Thus, while party contributions come with one set of policy rewards, members may additionally benefit from the involvement that accompanies interest group donations.

This final section examines whether members who receive more money from a sector are more effective in that policy area. The analyses draw on issue-by-issue legislative effectiveness scores (ILES) from Volden and Wiseman (2014) and data on contributions by sector from OpenSecrets (2022).[4] The sector data for both contributions and issue effectiveness span six different policy areas: agriculture, defense, energy, health, labor, and transportation. The time period extends from 1990 to 2022. Party leaders and committee chairs are again excluded from the analyses to allow for comparisons of similarly situated rank-and-file members. The number of observations ranges from 1,115 to 1,588 by Congress, for a total of approximately 23,500 observations.[5]

The analyses follow the same format as above. The dependent variable is the member's issue-by-issue legislative effectiveness score (agriculture, defense, etc.). The main independent variable is the total contributions received from the respective sector (agriculture, defense, etc.). Contributions from each sector are measured in $10,000s and in logged values (amounts are in 2021 dollars). One set of models includes the same control variables as above; another set includes member fixed effects.

The results are presented in table 7.4. Across models, those who receive more money from a respective sector have higher issue effectiveness scores. The relationship is positive and significant with total sector receipts and logged sector receipts (models 1 and 2) and when member fixed effects are included (models 3 and 4). A one standard deviation increase in total sector receipts is associated with a 0.4 increase in the member's respective issue effectiveness score (from 0.8 to 1.2). When predicted values are calculated from the model with member fixed effects (model 3), a

TABLE 7.4 **Sector Fundraising and Issue Effectiveness**

	(1)	(2)	(3)	(4)
	Total Receipts	Logged Receipts	Total Receipts	Logged Receipts
Sector Receipts (in $10,000s)	0.03**		0.04**	
	(0.00)		(0.01)	
Logged Sector Receipts		0.16**		0.17**
		(0.02)		(0.02)
Lagged Effectiveness Score	0.17**	0.18**	0.09	0.09
	(0.03)	(0.04)	(0.05)	(0.05)
Seniority	0.02**	0.03**	0.02	0.05*
	(0.01)	(0.01)	(0.02)	(0.02)
State Legislative Experience	–0.08	–0.09		
	(0.06)	(0.07)		
Experience × Legislative Prof.	0.01	0.03		
	(0.16)	(0.16)		
Majority Party	0.37**	0.37**	0.21	0.09
	(0.08)	(0.08)	(0.28)	(0.29)
Power Committee	–0.33**	–0.33**	–0.26**	–0.25**
	(0.05)	(0.05)	(0.08)	(0.08)
Distance from Median	–0.30*	–0.32*	–0.78	–1.07
	(0.15)	(0.15)	(0.77)	(0.79)
Female	0.18**	0.18**		
	(0.06)	(0.06)		
African American	–0.01	–0.03		
	(0.07)	(0.07)		
Latino	–0.02	–0.03		
	(0.09)	(0.10)		
Size of Congressional Delegation	–0.00	–0.00	0.00	0.01
	(0.00)	(0.00)	(0.02)	(0.02)
Vote Share	0.02	0.01	–0.01	–0.01
	(0.02)	(0.02)	(0.03)	(0.03)
Vote Share Squared	–0.00	–0.00	0.00	0.00
	(0.00)	(0.00)	(0.00)	(0.00)
Constant	–0.33	–1.60*	0.60	–1.17
	(0.58)	(0.63)	(1.16)	(1.15)
Observations	23,482	23,482	23,482	23,482
R^2	0.04	0.03	0.09	0.08
Member FE	No	No	Yes	Yes

Note: Results are from OLS regressions from 1990 to 2022, with Congress fixed effects. Standard errors are clustered by member. The sample excludes party leaders and committee chairs. The dependent variable is the lawmaker's issue-by-issue legislative effectiveness score. Models 3 and 4 include member fixed effects. $\dagger p < 0.10$, $*p < 0.05$, $**p < 0.01$.

similar shift is associated with a 0.4 increase in the legislator's issue effectiveness score as well (from 0.8 to 1.2). The results on the control variables are consistent with those in Volden and Wiseman (2014).

In addition, I explore differences in the relationship between sector contributions and issue effectiveness across sectors to see whether some

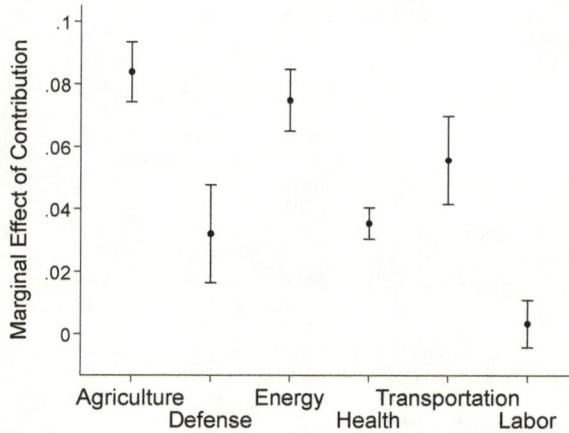

FIGURE 7.2. Marginal Effect of Sector Contributions on Issue Effectiveness Scores, across Sectors

Note: Values are calculated from model 3 in table 7.4, with sector receipts interacted with indicator variables for each sector.

sectors get more bang for their buck. I use indicator variables for each sector, and the main interest is the interaction between sector contributions and issue effectiveness scores. For ease of interpretation, the marginal effect of sector contributions on issue-by-issue effectiveness scores is plotted across the six sectors in figure 7.2. Predicted values are calculated from a model similar to model 3 in table 7.4, with member fixed effects and the same control variables, but where sector receipts are interacted with each sector.

Clear variation emerges across sectors. First, contributions from the agriculture and energy sectors appear to reap the largest policy returns. Contributions from the labor sector receive the lowest returns. The marginal effect of contributions on ILES is the smallest and not statistically different from zero for the labor sector. Across the defense, health, and transportation sectors, the marginal effect of contributions on issue effectiveness is positive and significant, though the magnitude differs slightly across sectors.[6] These data do not allow us to untangle whether issue-by-issue legislative effectiveness precedes or follows sector contributions, but the consistent association across nearly all sectors is notable.

The normative implications of these findings are mixed. On the one hand, effective lawmakers are critical for the functioning of Congress, especially in an era where partisan gridlock often hinders collaboration and stymies legislative action. And the results are consistent with prior work noting that lobbyists provide a legislative subsidy to lawmakers in their area of expertise (Hall and Deardorff 2006). At the same time, the core concern around the influence of contributions on legislator activity is that it leads to biased political outcomes. Future research should devote more attention to the association between sector contributions and issue effectiveness in light of the consequences for representational inequalities.

Summary

The previous chapters detailed how candidates, donors, journalists, and even voters use money as a focal point. This chapter demonstrated how money remains relevant after the election. Party leaders who allocate committee assignments and set the legislative agenda reward those who contribute to the party team in myriad ways. Top party donors are more likely to receive prestigious committee assignments, and their legislation fares better at key stages in the policymaking process. Members also benefit beyond the institutional rewards doled out by party leaders. Those who receive more donations from interest groups are more effective, on average, in specific policy areas. The office rewards of fundraising offer additional insight into why candidates and officeholders dial for more dollars even as more lawmakers are elected from safe seats.

The final empirical chapter steps back and illustrates what else can be gleaned from the use of fundraising as a focal point. The chapter takes a broader look at how disparities in fundraising matter for the quality of electoral competition. Fundraising is all or nothing in the vast majority of races, with winners faring dramatically better in the money chase. The attention, momentum, and perceived strength directed toward those at the top invites new questions about how resource-based measures of competition compare with those based on vote totals. Money provides a different vantage point into the nature of electoral competition. Resource disparities allow for further exploration of how equitable the *process* of running for office is in contemporary American elections.

CHAPTER EIGHT

Competition through a Fundraising Lens

In their final ratings of the 2020 cycle, the Cook Political Report rated twenty-seven House seats, or 6 percent of the lower chamber, as toss-ups where either party had a good chance of winning. In these races, the general election winner won with an average of 53 percent of the vote, and only three—French Hill (AR-2), Michelle Fischbach (MN-7), and John Katko (NY-24)—received more than 55 percent. An additional sixty-two seats were categorized as either competitive but leaning to one party or not competitive but had the potential to be. Forty, or about two-thirds, of these sixty-two winners received less than 55 percent of the vote.[1] A full 346, or 80 percent, of general elections were not expected to be competitive, and only eleven of these winners, or 3 percent, won with less than 55 percent of the vote.[2]

In 2020, a total of seventy-six winners, or 17 percent of House members, were elected with less than 55 percent of the vote. Low levels of general election competition are not new. The number of narrowly elected winners bottomed out in 2004, when only twenty-two representatives received less than 55 percent of the vote. Some observers have suggested that primaries offer another avenue for competition to thrive in the absence of close general elections. A recent article in the *Atlantic* fittingly titled "When Your Vote Doesn't Matter, Try Switching Ballots" encouraged voters whose party is sure to lose in November to participate in the opposite-party primary and help nominate less extreme choices (Robinson and Trende 2022). Scholars have also been optimistic about how primaries can inject competition into congressional elections (Hirano and Snyder 2019).

We care about electoral competition because it is one of the hallmarks of democratic government (Dahl 1956, 1971; Key 1949; Schlesinger 1966; Schumpeter 1942). The competitive struggle for the people's vote is so central to our understanding of democracy that the makeup of the ballot and the outcomes of elections have, mostly implicitly, come to dominate our depictions of the state of competition. Political scientists have evaluated close elections almost exclusively through vote totals at the end of the race. But how competitive the *process* is—whether candidates have access to resources—matters too. Money provides a window into how disparities in votes may mask even larger disparities in the process. In other words, our already uncompetitive elections may look even more uncompetitive through the lens of fundraising.

The all-or-nothing fundraising noted in chapter 2 means that advantage and disadvantage continue to compound during the cycle. Candidates at the top benefit from the get-go, while those at the bottom are priced out of services and unable to find campaign support. One 2022 candidate said, "I interviewed consultants out of Washington, and it's a $15,000 down payment before they'll even talk to you." Consultant services are "an à la carte kind of thing, where if you want somebody to do your social media, it's [this]. If you want somebody to do postcards and mail out, it's this. If you want somebody to do emails, it's this." She continued, "You have to pay to play, and we're talking hundreds of thousands of dollars. I've been told I would need five hundred thousand to a million dollars to have a chance in hell of winning this campaign, and it's not possible."

The previous chapters made the case that money matters in elections because it serves as a focal point for influential political actors and observers. A strong fundraising performance is beneficial in a variety of ways long before and well after the election. This chapter steps back and considers the implications for how level the playing field is. I look at fundraising disparities within races and ask how vote totals map onto the resources candidates have to arrive at those totals. Money provides a different vantage point to assess close electoral contests. While vote totals are the most commonly used metric of competition, money offers insights into how candidate war chests stack up during the campaign cycle.

The main question in this chapter is how measures of competition based on vote totals differ from those based on money. Some attention is given to general elections, but the focus is on primaries. I leverage preprimary receipts in seventeen thousand House primaries from 1980 to 2022 to construct new measures of competition with fundraising. The quality of competition looks markedly worse through the lens of resources than with vote shares. Fewer races are competitive, and the number of candidates declines. Open-seat primaries are often held up as bright spots, but the difference between vote share and fundraising measures is largest in these races. The disparity between the two measures is driven largely by financial long shots who outperform their receipt share at the ballot box.

Measuring Competition

Scholars have long studied the quality of electoral competition. For the past few decades, academics have raised concerns about the decline in close general elections.[3] The most commonly used measure is the number of contests won with 55 or 60 percent of the vote.[4] A 60 percent threshold perhaps used to be more appropriate when voters split their tickets for Republicans and Democrats. Today, however, a twenty-point general election margin is not seen as particularly close. With a narrower threshold, only 13 percent of general election winners won with less than 55 percent of the vote from 1980 to 2022.[5] And even a ten-point margin is not all that close when voters support candidates of their party around 90 percent of the time.

The number of competitive general elections is certainly much lower in the contemporary era than it was in the 1950s and 1960s. The lows in close outcomes in the early 2000s were followed by an increase in the 2010s and 2020s, but the share of competitive general elections is not especially high with any of these metrics. Across this period, 72 percent of general election winners won by at least twenty points; 87 percent won by at least ten points. The key difference today is that more of these winners are elected from safe partisan districts.[6] From 2012 to 2022, nearly 90 percent of those who won by at least twenty points were elected from safe districts, compared to 45 percent of those who won by at least twenty points from 1980 to 1988.[7]

The increase in lawmakers from safe districts has amplified the importance of primaries and sparked new interest in the quality of primary competition. Hirano and Snyder (2019) provide the most comprehensive study of primaries to date. They use four measures of competition: the percentage of primaries that were contested; the percentage where the winner received less than 57.5 percent of the total votes; the number of candidates in the race; and the votes cast for all losing candidates as a percentage of the total votes (Hirano and Snyder 2019, 39). They find that, across primaries from 1900 to 2016, the level of competition is highest in open-seat races and in constituencies with a partisan advantage. The authors have a positive view of primaries and conclude that primaries promote competition in lopsided partisan districts.

As the previous chapters demonstrated, multiple political actors use money as a signal of viability and strength. Fundraising provides a valuable window into the resources that candidates have to arrive at their respective vote totals. The strong association between money and election outcomes (detailed in chapter 6) adds validity to fundraising measures of competition, yet money and votes also differ in small but systematic ways that bear on our understanding of close elections. Figure 8.1 shows binned scatter plots of the relationship between primary receipt share and vote share for more than thirty-five thousand US House candidates across this four-decade period. The top graph includes all candidates, and the bottom graph excludes unopposed candidates.

Candidates who raise less than 10 percent of receipts still receive 15 percent of the vote, on average.[8] Indeed, the relationship between money and votes is weakest for those who are most likely to lose.[9] The correlation between receipt share and vote share among those who raise less than 10 percent of receipts is 0.12, compared to 0.77 for opposed candidates who raise more than 10 percent.[10] Moreover, long shots who raise little to no money make up a significant share of primary contenders: 44 percent of nonincumbents on the ballot raise less than 10 percent of primary receipts, and 27 percent did not file a report with the FEC, indicating that they raised less than $5,000.[11] Because long shots receive more votes than they do money, vote share measures are expected to result in a more optimistic view of competition than fundraising measures.

In addition, vote share measures are likely to differ more from fundraising measures in open-seat races, or the best-case scenarios of competition. Open seats attract the most candidates, but more amateurs run in these contests as well (Canon 1993). In open-seat primaries in safe districts, the average number of candidates who raise less than 10 percent of receipts is 2.6, compared to 0.5 in other primaries, and the share of candidates raising less than 10 percent of receipts is 39 and 17 percent, respectively. The top two candidates are more evenly matched than in other primaries, but the average difference between the top two vote-getters in contested safe open-seat primaries is twenty points, compared to twenty-nine points for the top two fundraisers.[12] The implication that vote share measures are

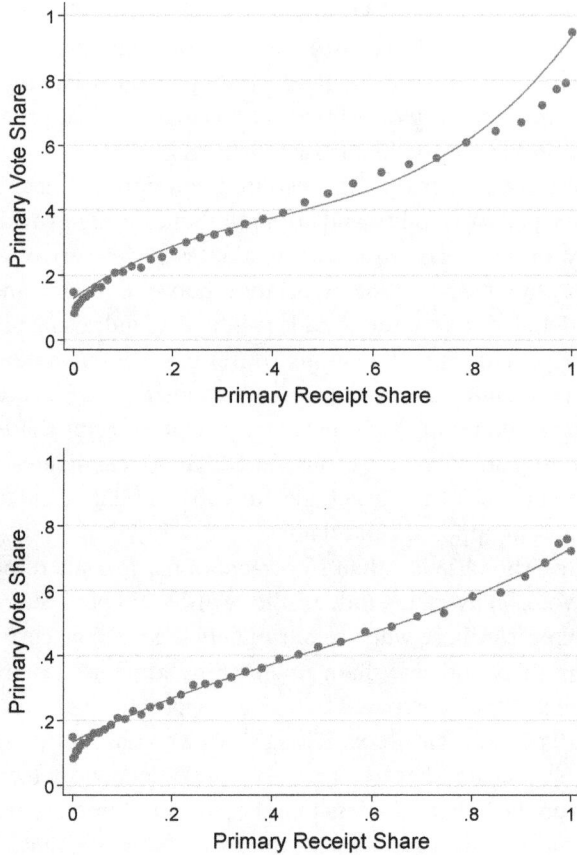

FIGURE 8.1. Relationship between Primary Receipt Share and Vote Share
All candidates (*top*), opposed candidates (*bottom*)

Note: Binned scatter plots of the relationship between primary receipt share and vote share for US House candidates from 1980 to 2022. The bottom graph excludes unopposed candidates.

most likely to diverge from fundraising measures in open seats is important because much of the optimism around primaries is driven by these races (Hirano and Snyder 2019).

I construct new measures of competition based on preelection fundraising totals. First, I create a binary measure of whether the race was competitive that considers the fundraising advantage of those at the top: whether the top fundraiser raised less than 57.5 percent of all preprimary receipts and whether the top fundraiser's share of receipts was within twenty points of the second-highest fundraiser.[13] I use both measures because, unlike in general elections with two candidates, a 55 or 60 percent threshold in primary elections does not necessarily indicate a narrow fundraising or victory margin since money and votes can be divided among more than two candidates.[14] Furthermore, winners are more likely to win with less than 57.5 percent of the vote but still prevail by a wide margin as the number of long shots increases.

Second, I use a weighted measure of the number of candidates in the race based on preprimary receipts. It is similar to Laakso and Taagepera's (1979) measure of the effective number of parties, where each party is weighted by being squared (see also Taagepera and Shugart 1993).[15] The advantage of using the effective number of parties is that it differentiates significant parties from less significant ones. I build on this approach and generate a fundraising-based measure of the effective number of candidates:

$$N_c = \frac{\left(\sum\limits_{i=1}^{n} f_{irt}\right)^2}{\sum\limits_{i=1}^{n} f_{irt}^2},$$

where f_{irt} is the amount of money raised by candidate i in race r at time t.[16] In races where campaign receipts are evenly distributed among candidates, the effective number of candidates is the same as the number of candidates on the ballot. In races where one candidate raises a large majority of receipts, the effective number of candidates is slightly larger than one. Because weighted values are almost always lower than unweighted values, our concern is where these values differ the most.

Shifting to the Race Level

The analyses follow the same structure as those in Hirano and Snyder (2019). Competition is measured at the race level, and primaries are divided into several types based on seat type and partisan leaning. I use the same dataset of House candidates from 1980 to 2022, and I draw on fundraising totals to measure competition and the number of candidates. The unit of analysis is the party primary by district and year. Only Republican and Democratic primaries are considered here.[17] There are 17,500 observations, but the number decreases to 17,100 with the fundraising measures due to missing values on preprimary receipts in about 2 percent of races.

The analyses focus on two factors that are known to affect primary competition: seat type and district partisanship. The primary is an open seat if no incumbent is in the race, incumbent-contested if an incumbent is in the primary, and challenger-party if an incumbent is in the opposite party primary. Like Hirano and Snyder (2019), partisan balance is coded as hopeless if the party received less than 42.5 percent of the district vote in the current or previous presidential election, competitive if the party received between 42.5 and 57.5 percent, and safe if the party received more than 57.5 percent.[18] I follow their classification of primary races into seven types: (i) safe open-seat primaries; (ii) safe incumbent-contested primaries; (iii) competitive open-seat primaries; (iv) competitive challenger-party primaries; (v) competitive incumbent-contested primaries; (vi) hopeless open-seat primaries; and (vii) hopeless challenger-party primaries.[19]

The first set of dependent variables are four binary indicators of whether the primary is competitive. The vote share measures are whether the winner received less than 57.5 percent of the vote and whether the winner's victory margin was within twenty points of the second-highest vote-getter.[20] The fundraising measures are whether the top fundraiser raised less than 57.5 percent of preprimary receipts and whether the top fundraiser's margin was within twenty points of the second-highest fundraiser.

The second set of dependent variables are three measures of the number of candidates in the race: the total number of candidates on the ballot, the effective number of candidates based on vote shares, and the effective number of candidates based on receipts. I also calculate the difference between the respective vote share and fundraising measures to examine where the two measures differ the most. Descriptive statistics of the competitive primary variables and distributions of the number of candidates variables are provided in Thomsen (2023).

Each model includes a dummy variable for open-seat and challenger-party primaries, with incumbent-contested races as the baseline. To measure the partisan tilt of the district, I include indicators for safe and competitive districts, with hopeless districts as the baseline. Seat type is interacted with party balance to analyze how competition varies across primary types. While fully self-funded candidates are rare, many candidates loan money to their campaigns. In other analyses, I exclude loans from the preprimary totals, and the results remain the same. I follow Hirano and Snyder's (2019) focus on seat type and district partisanship due to the overwhelming impact of these variables on competition, but all of the models include district and year fixed effects as well.

Descriptive Trends over Time

Before turning to the results, I plot the vote share and fundraising measures over time. The first set of graphs in figure 8.2 presents the percentage of primaries where the top vote-getter received less than 57.5 percent of the vote and where the top fundraiser raised less than 57.5 percent of receipts. The second set of graphs presents the total number of candidates on the ballot and the effective number of candidates with receipts.[21] The data are broken down by incumbent-contested, challenger-party, and open-seat primaries.

Two main patterns emerge. First, the fundraising measures reveal lower levels of competition across primaries. In open seats, 55 percent of races are competitive with the vote share measure, compared to 41 percent with the money measure. In challenger-party primaries, 19 percent of races are competitive with the vote share measure, versus 7 percent with fundraising. Very few incumbent-contested primaries are competitive, but the share is lower yet with the fundraising measure (6 versus 3 percent).[22] On average, the number of candidates on the ballot is 1.6 in incumbent-contested primaries, 1.5 in challenger-party primaries, and 3.8 in open seats. By comparison, the effective number of candidates with receipts is 1.1, 1.1, and 2.2, respectively.

Second, differences between the number of candidate measures are more pronounced in recent election cycles, particularly in open-seat primaries. The number of on-ballot candidates in open seats has risen sharply since 2008. From 1980 to 2006, the average number of candidates in incumbent-contested, challenger-party, and open-seat primaries is 1.4, 1.4, and 3.4, respectively. These figures increased to 2.0, 1.8, and 4.4, respectively, in the period from 2008 to 2022. The increase in the effective number of candidates is not nearly as stark. Similarly, in incumbent-contested races, the total number of candidates increased by 77 percent from 2008 to 2022, but the effective number of candidates increased by 17 percent. The change in the effective number of candidates is much more muted than the change in the number of candidates on the ballot.

While the highs and lows track similarly, the largest single-year differences between measures correspond to years in which top fundraisers fared worse. The worst year for top fundraisers was 1992, when 15 percent of top fundraisers lost (compared to the average of 8 percent), and their loss rates were relatively higher in 1994, 2010, 2018, 2020, and 2022 (but all under 12 percent). These years are widely considered to be wave elections

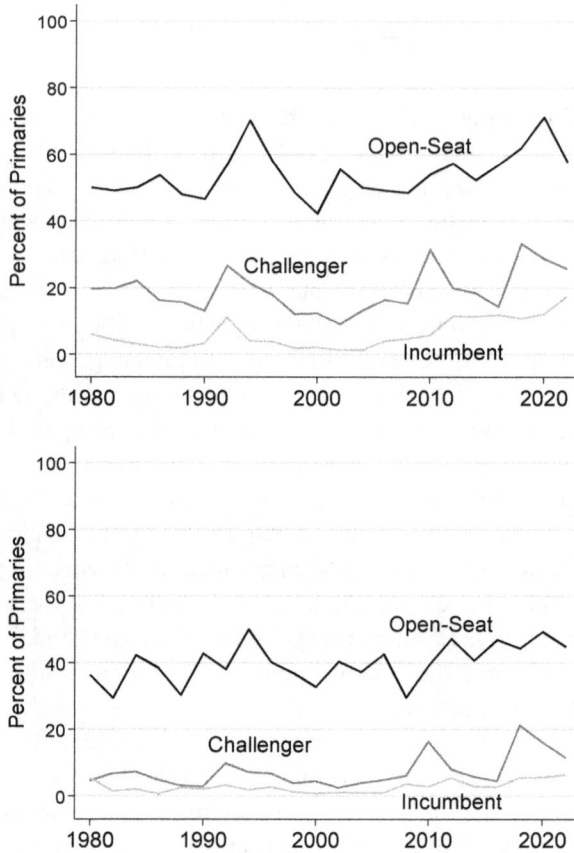

FIGURE 8.2. Measures of Primary Competition over Time and by Seat Type
From top down: < 57.5% of votes, < 57.5% of receipts, on-ballot candidates, effective candidates

Note: The first set of graphs shows the percentage of primaries where the winner received less than 57.5 percent of total votes and where the top fundraiser raised less than 57.5 percent of total receipts. The second set shows the number of candidates on the ballot and the effective number of candidates calculated with preprimary receipts.

or atypical with respect to victory patterns. Women were favored in 1992 and 2018, for example, and outsiders fared better in 2018 (Dittmar 2020; Porter and Treul 2025; Scott et al. 2019; Thomsen 2021). Top fundraisers are far more likely to win across this period, but atypical elections are useful contrasts because the outcomes differed from the norm. The trends provide initial support for the expectation that measures of competition based on vote shares differ from those based on money. The next section incorporates the partisan tilt of the district to further explore variation across primary types.

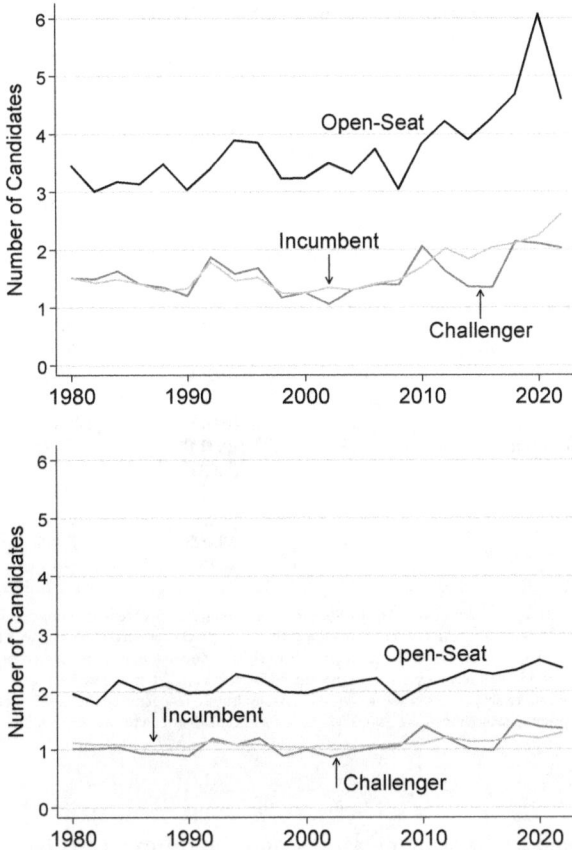

FIGURE 8.2. (*continued*)

Competition: Money versus Votes

As noted above, the main expectation is that vote share measures result in a more optimistic view of competition than measures based on money. Table 8.1 presents the results for whether the primary is competitive with the vote share and fundraising measures, and table 8.2 presents the results with the number of candidate measures.[23]

The results in table 8.1 illustrate that, across measures, open-seat primaries in safe districts are the most competitive, which is consistent with Hirano and Snyder's (2019) findings. The lower levels of competition in incumbent-contested primaries and in hopeless districts (the baseline categories) are unsurprising. Yet the size of the coefficients varies significantly with the

TABLE 8.1 **Likelihood of Competitive Primary with Votes and Receipts**

	(1)	(2)	(3)	(4)
			Competitive, 20-Pt Vote Margin	Competitive, 20-Pt Receipt Margin
	Competitive, 57.5% Votes	Competitive, 57.5% Receipts		
Open Seat	0.37**	0.24**	0.32**	0.20**
	(0.02)	(0.02)	(0.02)	(0.02)
Challenger Party	0.16**	0.07**	0.15**	0.06**
	(0.01)	(0.01)	(0.01)	(0.01)
Competitive District	0.06**	0.05**	0.05**	0.04**
	(0.01)	(0.01)	(0.01) ·	(0.01)
Open Seat × Competitive District	0.10**	0.12**	0.09**	0.10**
	(0.03)	(0.03)	(0.03)	(0.03)
Safe District	0.04**	0.04**	0.03*	0.03**
	(0.01)	(0.01)	(0.01)	(0.01)
Open Seat × Safe District	0.28**	0.31**	0.21**	0.24**
	(0.03)	(0.03)	(0.03)	(0.03)
Constant	0.09	−0.02	0.11	−0.03
	(0.06)	(0.03)	(0.08)	(0.02)
Observations	17,455	17,095	17,455	17,095
R^2	0.24	0.23	0.19	0.18

Note: Results are from OLS regressions from 1980 to 2022. Robust standard errors are in parentheses. The dependent variable in models 1 and 2 is whether the winner received less than 57.5 percent of total votes and whether the top fundraiser raised less than 57.5 percent of total receipts, respectively. The dependent variable in models 3 and 4 is whether the winner's victory margin is within twenty points of the second-highest vote-getter and whether the top fundraiser's fundraising margin is within twenty points of the second-highest fundraiser, respectively. The baseline categories are incumbent-contested primaries and hopeless districts. The models include district and year fixed effects. $\dagger p < 0.10$, $*p < 0.05$, $**p < 0.01$.

vote share and fundraising measures, and the difference is largest in open seats. Another notable pattern is that, even between the vote share measures (models 1 and 3), the likelihood that a primary is competitive is lower with the 20-point margin measure, because winning with less than 57.5 percent of the vote does not necessarily indicate a narrow 20-point margin.

The same patterns emerge in table 8.2. Across measures, the number of candidates increases in open-seat primaries in safe and competitive districts. The weighted measures calculated with votes as well as receipts (models 2 and 3) indicate that the unweighted measure of the number of on-ballot candidates includes a large number who fail to attract support from voters as well as donors. The coefficients are much smaller with the effective number of candidates measure based on votes (model 2), and the effective number of candidates based on preprimary receipts is lower yet (model 3). As in table 8.1, the magnitude of the difference across the number of candidate measures varies dramatically by primary type, with the largest difference emerging in open seats.

In addition, I calculated the difference between the vote share and fundraising measures to examine where they differ most. The dependent variables in the outcome models are whether the race is competitive with the 57.5 percent vote share and 20-point margin measure minus whether the race is competitive with the respective fundraising measure. The dependent variables in the number of candidate models are the total number of candidates with votes minus the effective number of candidates with receipts and the effective number of candidates with votes minus the effective number of candidates with receipts. The full models are provided in the appendix. Predicted values are plotted by primary type in figure 8.3.[24] The top graph shows the predicted probability that the primary is competitive with the 57.5 percent vote share measure but not the 57.5 percent fundraising measure. The bottom graph shows the expected difference between the number of candidates on the ballot and the effective number of candidates with receipts; positive (negative) values correspond to more (fewer) candidates with the vote share measures.

Both graphs indicate that competition looks better with vote share measures, but the disparity is smallest in incumbent-contested races and

TABLE 8.2 **Expected Number of Candidates with Votes and Receipts**

	(1)	(2)	(3)
	Total Number of Candidates, Ballot	Effective Number of Candidates, Votes	Effective Number of Candidates, Receipts
Open Seat	1.50**	0.99**	0.72**
	(0.10)	(0.06)	(0.04)
Challenger Party	0.23**	0.23**	0.12**
	(0.03)	(0.02)	(0.01)
Competitive District	0.47**	0.24**	0.22**
	(0.03)	(0.02)	(0.02)
Open Seat × Competitive District	0.52**	0.25**	0.30**
	(0.13)	(0.07)	(0.06)
Safe District	0.45**	0.22**	0.21**
	(0.04)	(0.02)	(0.02)
Open Seat × Safe District	1.96**	0.82**	0.85**
	(0.15)	(0.08)	(0.07)
Constant	2.20**	1.36**	1.01**
	(0.33)	(0.10)	(0.08)
Observations	17,455	17,455	17,095
R^2	0.37	0.34	0.33

Note: Results are from OLS regressions from 1980 to 2022. Robust standard errors are in parentheses. The dependent variable in model 1 is the total number of candidates on the ballot, and the dependent variable in models 2 and 3 is the effective number of candidates based on votes and receipts, respectively. The baseline categories are incumbent-contested primaries and hopeless districts. The models include district and year fixed effects. $†p < 0.10$, $*p < 0.05$, $**p < 0.01$.

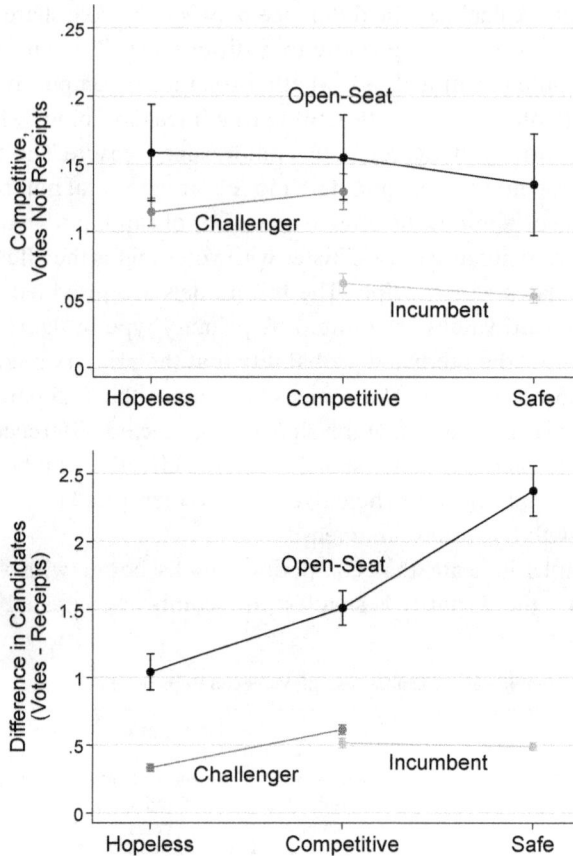

FIGURE 8.3. Difference between Vote Share and Fundraising Measures of Competition
Top, 57.5% of votes vs. receipts, *bottom*, on-ballot vs. effective

Note: Values are calculated from models 1 and 3 in table A.11. The top graph shows the probability the primary is competitive with the 57.5 percent vote share measure but not the respective fundraising measure. The bottom graph shows the difference between the number of candidates on the ballot and the effective number of candidates based on receipts.

largest in open seats. In open-seat primaries in safe districts, the probability that a primary is competitive with the vote share measure but not the fundraising measure increases by thirteen points with the 57.5 percent vote share measure (and by thirteen points with the 20-point margin measure; not shown). In competitive open seats, the probability increases by fifteen points with the 57.5 percent vote share measure (and by sixteen points with the 20-point margin measure). If unopposed primaries are excluded, the probability that an open-seat race is competitive with vote shares but not money increases by twenty-four points with the 57.5 percent measure.[25] The number of candidates results also reveal sizable differences between measures. The disparity between the total and effective number of candidates based on receipts reaches a height of 2.4 candidates in safe open-seat primaries (from 5.1 total to 2.7 effective) and 1.5 candidates in competitive open seats (from 3.6 total to 2.1 effective) (bottom graph). In other words, the number of candidates decreases by nearly *half* in safe open seats and by 40 percent in competitive open seats with the fundraising measure. Unweighted measures are often higher, but the difference between the effective number of candidates with votes and receipts is largest in open-seat primaries as well (not shown). The magnitude is smaller at 0.4 candidates, but it is substantively meaningful as the average effective number of candidates with votes and receipts is 2.5 and 2.1, respectively, in open seats.

These two measures of competition do not have quite the same implications for democracy. In particular, more candidates do not necessarily improve competition, but there is a strong association between the *effective* number of candidates and vote margins. In safe open seats, the average margin between the top two vote-getters in primaries with fewer than 2.7 effective candidates is thirty-eight points, compared to twelve points in primaries with more. In opposed incumbent-contested races, the average victory margin in primaries with fewer than the mean of 1.3 effective candidates is sixty points, compared to thirty points in primaries with more. The percentage of races with winning incumbents drops from 99.6 percent in opposed primaries with fewer than 1.3 effective candidates to 91.8 percent in primaries with more. In short, these measures are tapping into viability.

A Closer Look at the Mismatches

No preelection ratings exist at the primary stage from, for example, the Cook Political Report or Inside Elections to compare with the fundraising measures, but this section takes a closer look at the mismatches to see how they differ. There are 1,574 primaries where a primary is competitive with the 57.5 percent vote share measure but not with the fundraising measure (see the appendix). The top fundraiser's margin over the second-highest fundraiser in the mismatches is 64 points, on average.[26] The top vote-getter's average victory margin is 13 points and ranges from 0.02 to 44.5 points. Of the 1,574 mismatches, 355 are incumbent-contested races, and the incumbent won in 328, or 92 percent, of them. The discrepancy in incumbent-contested races is driven in large part by nonpartisan primaries (167 of 355), where the average number of long shots is 2.7, but incumbents nonetheless win by significant margins.

Of the 1,574 mismatches, 347 are open-seat races.[27] Top fundraisers win less often in more competitive races, and we can see if top fundraisers in these contexts are as likely to win when the measures match and when they do not. In the open-seat contests that are competitive with both the vote share and fundraising measures, the top fundraiser won in 57 percent of races, compared to 72 percent of races that are competitive with the vote share measure but not the fundraising measure. The top fundraiser's margin over the second-highest fundraiser in the open-seat mismatches is 54 points, on average, and the top vote-getter's margin is 13 points and ranges from 0.02 to 41 points. The average number of long shots in the open-seat mismatches is 2.2. Candidates at the bottom of the fundraising pack are able to obtain votes in a way that outperforms their fundraising totals, but they overwhelmingly lose at the ballot box.

How Long-Shot Candidates Influence Our Measures

We may be tempted to interpret the findings as good news because candidates can outperform a fundraising disadvantage at the ballot box. Yet the reason why vote share measures are expected to overstate the degree of competition is because of the entry of long-shot candidates.[28] This section examines whether the disparity between measures widens as the number of candidates with limited resources and a minimal chance of winning increases. The analyses are structured the same as above. Here the main independent variable is the number of long shots, or those who raise less than 10 percent of preprimary receipts.[29] I use indicator variables for the number of long shots, with zero as the baseline. Ninety-seven percent of primaries have fewer than four long shots so races with four or more are combined into one category.

The results are presented in table 8.3. The coefficient on the open-seat variable is still positive and significant in models 1 and 2, but the magnitude is much smaller than those on the number of long-shot candidates. For the most part, the difference between the vote share and fundraising measures increases with each additional long shot, although the size of the increase varies across models. In the number of candidate models (models 3 and 4), open seat is not even significant once the number of long

TABLE 8.3 **Relationship between Long Shots and Difference between Measures**

	(1)	(2)	(3)	(4)
	Difference in Competitive (57.5%)	Difference in Competitive (20-Pt Margin)	Difference in Candidates (Total-Effective)	Difference in Effective (Votes-Receipts)
One Long-Shot Candidate	1.63**	1.25**	0.97**	0.50**
	(0.09)	(0.08)	(0.01)	(0.01)
Two Long Shots	2.57**	1.56**	1.90**	0.77**
	(0.10)	(0.11)	(0.01)	(0.02)
Three Long Shots	2.86**	1.45**	2.83**	1.01**
	(0.13)	(0.17)	(0.02)	(0.04)
Four or More Long Shots	3.01**	1.63**	4.97**	1.37**
	(0.15)	(0.18)	(0.08)	(0.05)
Open Seat	0.54**	0.72**	0.02	0.02
	(0.20)	(0.19)	(0.03)	(0.03)
Challenger Party	0.79**	0.73**	−0.03**	0.05**
	(0.09)	(0.08)	(0.01)	(0.01)
Competitive District	−0.15	−0.02	0.01	−0.06**
	(0.09)	(0.09)	(0.01)	(0.01)
Open Seat × Competitive	−0.26	−0.10	0.07	−0.10**
	(0.23)	(0.23)	(0.04)	(0.04)
Safe District	−0.34**	−0.17	0.01	−0.07**
	(0.11)	(0.10)	(0.01)	(0.01)
Open Seat × Safe	−0.63*	−0.39	0.11*	−0.30**
	(0.27)	(0.28)	(0.06)	(0.05)
Constant			0.27	−0.04
			(0.14)	(0.06)
Cut Point 1	−3.76**	−3.79**		
	(0.45)	(0.58)		
Cut Point 2	3.88**	2.94**		
	(0.46)	(0.58)		
Observations	17,095	17,095	17,095	17,095
Log-likelihood	−5,444.80	−6,384.71	−9,755.10	−7,440.38

Note: The results in models 1 and 2 are from ordinal logistic regressions, and the results in models 3 and 4 are from OLS regressions (1980–2022). The dependent variable in models 1 and 2 is the difference between whether the primary is competitive with the 57.5 percent vote share and fundraising measures and the difference between whether the primary is competitive with the twenty-point victory and fundraising margin measures, respectively. The dependent variable in models 3 and 4 is the difference between the total and effective number of candidates with receipts and the difference between the effective number of candidates with votes and receipts, respectively. The baseline categories are incumbent-contested primaries, hopeless partisan districts, and primaries with zero long shots. †$p < 0.10$, *$p < 0.05$, **$p < 0.01$.

shots is taken into account. Much of what is driving the relationship between open-seat primaries and the disparity between vote share and fundraising measures is the number of long shots in the race.

Figure 8.4 shows the expected difference between measures by the number of long shots for safe open-seat primaries. Safe open-seat races have 2.6 long shots, on average. In races with three or more long shots, the likelihood a primary is competitive increases by twenty points with

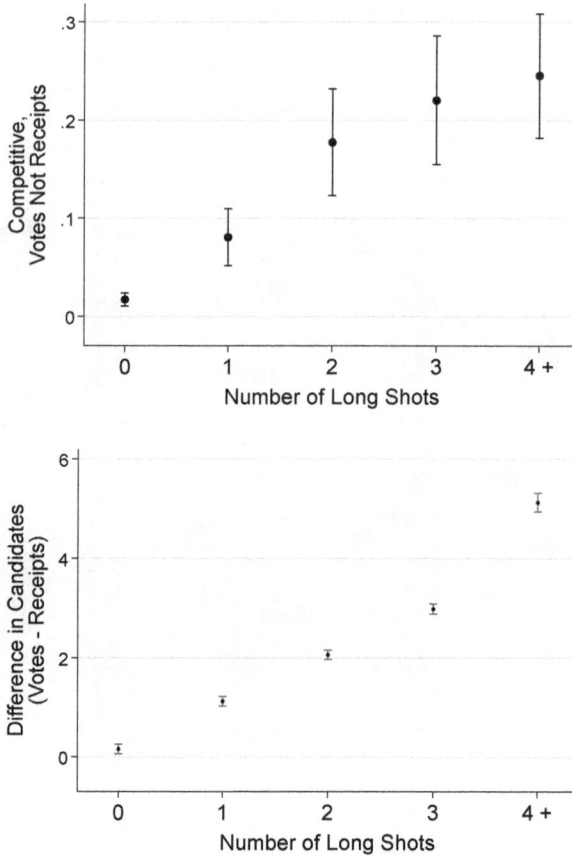

FIGURE 8.4. Difference between Measures, by Number of Long Shots
Top, 57.5% of votes vs. receipts, *bottom*, on-ballot vs. effective

Note: Predicted values are calculated from models 1 and 3 in table 8.3. The top graph shows the probability the primary is competitive with the 57.5 percent vote share measure but not the respective fundraising measure. The bottom graph shows the difference between the number of candidates on the ballot and the effective number of candidates with receipts.

the 57.5 percent vote share measure. Similarly, the disparity between the number of candidates on the ballot and the effective number with receipts increases by about one candidate with each additional long shot. Even the disparity between the two effective candidate measures, both of which are weighted, is 0.7 candidates in races with three or more long shots (not shown). The degree to which the measures differ is associated with the number of long shots, but vote share measures most often result in a better view of competition than measures based on money.

While the above analyses are at the race level, we can also look at the amount raised per primary vote to examine how much cheaper votes are for long shots. Vote prices differ dramatically, with opposed winners raising a median of $11 per primary vote and long shots raising a median of $0. Seat type has a significant impact, and competitive races come with a steeper price tag: the median amount raised by open-seat candidates is $12 per vote, and this increases to $16 in safe open seats. Non–long shots in open seats raise a median of $20 per vote, compared to $3 for long shots. In safe open seats, these values are $27 and $6, respectively. Incumbents raise a median of $15 per vote, compared to $0 for long shots in incumbent-contested races. Additional analyses demonstrate that long-shot candidates raise much less money per vote ($20 less, on average) than non–long shots. (All comparisons are limited to contested elections.)

One question for future research is why so many financial long shots run. The exponential increase in the cost of elections has not deterred candidates from entering the fray, even those who have little chance of success.[30] Candidates may miscalculate their ability to gain traction, and the broader media environment might play a role as well. Arceneaux et al. (2020) find that the density of Fox News in a congressional district altered the perceptions of high-quality potential Republican candidates and increased their likelihood of running for Congress. While their focus is on experienced challengers, it may be that media markets are associated with the entry of inexperienced candidates too. Regardless of their motivations, financial long shots are unlikely to be formidable in the current context.

Other Money-Based Measures of Competition

The analyses above used the same thresholds of vote shares and fundraising shares to measure competition. Receipt shares are appealing for some reasons—for example, certain geographic areas are more expensive than others, and norms around amounts of money have changed over time—but competition can be measured with money in other ways. Dollar amounts could be used if receipt shares might disguise the resources that candidates have. For example, if, in a two-candidate primary, one candidate raised $500,000 and the other raised $1.5 million, the race would not be considered competitive with these receipt share measures, but the second-highest fundraiser is nonetheless more viable than one who raised, say, $50,000.

Raising 25 percent of $2 million is very different from raising 25 percent of $200,000.

It is of course difficult to decide what the threshold should be, especially because these amounts have changed over time even in adjusted dollars. A lower threshold will result in more races being deemed competitive, but too low a threshold will not map onto the modal cases of what it takes to either be perceived as viable or be elected in November. I use decade-based amounts as a result, with the threshold set at the tenth percentile of how much nonincumbent general election winners raised in preprimary receipts in each decade. This value is $48,000 in the 1980s, $70,000 in the 1990s, $221,000 in the 2000s, $233,000 in the 2010s, and $367,000 in the 2020s (all in 2021 dollars). The average is much higher, but this value is a more conservative threshold.

Primaries are coded as competitive if at least two candidates raised more than this amount. Some differences do appear. With the dollar amount measure, 2,065 primaries are competitive, compared to 1,484 with the fundraising share measure (12 versus 9 percent of primaries, respectively).[31] Different kinds of races are competitive with each, however. In cases where the primary is competitive with the fundraising share measure but not the dollar amount measure (398 primaries), 71 percent are challenger-party primaries where candidates raise little money and are unlikely to win the general election. Two percent are incumbent-contested races, and 26 percent are open seats.

There are also cases where primaries are competitive with the dollar amount measure but not the fundraising share measure (979 races). About half of these are incumbent-contested primaries where incumbents can far outraise even competitors with a strong showing, 30 percent are open seats, and 20 percent are challenger-party primaries. Dollars and shares have different strengths. On the one hand, the dollar amount is notable, but if a candidate's haul dwarfs that of their opponent, their relative standing matters too. And perhaps competitive primaries in districts that heavily favor the other party are not ultimately serving an accountability purpose, though a similar critique could be levied at vote share measures if the candidate is a long shot in November.

The next task is to see whether vote share and fundraising measures differ in the same way by primary type when this dollar threshold is used. The first outcome of interest is the difference between whether the race is competitive with votes (one if the top vote-getter received less than 57.5 percent of the vote; zero otherwise) and money (one if at least two candidates raised above the dollar amount threshold; zero otherwise). The second is the difference between the effective number of candidates with vote shares and the number of candidates above the dollar threshold.

The patterns echo those above: competition looks better with votes than with money. The disparity is again smallest in incumbent-contested races and largest in open seats. The probability that a primary is competitive with the vote share measure but not the dollar threshold increases by between two and twenty percentage points in open seats. Even with the effective number of candidates vote share measure, the number of candidates increases by between 0.4 and 1.1 candidates in open seats. Thirty percent of primaries have zero candidates above the dollar threshold, whereas weighted receipt shares nonetheless result in more effective candidates even if the dollar values are low. More generally, the overall picture of competition is similar with dollars and fundraising shares, with close races the exception rather than the rule.

General Elections

While primary competition is our main concern, we might wonder how vote share measures compare to fundraising measures in general elections. The relationship between general election receipts and votes echoes that in the primary, with long shots who raise less than 10 percent of general election receipts receiving 29 percent of the vote, on average. In fact, the floor for long-shot candidates is even higher in general elections due to the significant impact of partisanship on voting behavior and the decline in split-ticket voting.[32] The ceiling for those who are almost certain to win is similarly lower than their receipt share, as candidates who raise more than 80 percent of receipts receive 75 percent of the vote, on average.

Vote share and fundraising measures have significant overlap in general elections as well. Races are either competitive or uncompetitive with both in 82 percent of general election contests from 1980 to 2022 (7,893 of 9,570). Of these 7,893 contests, 93 percent are uncompetitive with both, and 7 percent are competitive (7,325 and 568, respectively). However, the quality of competition is again higher with vote share measures than with fundraising measures. Of the 1,677 mismatches, 1,415 are competitive with votes but not receipts, and 262 are competitive with receipts but not votes. There are 405 open-seat general election contests in competitive districts. In these best-case scenarios of competition, the number of competitive races decreases from 276 with the vote share measure to 118 with the fundraising measure.

I construct the same analyses as above to examine the difference in competition between vote share and fundraising measures in general elections. I use the 57.5 percent threshold in four types of contests: incumbent-contested races and open-seat races in competitive and uncompetitive districts. The full models are provided in the appendix. For the competition variables, the difference is again largest in open seats. The probability that a race is competitive with the vote share measure but not the fundraising measure increases by thirty-three points in open-seat races in competitive districts. However, in contrast to the primary results, the difference between the number of candidate measures is smallest in open seats because both candidates are more viable (a difference of 0.26 candidates in competitive open seats). Primaries differ from general elections in key ways, but the results suggest that competition is better with votes than it is with money in both.

While it is difficult to know what truly counts as competition, fundraising measures offer a valuable alternative to vote shares. Money matters for whether candidates can obtain goods and services on the campaign trail and whether they are perceived as viable in the months before the election. In most elections today, the top fundraiser raises the lion's share of receipts; and even when the outcome is closer than we might expect, the ability to access the resources needed to mount a credible campaign tends to be lopsided. Although a small minority of candidates do overcome the odds through grassroots organizing efforts and prevail with less money, the ability to fundraise is clearly seen as an advantage by the vast majority of those who win.

Summary

Fundraising disparities provide new insight into how the final vote tallies correspond to the resources candidates have to arrive at those totals. This chapter has shown that when competition is viewed through the lens of fundraising, it looks worse than vote shares suggest. The likelihood that primaries are competitive decreases across race types with the fundraising measures, with the largest decline emerging in open seats—the best-case scenarios of competition. Financial disparities capture a crucial aspect of viability and visibility. Grappling more directly with resource inequities during the campaign cycle is particularly important because of the role that fundraising plays in running for and serving in office today.

The final chapter wraps up by reviewing the main findings of the book. I address various hurdles to campaign finance reform and discuss the need for dramatic change. The challenges run deep, but the unseemly amount of money in American politics may eventually prove to make the difference. The multimillion-dollar primary campaign and the ratcheting up of fundraising demands each cycle may be the impetus for a much-needed jolt to the system. We need to ask how the use of money as a signal and focal point is serving voters and the public. The findings in this book instead suggest that the widespread emphasis on money has a variety of negative consequences for who runs, who wins, how candidates spend their time, and who benefits most in office. The quality of American democracy suffers as a result.

CHAPTER NINE

Looking toward the Future

The central concern that runs through this book is that the rich will predominate in contests rooted in resources. As Sheila Krumholz, the former executive director of OpenSecrets, said in an interview, "Although small donors are making up a bigger portion of the money [in elections], it can't hold a candle to the power that one single wealthy billionaire can wield" (Wamp 2021). She also lamented the often myopic view of campaign finance and highlighted the broader dangers of money in politics:

> If we don't have limits, if one person can hand over $10 million to somebody who wants to run for Congress, what does that person owe to that donor? Is that donor effectively buying a seat in Congress? These are real questions that we need to grapple with. We're following the news every day. We're seeing who's running and where their money is coming from. But I don't think we often get a chance to sit back and say where are we on that scale of freedom of speech versus corruption or the appearance of corruption. And the appearance of corruption is important because we don't want people to grow so cynical that they think everybody is bought and sold.

The reality is that donors carry significant weight in American politics. They influence who appears on the ballot, who wins elections, and which members are more prominent in the legislative process. The amount of money spent in elections is staggering. The record-breaking fundraising totals in each election cycle should give the public and lawmakers pause and reinvigorate discussions on how to curb the flow of money. Moreover, the unpopularity of fundraising among officeholders means that the issue has potential to attract the bipartisan support—and perhaps from strange bedfellows—that is necessary for real and meaningful campaign finance reform.

The pathway to reform is an uphill one, but Americans are overwhelmingly supportive of change. A Pew Center report shows that 77 percent of the public agrees there should be limits on how much money individuals and organizations can spend on campaigns, compared to just 20 percent who say individuals and organizations should be able to spend as much as they want. Partisan gaps are apparent but not especially pronounced: 71 percent of Republicans and Republican leaners support spending limits, versus 85 percent of Democrats and Democratic leaners. Nearly two-thirds of Americans say new laws could be effective in reducing the role of money in politics (Pew 2018). In short, a majority of the public is already on board.

This chapter starts by providing a brief overview of the history of campaign finance regulation. I then review commonly discussed pathways to reform and highlight the "leveling up" approach that has gained prominence in recent years. While this school of thought is rooted in practical concerns and is undoubtedly influenced by the serious obstacles that stand in the way of change, the hope is that the reform agenda moves closer toward spending limits. There is simply too much money in American politics, and it gives the wealthy and those at the top of the income strata an outsized influence. Elections play a critical role in responsiveness and accountability, and the intense focus on money is damaging for democratic legitimacy.

I conclude by recapping the takeaways and lessons of this book. A broader goal is to offer a new way of thinking about the impact of money in politics. The central argument is that the value of money is rooted in its use as a signal and focal point. Fundraising is the "performance" that spectators watch. The chapters shed light on the mechanisms through which money matters on the campaign trail and in Washington. Candidates, donors, journalists, and party leaders all prop up and perpetuate the money-driven ecosystem of politics. It is understandable why those who want to win compete on the field deemed to matter most. Yet the emphasis on money has a variety of negative consequences for American democracy. It seems like there has to be a better way.

How We Got Here: A Brief History

Money has long been suspected to have a corrosive influence on politics. The origins of modern campaign finance regulation date back to the Progressive Era. In his 1904 annual address to Congress, President Theodore

Roosevelt advocated for "provisions for the publication not only of the expenditures for nominations and elections of all candidates but also of all contributions received and expenditures made by political committees." Roosevelt, who himself was accused of accepting corporate contributions, went further in his 1905 and 1906 addresses and said that "all contributions by corporations to any political committee or for any political purpose should be forbidden by law" (The Miller Center 2020). In response, Congress enacted the Tillman Act of 1907, the first legislation that banned corporate contributions to national campaigns.

The Tillman Act was a step toward regulation, but because candidates were not required to file disclosures, there was no way to enforce the law. In 1910, Congress enacted the Federal Corrupt Practices Act, which set spending limits for political parties in House general elections and required party committees to file postelection reports of candidate contributions and expenditures. The law was similarly unenforced. Congress passed subsequent amendments in 1911 and 1925. The 1911 amendments mandated financial disclosures from candidates and set limits on the amount that both House and Senate candidates could spend. House campaign expenditures were limited to $5,000 and Senate expenditures to $10,000, or $143,000 and $285,000, respectively, in 2021 dollars. The amendments also extended the requirements to primary elections.

In 1921, the Supreme Court ruled in *Newberry v. U.S.* that the Federal Corrupt Practices Act was unconstitutional because Congress does not have the authority to regulate party primaries or nominations. The spending limits in primaries were struck down as a result. In 1925, Congress again amended the act to require quarterly disclosures and the reporting of contributions greater than $100. The spending limit for House candidates in general elections remained at $5,000, and the Senate limit was increased to $25,000 ($77,000 and $387,000, respectively, in 2021 dollars). But the law continued to lack enforcement mechanisms. There was no regulatory body to oversee reporting and no penalties for failure to comply.

Spending limits were thus never subjected to major tests of constitutionality, but later Supreme Court decisions that concerned the disenfranchisement of Black voters in primaries extended Congress's authority to the realm of nominations. In the 1941 case *United States v. Classic*, the court overruled *Newberry* and held that Congress has the power to regulate primary elections and nominations if they were "made an integral part of the election machinery." The reasoning set the pathway for the court's 1944 ruling in *Smith v. Allwright*, which held that primaries for federal or state office were subject to the Constitution.

The Federal Corrupt Practices Act was the main law that governed campaign finance until the passage of the Federal Election Campaign Act in 1971. The FECA and the 1974 amendments were a major development in campaign finance reform. They included provisions for limits on contributions to candidates, expenditure ceilings for candidates and parties, disclosure requirements, public funding for presidential campaigns, and the creation of the Federal Election Commission, an independent agency that would enforce the law and administer compliance. Senate candidates were limited to $100,000 or $0.08 per eligible voter for primaries and $150,000 or $0.12 per eligible voter for general elections ($550,000 and $824,000, respectively, in 2021 dollars). House candidates were limited to $70,000 for both primary and general elections ($385,000 in 2021 dollars).

The constitutionality of the FECA was challenged before the Supreme Court in *Buckley v. Valeo* in 1976.[1] The questions put before the court highlight the tension between, on the one hand, limiting the amount of information that the public may have about candidates and, on the other, allowing the donor class to have undue influence on the political process and, as Justice White wrote in his dissent, "enjoy political favor if the candidate is elected."

In its opinion, the court drew a distinction between contributions and expenditures and concluded that limits on expenditures present far more significant restraints on "the quantity and diversity of political speech." This distinction provided the basis for striking down expenditure limits but retaining limits on contributions (Schneider 1976). The decision noted that "it is of particular importance that candidates have the unfettered opportunity to make their views known so that the electorate may intelligently evaluate the candidates' personal qualities and their positions on vital public issues before choosing them on election day." The court emphasized that a "candidate, no less than any other person, has a First Amendment right to engage in the discussion of public issues and vigorously and tirelessly to advocate his own election."

The Supreme Court has adhered to the free speech argument in the decades since, and *Buckley* has been extended to other cases. The principle that spending limits of any sort are unconstitutional was, as FEC Commissioner Ellen Weintraub put it, "supercharged" by the landmark case *Citizens United v. Federal Election Commission* in 2010, when the court held that the prohibition of independent expenditures by corporations and unions violated the First Amendment's protection of free speech. The ruling in *McCutcheon v. Federal Election Commission* in 2014 further cemented aggregate limits on individual giving as unconstitutional. In 2022, the court affirmed a district court's ruling that the $250,000 limit on the repayment of candidate loans with postelection contributions is unconstitutional because it burdens the First Amendment rights of candidates and donors. Adherence to this doctrine is likely to persist for the foreseeable future.

Pathways to Reform

Calls for campaign finance reform have gained some momentum as the amount of money in politics reaches unseemly highs. As discussed above, spending limits have faced fierce resistance from the Supreme Court for nearly fifty years, and change is unlikely to occur through the courts. The prevailing reform promoted today is thus a fundraising system weighted toward small donors, or as Pildes (2021) writes, "'leveling up' campaign dollars by providing public funds to candidates rather than trying to 'level down' by imposing caps on election spending." A recent report from the Brennan Center similarly notes, "Small donor public financing is an antidote to big money politics and the single most effective way to respond to *Citizens United* and other court cases that have swept aside campaign finance safeguards" (Fowler and Weiner 2019, 2).

An additional challenge is that legislative action needs to be initiated by the very politicians who have an upper hand in the game of politics as it is currently, though Democratic candidates and elected officials have been more vocal about reform. In March 2019, the Democratic House majority passed H.R.1, a bill that proposed an array of changes to current campaign finance regulations. One of the specific reforms was to provide government matching for small donations. The maximum donation that could be matched would be capped at $200 to shift the balance of fundraising toward small donors. The program would be funded by criminal fines from corporate defendants and not by taxpayer dollars. H.R.1 also expressed support for a constitutional amendment to overturn the *Citizens United* decision. However, the bill stalled in the Senate and has not progressed since.

Politicians are constrained by the broader context, but the reforms that have gained the most traction fail to address the larger problem: the need to regulate the amount of money in politics. In a recent *Politico* article, Commissioner Weintraub notes, "The idea of reversing *Citizens United* has captured some of the public's imagination, but flipping *Citizens United* achieves little as long as the *Buckley* decision stands." The path to over-turning *Buckley* by a constitutional amendment is a difficult one. It would require coordination among elected officials who want to curb spending but may have distinct electoral, policy, and partisan motivations for doing so. The future of campaign finance may instead see a layering of new rules on top of existing ones (Schickler 2001), not unlike its trajectory in the twentieth century, but we should be wary of a "leveling up" solution in a country where spending is already an outlier.

Moreover, the increase in dark money, or political money routed through Internal Revenue Service (IRS)–governed nonprofit organizations, provides further motivation to limit spending. While the hyperattention to regulated money comes with its own set of problems, the complete lack of transparency associated with dark money comes with many more (e.g., Schnakenberg et al. 2023; Wood 2021, 2023). These organizations are subject to far less stringent disclosure rules. As Oklobdzija's (2024) work shows, the result is that a nontrivial amount of campaign cash in the last decade has gone underground. Dark money is of course difficult to study, but future research should give additional attention to how this source of money chips away at the integrity of elections as well.

Spending limits will not eliminate the influence of money, and Weschle (2022) draws attention to how money seeps into politics in different forms. Yet there is ample evidence of the benefits of spending limits for elections and representation. A study of mayoral elections in Brazil finds that limiting campaign spending increases competition and generates a larger pool of candidates that is less wealthy (Avis et al. 2017). Stricter spending limits also reduce the incumbency advantage and cause mayors to be less likely to be reelected. In a rich analysis of UK elections from 1885 to 2019, Fouirnaies (2021) finds when the level of permitted spending increases, the cost of campaigns increases, the pool of candidates shrinks, elections become less competitive, and the advantages enjoyed by incumbents are amplified.[2]

The most dramatic reform would be to decrease the cost of running for office, not to allow more people to pay. Smaller, albeit less transformative, changes are possible too. While candidates are unlikely to alter their behavior absent a disruption in incentives, other actors could more deliberately shift course. Journalists could avoid the temptation to cite dollars and instead dive deeper into other candidate attributes. Money is easy, convenient, and cheap to access, but factors like experience and qualifications are important for voters to know. Similarly, party leaders might sever the connection between fundraising and party rewards. Like candidates, leaders also operate in and are constrained by the money-driven ecosystem of politics, but it is worth thinking about other actionable steps that could diminish the emphasis on and meaning of money.

Summing Up: Takeaways and Insights

It seems increasingly untenable to say that money doesn't matter in politics. Money is one of the most widely used signals of viability, strength, and support. Several key actors and spectators—candidates, donors, journalists, and party leaders—turn to dollars as a focal point. Candidates today start raising money earlier and earlier in the cycle. They strive to post strong early totals to convey the correct impression about their campaign, and those who fall short are more likely to drop out. Donors steer their money to candidates with a strong track record of fundraising. Journalists increasingly reference dollars to indicate electability in their coverage of races. Party leaders reward better fundraisers with institutional and policy rewards in office.

Approaching dollars in this way changes how we understand the value of money. Most studies have examined the impact of money on votes at the ballot box or votes in office. This book suggests that the power of money is different. Money serves as a focal point long before the election and well after the votes have been cast. Congressional elections are low-information contexts. Candidates and officeholders who raise large sums of money are seen as viable and worthy of attention, which results in a feedback loop where they are deemed more formidable to other candidates, more appealing to donors seeking to give their money efficaciously, more competitive to journalists who cover frontrunners, and more electable to party leaders whose goal is to win majorities.

A key part of this story is that we have to look beyond the ballot to capture the meaning of money. Early money is critical because it serves as a first impression and molds expectations about what is likely to follow. Fundraising ability is the main heuristic used to judge candidates and officeholders, and raising money is a top priority for those who want to win or retain power. This book does not delve into the many attributes for which money serves as a proxy, nor does it attempt to tease out which attribute is most central. Rather, the goal is to provide a new vantage point into how money matters and offer a new perspective into why candidates and officeholders dial for more and more dollars with each election cycle.

The analyses in this book provide the most comprehensive study of money, and of early money in particular, across more than four decades of elections. This historical lens is vital because the political and electoral landscape has changed in profound ways during this period. For one, the time horizon of congressional elections has shifted, with more of the action now happening earlier in the campaign cycle. Primary elections have become increasingly relevant in the selection of officeholders as more lawmakers are selected from safe partisan districts. Scholars and practitioners have given more attention to primaries in recent years, because for many lawmakers, their most serious competition would happen well before November.

In addition, technological innovations have transformed the nature of campaign finance reporting. FEC reports have been publicly available for decades, but with the rise of the internet, transparency is now coupled with accessibility. Anyone and everyone can access detailed fundraising and spending data in seconds. The days of paper filings and handwritten reports are long gone. The correct fundraising impression matters because those who want to follow the money are able to, and they can do so more easily than ever before. In an era where "big data" reigns, campaign dollars are measurable and comparable across candidates. These changes provide an important backdrop for why money has become an increasingly salient metric.

The intense focus on money raises a number of concerns for American democracy. First, an elite donor class structures the selection of our representatives by steering resources and momentum to some candidates over others. Candidates and officeholders respond to growing fundraising demands by raising more money, and they spend a lot of time talking with donors. A host of studies have found that donors are unrepresentative of the public in many ways: they are older, wealthier, whiter, better educated, and more ideologically extreme than nondonors (e.g., Bafumi and Herron 2010; Barber 2016; Bonica 2014; Bonica and Grumbach 2023; Grumbach and Sahn 2020; Hill and Huber 2017; Pew 2018). Worse yet, more and more money comes from a sliver of very rich megadonors (Bonica et al. 2013; Page and Gilens 2020). It is unsurprising that economic inequality has been fueled by government policies (Hacker and Pierson 2010a,b).

Second, fundraising is a central reason why so many candidates do not run and why our institutions are unrepresentative of the public. Carnes (2018) finds that the high price tag of running for office keeps working-class individuals out of politics, and Bonica (2020) shows that lawyers' early money advantage explains why they are so much more likely to win. For those in office, the constant need to fundraise—from nearly anywhere and anyone—has negative consequences for representation. Canes-Wrone and Miller (2022) find that lawmakers who receive more out-of-district contributions are more responsive to the national donor base. Unlike Mayhew's (1974a) reelection seekers, fundraising outside of the district is a key aspect of representation in the current money-driven era.

Finally, we should be critical of the emphasis on money because of its implications for perceptions of democratic legitimacy. Majorities of Democrats and Republicans say that donors have more influence in politics (Lessig 2011; Pew 2018; Primo and Milyo 2020). Unsurprisingly, donors have a more optimistic view of legislator responsiveness: 37 percent of Americans say that their representative would help them with a problem if they contacted them, compared to 53 percent of those who donated money and 63 percent of donors who gave more than $250 (Pew 2018). The widespread acceptance of and belief in donor influence undermines basic principles of democratic government. Campaign finance reform may come with its own set of unintended consequences, but most Americans believe it would be a step in the right direction.

The unseemly amount of money in politics may be the straw that breaks the camel's back. It is increasingly hard to ignore the hundreds of millions of dollars that flood into the most high-stakes elections each cycle. In Georgia's 2022 Senate race alone, the two major-party candidates raised a quarter of a *billion* dollars combined (OpenSecrets 2023b). While the Supreme Court has long been resistant to reform, there is widespread dissatisfaction with the status quo. Members of Congress hate fundraising; political candidates hate fundraising; and the public is overwhelmingly supportive of spending limits for candidates, organizations, and political parties. The forces for resistance are well known, but optimists can point to other ingredients that might precipitate change. Leaning out from money would be better for candidates and lawmakers, for the policymaking process, and most importantly, for American democracy.

Appendixes

Appendix to Chapter 1

Fundraising Data in US House Elections, 1980–2022

The main dataset in the book includes more than thirty-five thousand US House candidates who filed fundraising reports with the Federal Election Commission (FEC) and/or were on the primary or general election ballot from 1980 to 2022. I collected the full sample of on-ballot primary candidates from the America Votes series, the FEC website, and State Board of Elections' websites. Those who were not on the ballot but raised money are from the FEC database. Dropouts are included if they raised money in the same election cycle they registered with the FEC. Incumbents who raised money but retired are excluded. The dataset includes all fundraising reports filed by each candidate in the cycle. There are eight reporting quarters and several other election-specific reports that candidates have to file if they raise more than the $5,000 minimum (e.g., preprimary, pregeneral, postgeneral; see the FEC website for a full list).

The dataset includes the FEC candidate identifier, the FEC committee identifier (when available), and the DIME identifier for each candidate to facilitate merges across datasets (Bonica 2014). All of the preelection and quarterly fundraising data are from FEC reports. The dataset includes overall fundraising totals from the FEC and DIME, which allows for additional checks on preprimary values. Virtually all of those in the DIME dataset who raised no money overall did not file preprimary reports, which increases our confidence in the zero values of preprimary receipts in these cases.

There are significant challenges associated with collecting fundraising data. The first hurdle was merging the candidates with FEC data, which was made possible with the identifiers noted above. Of the 35,400 primary candidates in the dataset, 27,200 raised some money before the primary election. Another 6,600 raised no money during the election cycle, and approximately 1,600 candidates did not raise money before the primary but did so before the general. The preprimary figures were further validated by summing all of the reports filed by the candidate in a cycle and matching these totals to their overall FEC totals. This ensures that the zero values in the preprimary stage are zero values rather than errors.

Of the full sample of candidates, all but five candidates are exact matches with the totals reported by the FEC. The FEC occasionally errs in the totals they report, and the cases where the totals are different were left that way due to likely administrative errors by the FEC. In other analyses, I examined the relationship between preprimary receipts as a share of a candidate's own receipts for all primary winners who advanced to the general election. Preprimary receipts comprise a larger share of a primary winner's total receipts in states with later primaries, which is consistent with expectations.

A second challenge is related to FEC reporting requirements. The FEC has collected quarterly and preprimary reports since 1980, but the document did not instruct candidates to provide the total amount raised in the entire preprimary period (election cycle-to-date) until 2002. Thus, from 2002 on, I use the preprimary total reported by the candidate. From 1980 to 2000, I use the sum of the amount reported in each quarterly period before the primary and the amount in the preprimary report, which covers the first day of the current quarterly period through the twentieth day before the election. In the 1980s and 1990s, candidates sometimes filed midyear reports instead of quarterly reports. Candidates who did not file a preprimary report or any quarterly report before the primary are coded as raising no money.

I validated these measures with the post-2002 preprimary totals provided by the candidates. The preprimary totals that I generated with quarterly and preprimary reports are correlated with the preprimary totals reported by the candidates at 0.99 so I am confident in the validity of these totals in the pre-2002 period. Around 2,600 candidates, or 7 percent of the sample, filed reports with multiple committees in a cycle; the quarterly and preelection receipts filed with each committee are included in the dataset. For these individuals, I used the totals that I calculated with quarterly and preelection reports. All totals thus reflect candidate totals, rather than committee totals.

There are zero missing values on preprimary receipt amounts because candidates are coded as raising zero receipts if they do not file a report with the FEC. When preprimary receipts are measured as the share of total receipts, primary winners who were unopposed are coded as raising all of the money in the primary. As a result, there are about 1,500 unopposed candidates who reported zero fundraising but raised 100 percent of preprimary receipts. In addition, there are 900 candidates, or about 2.6 percent of the sample, who ran in opposed races where not one candidate reported raising money and thus have missing values on their share of primary receipts and zero values on preprimary receipts.[1]

The dataset includes prior office experience for all of the candidates so I can examine both money and experience. I have worked with dozens of research assistants at Duke University, Syracuse University, Princeton University, and the University of California, Irvine, to collect prior experience. I have taken several steps to ensure the accuracy of these data. First and foremost, I have at least two values of experience for each candidate. I hire multiple research assistants to collect experience for the same candidate, and I compare these values and recollect them when they are different.

Several scholars have also generously provided or made their data publicly available. I have used Gary Jacobson's data on general election candidates for the entire period, as well as data on primary candidates from Porter and Treul (2025) from 1980 to 1988, from Hassell (2018) from 2004 to 2014, and from Pettigrew et al. (2014) from 2000 to 2010. When two datasets had the same value on experience, I used that value without independently collecting it (for example, a primary candidate in 2006 could have values from Pettigrew et al.'s data and Hassell's data, but it is a small subset of the 1980–2022 period where two of these datasets overlapped). When there was only one value from one of these, I collected the data independently and validated it with theirs.

I additionally use unique identifiers to further validate the data. My dataset has both DIME identifiers and FEC identifiers, and I created my own identifiers because DIME identifiers are occasionally different for the same candidate. This allows for consistency in whether repeat candidates are coded as experienced or inexperienced over time. For example, if a candidate is first coded as experienced and then later as inexperienced, I would recollect this data to confirm. However, if a candidate is first coded as inexperienced and later as experienced, this may not be an error if they held office in the meantime. I am grateful to the scholars who have shared their data and the many research assistants who have helped collect these data and ensure their accuracy.

Interview Data

I interviewed twelve US House candidates, two journalists, and one FEC staffer. Eight of the twelve candidates ran in the 2022 election, and they vary geographically in where they ran (Northeast, South, Midwest, and West), the amount of money they raised, and their primary vote shares. Two raised more than a million dollars before the primary, and five reported more than $100,000 in preprimary receipts. Five of the twelve filed to run and raised money but dropped out before the election (between 1998 and 2022).

For the non-2022 candidates, I found the email addresses of a subset who raised more than $100,000 and had prior political experience. I emailed them in April 2020 and requested a thirty-minute phone conversation; I spoke with all of those who responded.

The 2022 candidates reached out to me. I (along with my collaborator Ryan Mundy, as discussed in chapter 3) conducted a survey of 2022 House candidates. I included my email address and phone number in the initial email to approximately 1,200 candidates. Several emailed me to express their views on the survey or the project. (I corresponded with many more who emailed to confirm that they completed the survey or note that they would not complete the survey for various reasons.) I asked some, and all of those who raised more than $100,000, if they would be willing to discuss their experiences with fundraising in a thirty-minute phone conversation. All of the interviews were recorded and transcribed. I ensured anonymity to all candidates prior to the interview, and no identifying information is used in the book.

I interviewed two political journalists, and I was put in touch with these individuals through the candidates that I spoke with or through media requests that were made to me. These interviews lasted approximately thirty minutes, and the interviews were recorded and transcribed. Finally, I interviewed a longtime staffer at the FEC who has over two decades of experience at the agency and detailed knowledge of how campaign finance reporting has changed over time. I reached back out to everyone I interviewed for their approval of the specific quotes included in the book. I wanted candidates to feel like they could speak candidly about their experiences and all interviewees to feel like their views were properly represented.

Appendix to Chapter 3

The survey was created in Qualtrics. Participants received a link to the online survey.

The text of the questions in chapter 3 is provided below.

1. Are (or were) you a candidate for the US House of Representatives (in the 2021–22 cycle)?

   ○ Yes, I was (or am currently) a candidate and either won or lost in the primary election
   ○ Yes, I was a candidate but I ended my campaign before the primary election
   ○ No, I was never a candidate for the US House of Representatives in the 2021–22 cycle

2. Are you the candidate or a member of the campaign staff? We would prefer the candidate to complete the survey if possible, but we would still be grateful for a staff member's perspective if the candidate is unable to do so.

   ○ I am the candidate
   ○ I am on the campaign staff

3. How many hours per week did (or do) you typically spend on the following campaign activities?

   Personally contacting voters one-on-one (such as knocking on doors) _____
   Raising money _____

Attending public meetings or events to speak to groups of voters _____
Meeting privately with community leaders _____
Meeting privately with local or national party leaders _____

4. How important do you think fundraising is for congressional candidates today?

o	o	o	o	o
Not at all important	Slightly important	Moderately important	Very important	Extremely important

5. Why do you think fundraising is important? Select all that apply.

   o Pays for staff and infrastructure (such as offices and supplies)
   o Pays for advertisements
   o Pays for campaign consultants
   o Conveys support in media coverage
   o Helps with later fundraising
   o Attracts support from party leaders
   o Other _____

6. How hard was it to raise money compared to your expectations?

o	o	o	o	o
Much harder than expected	Somewhat harder than expected	In line with expectations	Somewhat easier than expected	Much easier than expected

7. Who donated most of your campaign contributions in the first three months of your campaign? Select all that apply.

   o Friends and acquaintances in your district
   o People in your professional networks
   o Followers on social media from outside of your district
   o Local party donors
   o National party donors
   o Local fundraising events
   o Other _____

8. How did each of the following influence your ability to raise money?

	Made fundraising much harder	Made fundraising somewhat harder	Made fundraising somewhat easier	Made fundraising much easier	No effect
Online fundraising platforms (such as ActBlue or WinRed)	○	○	○	○	○
Social media like Facebook and Twitter	○	○	○	○	○
Local campaign events	○	○	○	○	○
Endorsements from interest groups	○	○	○	○	○
Endorsements from party leaders	○	○	○	○	○

9. How successful do you think you were at:

	Very unsuccessful	Somewhat unsuccessful	Somewhat successful	Very successful
Raising money for your campaign	○	○	○	○
Receiving endorsements from interest groups	○	○	○	○
Building a strong campaign organization	○	○	○	○
Hiring knowledgeable campaign consultants	○	○	○	○
Convincing likely voters to vote for you in the primary	○	○	○	○
Receiving campaign support from party leaders	○	○	○	○

10. Please name the candidate in your **primary race** who you viewed as your strongest competitor. _____

11. How successful do you think your strongest primary competitor was (or is) at:

	Very unsuccessful	Somewhat unsuccessful	Somewhat successful	Very successful
Raising money for your campaign	o	o	o	o
Receiving endorsements from interest groups	o	o	o	o
Building a strong campaign organization	o	o	o	o
Hiring knowledgeable campaign consultants	o	o	o	o
Convincing likely voters to vote for you in the primary	o	o	o	o
Receiving campaign support from party leaders	o	o	o	o

12. Please indicate whether any of the following contacted you to encourage or discourage you in running for the US House. If the group did not contact you at all about running, please mark the "No contact" circle.

	Discouraged	Encouraged	No contact
The national political party committee	o	o	o
The state political party	o	o	o
The political party in the district or county	o	o	o
Local community leaders	o	o	o
Family or friends	o	o	o
National interest groups	o	o	o
Local interest groups	o	o	o
Members of the media	o	o	o

13. Which of the following sources of information did you use to help you assess your chances of winning the primary or general election? Select all that apply.

- o Your national political party
- o Your state political party
- o Your local political party
- o Newspaper or other media assessments
- o Political polls conducted by you
- o Political polls conducted by others
- o Campaign consultants

- o Donors to your campaign
- o Endorsements from politicians or interest groups
- o Other _____

14. Do you think the attributes below help candidates in your party win elections?

	Hurts candidates a lot	Hurts candidates a little	Helps candidates a little	Helps candidates a lot	No effect
Ability to raise money to fund their campaign	o	o	o	o	o
Ability to fund their campaign personally	o	o	o	o	o
Having prior experience in elected office	o	o	o	o	o
Having strong ties in the community	o	o	o	o	o
Being a racial minority	o	o	o	o	o
Being a woman	o	o	o	o	o

15. How would you describe your ideology?

o	o	o	o	o	o	o
Extremely liberal	Liberal	Slightly liberal	Middle-of-the-road	Slightly conservative	Conservative	Extremely conservative

16. What is your race or ethnicity?

- o White
- o Black or African American
- o Hispanic or Latino
- o American Indian or Alaska Native
- o Asian
- o Native Hawaiian or Pacific Islander
- o Rather not say

17. What is your gender?

- o Male
- o Female

    o Non-binary
    o Rather not say

18. What is your age?

    o Under 30
    o 30–39
    o 40–49
    o 50–59
    o 60–69
    o 70–79
    o 80 or older
    o Rather not say

19. What is your current household income?

    o Less than $30,000
    o $30,000–$49,999
    o $50,000–$74,999
    o $75,000–$99,999
    o $100,000–$149,999
    o More than $150,000
    o Rather not say

20. What is your occupation? If you are retired or if holding elected office is your main occupation, what was your last main occupation before that? _____

21. What is the highest degree or level of school you have completed?

    o Less than high school
    o High school graduate
    o Some college
    o 2 year degree
    o 4 year degree
    o Professional degree
    o Doctorate
    o Rather not say

Appendix to Chapter 4

Dropouts include nonincumbents who raised money (at least $1,000 in the cycle they registered with the FEC) but were not listed on the ballot. Another option was to look at those who filed paperwork to run within their states, but this was less desirable for several reasons. First, most states do not keep historical records of those who filed to run for office. Second, filing records are stored at the county level in some cases and at the state level in others. New York, for example, retains their records for two years after the election, and New Yorkers who file to run in congressional districts that fall within a single county do so at the county level while those in districts that cross county borders file at the state level. Third, differences in filing deadlines across states means that the pool of filers in states with earlier deadlines is likely to be larger and more reflective of the pool of FEC filers than the pool of filers in states with later deadlines as some may have decided to exit the race by that point. The pool of FEC filers thus provides the best opportunity to examine dropouts systematically across states and over time.

Candidates who raise more than $5,000 are required to file with the FEC, and this law has been in place since 1979. Not all who file meet the threshold, but the act of filing conveys an intention to do so. The FEC filers who raise no money and drop out are excluded as they are unlikely to be seen as threats. Incumbent members of Congress who filed with the FEC but retired before the primary are not considered dropouts. Retirements are conceptually different from nonincumbents who decide not to run.

In addition, candidates who withdraw before the election but are listed on the ballot are counted as on-ballot candidates. It is difficult to know the number of candidates who dropped out but were on the ballot. A team of research assistants traced postcandidacy trajectories for 488 experienced

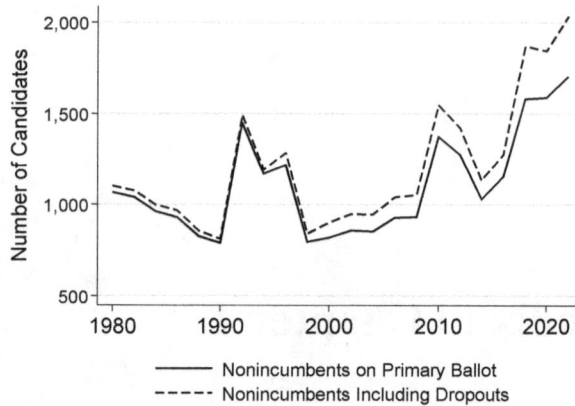

FIGURE A.1. Number of Nonincumbents with and without Dropouts, 1980–2022

Note: The solid line shows the number of nonincumbents on the primary ballot. The dashed line shows the number of nonincumbents when dropout candidates are included. Dropouts are those who filed with the FEC and raised money but were not on the ballot. On-ballot candidates were collected from the America Votes series, the FEC, and state board of elections' websites.

dropouts and 250 experienced losers in the same races (1980–2016). Of the 250 losers, they found 9 who dropped out (3.6 percent). The number of dropouts is thus a slight underestimate, but I use the criteria of being voted on for consistency. The total number of nonincumbents, calculated with and without dropouts, is shown in figure A.1.

To measure early money, I use the amount in the candidate's first fundraising report as a share of the leading early fundraiser's total. This measure captures our interest in the first impression, but I used other measures of early money as well. I used the candidate's first report share of total first report receipts (rather than just the leading fundraiser's) and the total amount in their first report (in 2021 dollars). I also used the candidate's share of individual contributions in the first ninety days of fundraising, rather than the first report, due to differences in the amount of time in the race for those who enter earlier or later in the quarter. The latter analysis is limited to 2004 to 2018, but the results are the same across measures (table A.1).

Bonica (2017) uses the amount raised in the candidate's first ninety days after the statement of candidacy date as a share of the leading fundraiser's total, but some candidates do not fundraise immediately, and others report totals prior to the statement of candidacy. I considered using the change in the candidate's receipt share (from the quarter of entry to

TABLE A.1 **Alternative Measures of Early Money**

	(1)	(2)	(3)
	Sum Q1	Amount Q1	90 Days
Early Fundraising Share	−1.77**		
	(0.10)		
Experienced	0.79**	0.65**	1.04**
	(0.08)	(0.07)	(0.11)
Experienced × Early Fundraising Share	−1.30**		
	(0.17)		
Q1 Receipts (in $100,000s)		−0.05*	
		(0.02)	
Experienced × Q1 Receipts (in $100,000s)		−0.41**	
		(0.05)	
First 90 Day Share (Indiv Contribs)			−1.27**
			(0.11)
Experienced × First 90 Day Share (Indiv Contribs)			−1.15**
			(0.19)
Open Seat	0.62**	0.32**	0.67**
	(0.10)	(0.10)	(0.15)
Challenger Party	0.52**	−0.02	0.50**
	(0.09)	(0.09)	(0.14)
Competitive District	0.46**	0.66**	0.60**
	(0.06)	(0.07)	(0.09)
Safe District	0.42**	0.56**	0.33*
	(0.10)	(0.10)	(0.16)
Open Seat × Safe District	0.15	0.23	0.35
	(0.14)	(0.14)	(0.21)
Preprimary Endorsements	0.16	0.05	0.25
	(0.16)	(0.16)	(0.26)
Primary Election Month	0.03	0.03	0.11**
	(0.03)	(0.03)	(0.04)
Number of State Legislators	0.13	0.12	0.09
	(0.24)	(0.24)	(0.28)
Number of Candidates	−0.32**	−0.19**	−0.32**
	(0.03)	(0.02)	(0.03)
Woman	−0.13*	−0.15*	−0.19*
	(0.06)	(0.06)	(0.09)
Republican	−0.08	−0.08	−0.06
	(0.05)	(0.05)	(0.08)
Constant	−4.59*	−5.25**	−3.80†
	(1.94)	(1.97)	(2.30)
Observations	25,680	25,680	9,625
Log-likelihood	−6,393.41	−6,693.65	−2,985.98

Note: Results are from logistic regressions from 1980 to 2022. Standard errors are clustered at the race level. The dependent variable is whether the candidate dropped out of the race. The models include state and year fixed effects. $†p < 0.10$, $*p < 0.05$, $**p < 0.01$.

the next quarter), but other analyses of news coverage of dropout dates showed that 60 percent of experienced dropouts exited before the end of the next quarter. A subsequent decline in fundraising would thus follow, rather than precede, the dropout decision. Finally, I examined candidate loans to see how early money from loans matters for exit decisions. The main results are the same; however, those with a higher loan ratio are more likely to drop out, and candidates who loaned $50,000 or $100,000 in their first quarter are also more likely to do so (table A.2). The fact that the patterns are the same across measures provides additional confidence in the results.

TABLE A.2 **Early Money, Experience, and Candidate Exit, With Loans**

	(1)	(2)	(3)	(4)
	Loan Ratio	Loan Ratio × Experienced	Self Loan, $50,000	Self Loan, $100,000
Loan Ratio of Early Fundraising	0.01*	0.01*		
	(0.00)	(0.00)		
Experienced × Loan Ratio		0.02		
		(0.14)		
Loaned Self More than $50,000			0.41**	
			(0.10)	
Loaned Self More than $100,000				0.47**
				(0.13)
Early Fundraising Share	−0.92**	−0.92**	−0.99**	−0.98**
	(0.08)	(0.08)	(0.08)	(0.08)
Experienced	0.85**	0.84**	0.85**	0.85**
	(0.08)	(0.08)	(0.08)	(0.08)
Experienced × Early Fundraising Share	−1.02**	−1.02**	−1.02**	−1.03**
	(0.13)	(0.13)	(0.13)	(0.13)
Open Seat	0.53**	0.53**	0.52**	0.52**
	(0.10)	(0.10)	(0.10)	(0.10)
Challenger Party	0.32**	0.32**	0.34**	0.33**
	(0.09)	(0.09)	(0.09)	(0.09)
Competitive District	0.54**	0.54**	0.52**	0.53**
	(0.06)	(0.06)	(0.06)	(0.06)
Safe District	0.49**	0.49**	0.47**	0.47**
	(0.10)	(0.10)	(0.10)	(0.10)
Open Seat × Safe District	0.14	0.14	0.14	0.14
	(0.14)	(0.14)	(0.14)	(0.14)
Preprimary Endorsements	0.12	0.12	0.13	0.13
	(0.16)	(0.16)	(0.16)	(0.16)
Primary Election Month	0.03	0.03	0.03	0.03
	(0.03)	(0.03)	(0.03)	(0.03)
Number of State Legislators	0.12	0.11	0.11	0.11
	(0.24)	(0.24)	(0.24)	(0.24)
Number of Candidates	−0.25**	−0.25**	−0.26**	−0.25**
	(0.02)	(0.02)	(0.02)	(0.02)
Woman	−0.13*	−0.13*	−0.13*	−0.13*
	(0.06)	(0.06)	(0.06)	(0.06)

TABLE A.2 (*continued*)

	(1)	(2)	(3)	(4)
	Loan Ratio	Loan Ratio × Experienced	Self Loan, $50,000	Self Loan, $100,000
Republican	−0.08	−0.08	−0.09	−0.09
	(0.05)	(0.05)	(0.05)	(0.05)
Constant	−4.77*	−4.77*	−4.69*	−4.70*
	(1.95)	(1.95)	(1.95)	(1.95)
Observations	25,680	25,680	25,680	25,680
Log-likelihood	−6,561.18	−6,561.17	−6,553.21	−6,554.91

Note: Results are from logistic regressions from 1980 to 2022. Standard errors are clustered at the race level. The dependent variable is whether the candidate dropped out of the race. The models include state and year fixed effects. The fundraising measures are the same as table 1 in chapter 6. †$p < 0.10$, *$p < 0.05$, **$p < 0.01$.

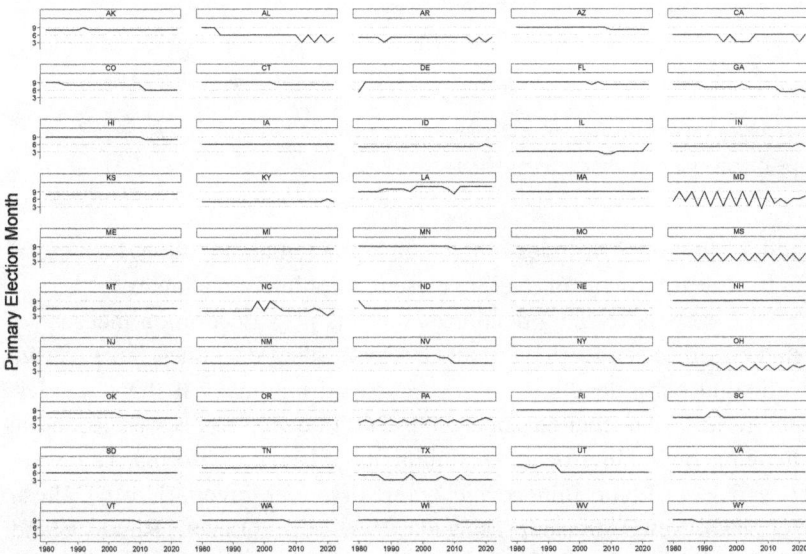

FIGURE A.2. State Primary Election Months, over Time

Note: Primary election dates are from Boatright (2013).

The analyses in chapter 4 also leverage variation in primary election dates and filing deadlines. The following states did not change the month of the primary election across this period: Iowa, Kansas, Massachusetts, Michigan, Missouri, Montana, Nebraska, New Hampshire, New Mexico, Oregon, Rhode Island, South Dakota, Tennessee, and Virginia. The sample in model 1 in table 2 includes candidates in these states; the sample in

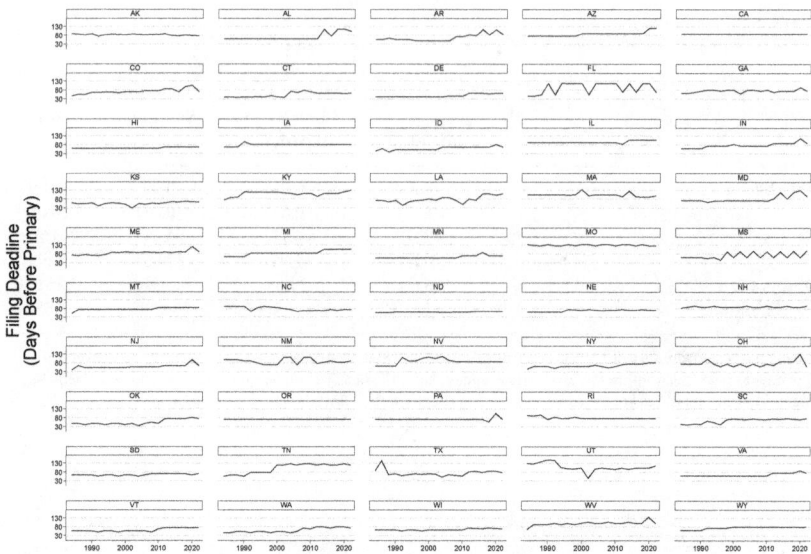

FIGURE A.3. State Primary Ballot Deadlines, over Time

Note: Primary election filing deadlines are from Boatright (2013).

model 2 in table 2 includes candidates in the remaining states. I am grateful to Rob Boatright for making these data publicly available.

With respect to filing deadlines, there is no agreed-upon measure of what constitutes a large or small change in filing deadlines, but I considered state filing deadlines to have changed minimally if there was less than a thirty-day change since 2000. The following states were coded as changing their filing deadline minimally: Alaska, California, Delaware, Hawaii, Iowa, Idaho, Illinois, Michigan, Missouri, Montana, North Dakota, Nebraska, New Hampshire, Nevada, New York, Oregon, Rhode Island, South Carolina, South Dakota, Tennessee, Virginia, Vermont, Wisconsin, and Wyoming. Model 2 in table 2 includes candidates in these states; model 3 in table 2 includes candidates in the remaining states.

Appendix to Chapter 5

Text of Conjoint Survey

Note: The survey was conducted by YouGov in February 2019. Respondents were validated primary voters who donated to a political campaign. Each respondent evaluated seven pairs of primary candidates. Figure A.4 shows the sample text of a candidate pair for a Democratic primary voter.

(Comparison 1 of 7)

Both candidates share your party affiliation, but there are important differences between them. We are interested in your views of the candidates and which candidate you would support in a <u>primary election</u>.

	Democratic Candidate A	Democratic Candidate B
Policy Position:	More moderate than most Democrats in Congress	Rarely works across the aisle with Republicans
Previous Political Experience:	City Council	State Legislator
Outside Support:	Has received many endorsements from local leaders	Has received few endorsements from local leaders
Gender:	Female	Male
Age:	55	45
Expected General Election Opponent:	A Republican incumbent who almost always votes with their own party	

Based on the limited information above, which candidate are you more likely to choose?

◯ Candidate A

◯ Candidate B

How would you evaluate **Candidate A**?

Very unfavorable   1 — 2 — 3 — 4 — 5 — 6 — 7   Very favorable

Based on your best guess, how liberal or conservative is **Candidate A**?

Very liberal   1 — 2 — 3 — 4 — 5 — 6 — 7   Very conservative

How would you evaluate **Candidate B**?

Very unfavorable   1 — 2 — 3 — 4 — 5 — 6 — 7   Very favorable

Based on your best guess, how liberal or conservative is **Candidate B**?

Very liberal   1 — 2 — 3 — 4 — 5 — 6 — 7   Very conservative

>

	(1)	(2)	(3)
	All Donors	Republican Donors	Democratic Donors
Raised a Lot of Money	0.13**	0.11**	0.16**
	(0.02)	(0.02)	(0.02)
Few Local Endorsements	0.04*	0.04	0.05
	(0.02)	(0.02)	(0.02)
Many Local Endorsements	0.18**	0.15**	0.20**
	(0.02)	(0.02)	(0.02)
Moderate	−0.20**	−0.26**	−0.15**
	(0.02)	(0.03)	(0.03)
Rarely Works across the Aisle	−0.24**	−0.22**	−0.25**
	(0.02)	(0.03)	(0.02)
Often Works across the Aisle	−0.18**	−0.25**	−0.12**
	(0.02)	(0.03)	(0.03)
Mayor	0.07**	0.05*	0.09**
	(0.01)	(0.02)	(0.02)
State Legislator	0.11**	0.11**	0.11**
	(0.01)	(0.02)	(0.02)
Female	0.07**	0.00	0.14**
	(0.01)	(0.02)	(0.02)
45 Years Old	0.03	0.05*	0.03
	(0.02)	(0.02)	(0.02)
55 Years Old	0.00	0.03	−0.02
	(0.02)	(0.02)	(0.02)
65 Years Old	−0.07**	−0.02	−0.11**
	(0.02)	(0.02)	(0.02)
Bipartisan Incumbent	0.00	−0.00	0.01
	(0.00)	(0.00)	(0.00)
Constant	0.48**	0.54**	0.42**
	(0.02)	(0.03)	(0.03)
Observations	6,972	3,178	3,794
R^2	0.07	0.07	0.09

Note: Results are from OLS regressions, with robust standard errors clustered by respondent. Data are from a 2019 YouGov survey of validated primary voters. Baseline categories are raised virtually no money, ideologue, city councilor, male, thirty-five years old, and partisan incumbent. $\dagger p < 0.10$, $*p < 0.05$, $**p < 0.01$.

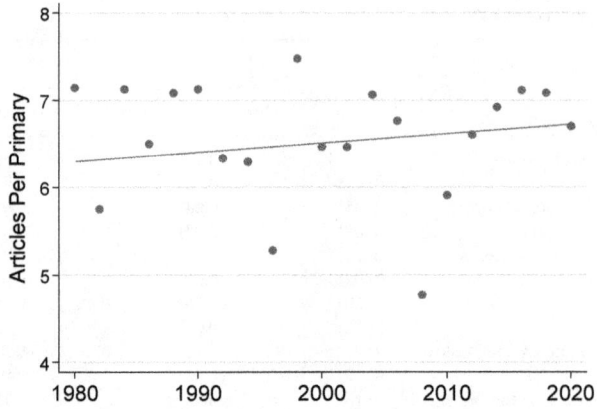

FIGURE A.4. Mean Number of Newspaper Articles per Primary Race, by Year

Note: Average number of newspaper articles per primary by election year.

Appendix to Chapter 6

The results from the replication are shown in table A.4. The dependent variable is the challenger's general election vote share. The main independent variables are challenger expenditures, incumbent expenditures, challenger-party strength, challenger quality, and challenger party. Expenditures are measured in logged values (following Green and Krasno 1988, 899). Challenger-party strength is either the vote share received by the challenger's party in the previous House election or district presidential vote share for the challenger's party in the current or previous presidential election. Quality is coded one if the challenger has held elected office. Green and Krasno (1988) also include interactions between challenger spending and challenger-party strength and between challenger spending and quality.

The relationships are consistent with those in Jacobson (1990) and Green and Krasno (1988), though these data are from a larger sample of elections, so some differences are expected. Partisanship has played an increasingly important role in shaping general election outcomes since this earlier work was conducted, but we can see that similarities remain. Challenger receipts have a positive and significant impact on challenger vote share across models. The negative and significant coefficients on incumbent receipts in the two-stage least squares models in columns 2 and 4 conform to those in Jacobson (1990) and Green and Krasno (1988). One issue in this debate was how incumbent spending compared to challenger spending, and the magnitude of the effect of challenger spending here is much larger than that for incumbent spending.

Table A.5 provides the main replication but includes decade interactions. Model 1 includes interactions between challenger and incumbent spending and decade, and models 2 and 3 include an additional interaction

TABLE A.4 **OLS and TSLS Estimates of the Effects of Campaign Spending in General Elections**

	(1)	(2)	(3)	(4)
	Jacobson, OLS	Jacobson, TSLS	G and K, OLS	G and K, TSLS
Challenger Spending	2.14**	2.22**	3.04**	2.93**
	(0.05)	(0.06)	(0.14)	(0.16)
Incumbent Spending	0.61**	−1.19**	0.70**	−1.10**
	(0.12)	(0.20)	(0.13)	(0.20)
Challenger Party Strength	4.33**	5.11**	5.06**	5.71**
(CPS, in 10s)	(0.09)	(0.11)	(0.14)	(0.16)
Challenger Quality	1.31**	1.72**	0.43	0.46
	(0.18)	(0.20)	(0.44)	(0.48)
Party (Democrat)	0.31*	0.72**	0.21	0.64**
	(0.14)	(0.15)	(0.14)	(0.15)
Challenger Spending × CPS			−0.27**	−0.23**
			(0.04)	(0.04)
Challenger Spending ×			0.24*	0.34**
Challenger Quality			(0.10)	(0.11)
Constant	10.14**	16.51**	7.55**	14.40**
	(0.61)	(1.13)	(0.72)	(1.25)
Observations	6,455	4,973	6,455	4,973
R^2	0.68	0.67	0.68	0.67

Note: Results are from OLS and TSLS regressions from 1982 to 2022. Standard errors are in parentheses. Models 1 and 2 follow Jacobson (1990, 339), and models 3 and 4 follow Green and Krasno (1988, 899). The dependent variable in the challenger's vote share in the general election. Challenger and incumbent expenditures are logged values. Like previous work, $5,000 is first added to each candidate's total expenditures; I follow Green and Krasno (1990, 372) and subtract the log of $5,000 (8.517) from the logged totals. The models include year fixed effects. †$p < 0.10$, *$p < 0.05$, **$p < 0.01$.

TABLE A.5 **TSLS Estimates of the Effects of Campaign Spending, with Decade Interactions**

	(1)	(2)	(3)
	No CPS Interactions	CPS = Vote for Prior Challenger	CPS = Pres Vote for Chall Party
Challenger Spending	3.40**	3.48**	3.86**
	(0.20)	(0.20)	(0.19)
Challenger Spending × 1990s	−0.20	−0.29	−0.30
	(0.17)	(0.18)	(0.16)
Challenger Spending × 2000s	−0.70**	−0.99**	−1.05**
	(0.17)	(0.17)	(0.15)
Challenger Spending × 2010s	−0.33*	−0.53**	−1.20**
	(0.17)	(0.17)	(0.16)
Challenger Spending × 2020s	−1.01**	−1.34**	−2.12**
	(0.21)	(0.22)	(0.21)
Incumbent Spending	−1.98**	−0.93*	1.71**
	(0.43)	(0.43)	(0.38)
Incumbent Spending × 1990s	0.38	−0.36	−1.10*
	(0.58)	(0.59)	(0.55)
Incumbent Spending × 2000s	1.94**	0.11	0.39
	(0.62)	(0.62)	(0.56)

TABLE A.5 (*continued*)

	(1)	(2)	(3)
	No CPS Interactions	CPS = Vote for Prior Challenger	CPS = Pres Vote for Chall Party
Incumbent Spending × 2010s	0.89	−0.46	−2.44**
	(0.62)	(0.63)	(0.57)
Incumbent Spending × 2020s	1.20	−0.09	−2.04**
	(0.66)	(0.66)	(0.59)
Challenger Party Strength (CPS)	5.69**	4.25**	2.20**
	(0.16)	(0.27)	(0.16)
CPS × 1990s		0.85**	1.33**
		(0.32)	(0.20)
CPS × 2000s		2.37**	1.87**
		(0.32)	(0.20)
CPS × 2010s		1.79**	3.69**
		(0.32)	(0.21)
CPS × 2020s		2.17**	5.14**
		(0.41)	(0.33)
Quality Challenger	0.52	0.43	0.39
	(0.49)	(0.49)	(0.46)
Party (Democrat)	0.62**	0.56**	0.91**
	(0.16)	(0.16)	(0.15)
Challenger Spending × CPS	−0.23**	−0.21**	−0.20**
	(0.05)	(0.05)	(0.03)
Challenger Spending × Quality	0.30**	0.32**	0.22*
	(0.12)	(0.12)	(0.11)
Constant	15.39**	14.60**	4.90**
	(1.91)	(1.89)	(1.73)
Observations	4,973	4,973	5,643
R^2	0.66	0.67	0.69

Note: Results are from TSLS regressions from 1982 to 2022. Standard errors are in parentheses. The dependent variable is the challenger's vote share in the general election. Challenger and incumbent expenditures are logged values; I follow Green and Krasno (1990, 372) and subtract the log of $5,000 (8.517) from the logged totals.
†$p < 0.10$, *$p < 0.05$, **$p < 0.01$.

between challenger-party strength and decade. In models 1 and 2, we can similarly see that the marginal effect of challenger spending decreases in the 2000s, 2010s, and 2020s, whereas the effect of challenger-party strength increases over time (models 2 and 3).

Table A.6 presents the primary election outcome models with decade interactions. The sample is broken down by all primaries (models 1 and 2) and those in safe or competitive open seats (models 3 and 4). In the victory models, the money and experience interactions are insignificant across decades. The predicted vote share of top fundraisers declines by 2 percentage points in both the 2000s and 2010s, though the magnitude is small:

TABLE A.6 **Money, Experience, and Primary Outcomes, with Decade Interactions**

	(1)	(2)	(3)	(4)
	Win Primary	Primary Vote Share	Win Primary	Primary Vote Share
Top Fundraiser	0.49**	0.23**	0.53**	0.24**
	(0.02)	(0.01)	(0.03)	(0.01)
Top Fundraiser × 1990s	−0.04	−0.02*	−0.09*	−0.04**
	(0.02)	(0.01)	(0.04)	(0.01)
Top Fundraiser × 2000s	−0.02	−0.02*	−0.01	−0.02
	(0.02)	(0.01)	(0.04)	(0.01)
Top Fundraiser × 2010s	−0.01	−0.02*	0.02	−0.01
	(0.02)	(0.01)	(0.04)	(0.01)
Top Fundraiser × 2020s	−0.03	−0.03**	−0.01	−0.01
	(0.03)	(0.01)	(0.05)	(0.02)
Experienced	0.17**	0.09**	0.16**	0.10**
	(0.02)	(0.01)	(0.03)	(0.01)
Experienced × 1990s	0.01	−0.00	0.05	0.01
	(0.02)	(0.01)	(0.04)	(0.01)
Experienced × 2000s	0.03	−0.00	0.05	0.01
	(0.03)	(0.01)	(0.04)	(0.01)
Experienced × 2010s	0.00	−0.01	−0.01	−0.02
	(0.02)	(0.01)	(0.04)	(0.01)
Experienced × 2020s	−0.05	−0.01	−0.03	−0.01
	(0.03)	(0.01)	(0.04)	(0.01)
Open Seat	−0.03**	−0.04**		
	(0.01)	(0.00)		
Competitive District	−0.02	−0.01*		
	(0.01)	(0.00)		
Safe District	−0.03**	−0.02**	−0.02	−0.03**
	(0.01)	(0.00)	(0.02)	(0.01)
Loan Ratio	−0.00	−0.00	−0.14**	−0.05**
	(0.00)	(0.00)	(0.02)	(0.01)
Number of Candidates	−0.02**	−0.03**	−0.01**	−0.02**
	(0.00)	(0.00)	(0.00)	(0.00)
Woman	0.08**	0.04**	0.02	0.03**
	(0.01)	(0.00)	(0.01)	(0.00)
Republican	0.01	0.01*	0.00	0.01*
	(0.01)	(0.00)	(0.01)	(0.00)
Constant	0.22**	0.37**	0.29**	0.29**
	(0.06)	(0.02)	(0.11)	(0.04)
Observations	13,924	13,924	5,135	5,135
R^2	0.31	0.58	0.35	0.62

Note: Results are from logistic and OLS regressions from 1980 to 2022. Standard errors are in parentheses. The dependent variable in models 1 and 3 is whether the candidate won the primary, and the dependent variable in models 2 and 4 is the candidate's primary vote share. The sample is limited to contested primaries. Models 3 and 4 are limited to open-seat primaries in safe or competitive districts. All models include district and year fixed effects. †$p < 0.10$, *$p < 0.05$, **$p < 0.01$.

being a top fundraiser increases vote shares by 22.4 points in the 1980s and by 20.6 points in the 2010s. Similar patterns are apparent in open-seat primaries in safe or competitive districts, though top fundraisers' vote shares were a few points lower in the 1990s. Yet it is important to note that although the relationship between fundraising and primary outcomes is similar across this period, the salience of primaries and the stakes of early fundraising have changed.

Appendix to Chapter 7

TABLE A.7 **Relationship between Party Contributions and Committee Assignments, Newly Elected Members (by Party)**

	(1)	(2)	(3)	(4)
	Republicans, Power Committee	Republicans, Portfolio Score	Democrats, Power Committee	Democrats, Portfolio Score
Top 20 Percent of Party Donors	0.10†	0.19*	0.03	0.03
	(0.05)	(0.09)	(0.05)	(0.08)
Experienced Candidate	0.11**	0.07	−0.01	0.00
	(0.04)	(0.07)	(0.05)	(0.07)
Open Seat	−0.06	−0.18*	0.03	−0.02
	(0.05)	(0.07)	(0.04)	(0.06)
Safe District	0.05	−0.06	0.04	0.06
	(0.05)	(0.07)	(0.04)	(0.06)
Moderate	−0.10	0.47**	−0.03	−0.01
	(0.10)	(0.15)	(0.06)	(0.09)
Woman	−0.13†	0.02	0.02	0.03
	(0.07)	(0.11)	(0.04)	(0.07)
Constant	0.10	0.21	0.09	−0.19†
	(0.11)	(0.17)	(0.07)	(0.11)
Observations	477	477	358	358
R^2	0.05	0.12	0.03	0.05

Note: Results are from OLS regressions from 1992 to 2016, with Congress fixed effects. The dependent variable in models 1 and 3 is whether the MC received a prestigious committee assignment (Appropriations, Budget, Energy and Commerce, Ways and Means). The dependent variable in models 2 and 4 is the member's committee portfolio score. †$p < 0.10$, *$p < 0.05$, **$p < 0.01$.

TABLE A.8 **Relationship between Party Contributions and Committee Assignments, Transferring Incumbents (by Party)**

	(1)	(2)	(3)	(4)
	Republicans, Power Committee	Republicans, Portfolio Score	Democrats, Power Committee	Democrats, Portfolio Score
Top 20 Percent of	0.09	0.28	0.18*	0.60**
Party Donors	(0.09)	(0.19)	(0.08)	(0.15)
Safe District	−0.02	−0.18	−0.11*	−0.05
	(0.06)	(0.14)	(0.06)	(0.11)
Seniority	−0.04*	−0.07*	−0.01	−0.02
	(0.02)	(0.04)	(0.01)	(0.03)
Moderate	−0.16	−0.15	−0.19*	−0.17
	(0.13)	(0.29)	(0.08)	(0.16)
Woman	0.04	0.04	−0.08	−0.17
	(0.09)	(0.20)	(0.07)	(0.13)
Constant	0.69**	0.91**	0.69**	0.64**
	(0.15)	(0.33)	(0.09)	(0.17)
Observations	308	308	345	345
R^2	0.13	0.10	0.14	0.15

Note: Results are from OLS regressions from 1992–2016, with Congress fixed effects. The dependent variable in Models 1 and 3 is whether the MC received a prestigious committee assignment (Appropriations, Budget, Energy and Commerce, Ways and Means). The dependent variable in models 2 and 4 is the member's committee portfolio score. †$p < 0.10$, *$p < 0.05$, **$p < 0.01$.

TABLE A.9 **Relationship between Sector Fundraising and Issue Effectiveness**

	(1)	(2)
	Total Receipts	Logged Receipts
Sector Receipts (in $10,000s)	0.08**	
	(0.00)	
Logged Sector Receipts		0.38**
		(0.03)
Defense × Sector Receipts (in $10,000s)	−0.05**	
	(0.01)	
Energy × Sector Receipts (in $10,000s)	−0.01	
	(0.01)	
Health × Sector Receipts (in $10,000s)	−0.05**	
	(0.01)	
Transportation × Sector Receipts (in $10,000s)	−0.03**	
	(0.01)	
Labor × Sector Receipts (in $10,000s)	−0.08**	
	(0.01)	
Defense × Logged Sector Receipts		−0.29**
		(0.04)
Energy × Logged Sector Receipts		−0.03
		(0.05)
Health × Logged Sector Receipts		−0.03
		(0.05)
Transportation × Logged Sector Receipts		−0.17**
		(0.05)
Labor × Logged Sector Receipts		−0.35**
		(0.04)
Defense	0.43**	3.13**
	(0.07)	(0.45)
Energy	0.22**	0.41
	(0.07)	(0.48)
Health	0.26**	0.18
	(0.07)	(0.52)
Transportation	0.14	1.68**
	(0.08)	(0.52)
Labor	0.44**	3.59**
	(0.08)	(0.46)
Constant	−0.27	−3.63**
	(1.22)	(1.28)
Observations	23,482	23,482
R^2	0.10	0.09

Note: Results are from OLS regressions from 1990 to 2022, with member fixed effects. Standard errors are clustered by member. The dependent variable is the lawmaker's issue-by-issue legislative effectiveness score. Agriculture is the baseline category. †$p < 0.10$, *$p < 0.05$, **$p < 0.01$.

Appendix to Chapter 8

TABLE A.10 **Descriptive Statistics of Competitive Primary Variables**

Less Than 57.5% of Votes	Less Than 57.5% of Receipts		
	Uncompetitive	Competitive	Total
Uncompetitive	14,037	302	14,339
Competitive	1,574	1,182	2,756
Total	15,611	1,484	17,095

20-Point Victory Margin	20-Pt Receipt Margin		
	Uncompetitive	Competitive	Total
Uncompetitive	14,274	451	14,725
Competitive	1,534	836	2,370
Total	15,808	1,287	17,095

Note: Entries show the number of competitive and uncompetitive primaries with each measure (i.e., whether the top vote-getter received less than 57.5 percent of total votes and whether the top fundraiser raised less than 57.5 percent of total receipts; whether the top vote-getter's victory margin is within twenty points of the second-highest vote-getter and whether the top fundraiser's fundraising margin is within twenty points of the second highest fundraiser). With the 57.5 percent measures, 89 percent of races are either competitive or uncompetitive with both; 9 percent of races are competitive with the vote share measure but not the fundraising measure; and 2 percent are competitive with the fundraising measure but not the vote share measure. The values on the difference measure is 0 when both are the same, 1 when the race is competitive with the vote share measure but not the fundraising measure, and -1 when the race is competitive with the fundraising measure but not the vote share measure. Sixty percent of the primaries in which the two measures are the same are unopposed (9,200 of 15,218).

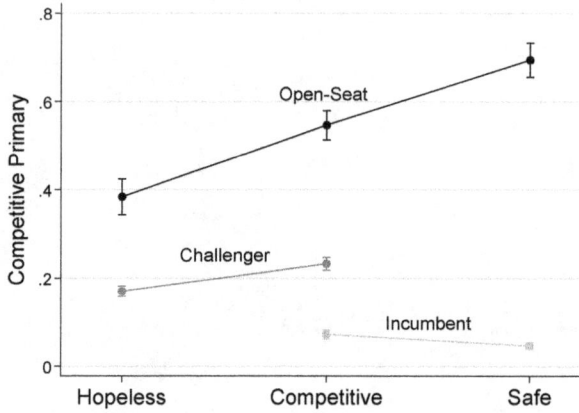

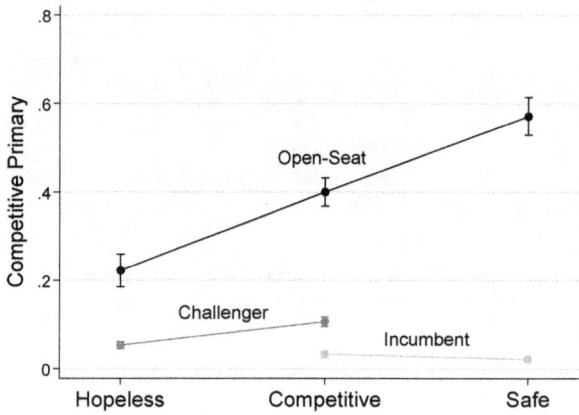

FIGURE A.5. Likelihood of Competitive Race by Primary Type with Vote Share and Fundraising Measures

< 57.5% of votes (*top*), < 57.5% of receipts (*bottom*)

Note: Values are calculated from models 1 and 2 in table 8.1. The dependent variable in the top and bottom graphs is whether the winner received less than 57.5 percent of the vote and whether the top fundraiser received less than 57.5 percent of all receipts, respectively.

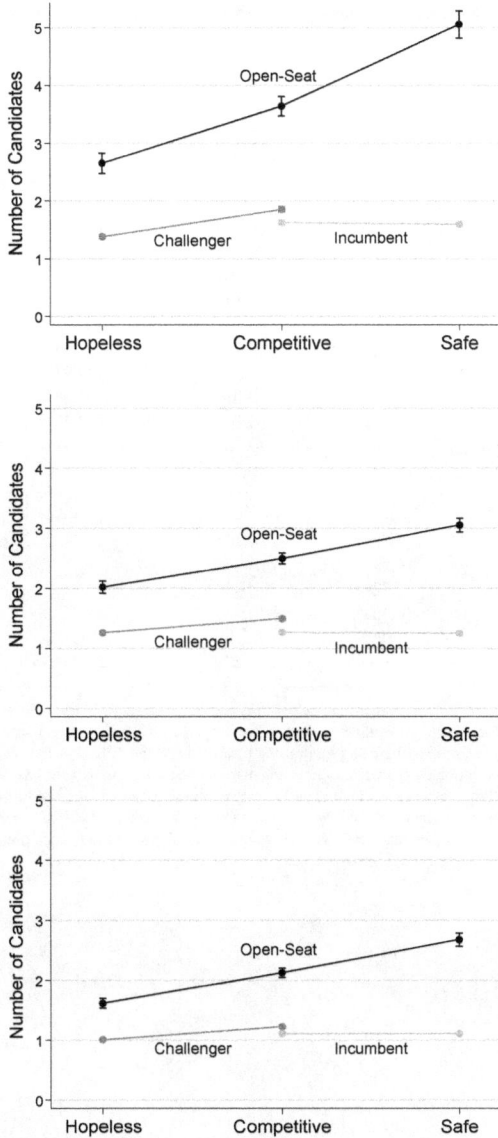

FIGURE A.6. Expected Number of Candidates by Primary Type with Vote Share and Fund-raising Measures

On-ballot candidates (*top*), effective candidates (votes) (*middle*), effective candidates (receipts) (*bottom*)

Note: Values are calculated from the models in table 8.2. The dependent variable in the top graph is the total number of candidates on the ballot, and the dependent variable in the middle and bottom graphs is the effective number of candidates based on votes and receipts, respectively.

TABLE A.11 **Difference between Vote Share and Fundraising Measures of Competition**

	(1)	(2)	(3)	(4)
	Difference in Competitive (57.5%)	Difference in Competitive (20-Pt Margin)	Difference in Candidates (Total-Effective)	Difference in Effective (Votes-Receipts)
Open Seat	1.25**	1.13**	0.80**	0.28**
	(0.18)	(0.19)	(0.07)	(0.04)
Challenger Party	0.86**	0.79**	0.10**	0.10**
	(0.08)	(0.08)	(0.02)	(0.01)
Competitive District	0.15	0.14	0.28**	0.04**
	(0.09)	(0.09)	(0.02)	(0.01)
Open Seat × Competitive	–0.16	–0.04	0.20*	–0.06
	(0.22)	(0.23)	(0.09)	(0.04)
Safe District	–0.03	0.01	0.26**	0.03
	(0.11)	(0.10)	(0.03)	(0.02)
Open Seat × Safe	–0.16	–0.16	1.08**	–0.04
	(0.25)	(0.27)	(0.11)	(0.05)
Constant			1.16**	0.32**
			(0.30)	(0.08)
Cut Point 1	–4.76**	–4.42**		
	(0.46)	(0.54)		
Cut Point 2	2.32**	2.06**		
	(0.46)	(0.54)		
Observations	17,095	17,095	17,095	17,095
Log-likelihood	–6,066.24	–6,651.68	–24,163.35	–11,717.90

Note: The results in models 1 and 2 are from ordinal logistic regressions, and the results in models 3 and 4 are from OLS regressions (1980–2022). The dependent variable in models 1 and 2 is the difference between whether the primary is competitive with the 57.5 percent vote share and fundraising measures and the difference between whether the primary is competitive with the twenty-point victory and fundraising margin measures, respectively. The dependent variable in models 3 and 4 is the difference between the total and effective number of candidates (based on receipts) and the difference between the effective number of candidates based on votes and receipts, respectively. Positive coefficients indicate that primaries are more competitive with vote share measures than with fundraising measures. The models include district and year fixed effects. $\dagger p < 0.10$, $*p < 0.05$, $**p < 0.01$.

TABLE A.12 **Difference between Vote Share and Fundraising Measures of Competition, General Elections**

	(1)	(2)	(3)
	Difference in Competitive (57.5%)	Difference in Candidates (Total-Effective)	Difference in Effective (Votes-Receipts)
Open Seat	0.46**	−0.07**	−0.04**
	(0.14)	(0.02)	(0.01)
Competitive District	0.67**	−0.08**	−0.02*
	(0.07)	(0.01)	(0.01)
Open Seat × Competitive District	0.45*	−0.16**	−0.13**
	(0.19)	(0.02)	(0.02)
Constant		0.42**	0.22**
		(0.08)	(0.05)
Cut Point 1	−4.84**		
	(0.54)		
Cut Point 2	1.38**		
	(0.53)		
Observations	9,570	9,570	9,570
Log-likelihood	−4,423.13	−3,568.72	−1,136.70

Note: The results in model 1 are from ordinal logistic regressions, and the results in models 2 and 3 are from OLS regressions (1980–2022). The dependent variable in model 1 is the difference between whether the general election is competitive with the 57.5 percent vote share and fundraising measures. The dependent variable in models 2 and 3 is the difference between the total and effective number of candidates (based on receipts) and the difference between the effective number of candidates based on votes and receipts, respectively. The models include district and year fixed effects. $\dagger p < 0.10$, $*p < 0.05$, $**p < 0.01$.

Notes

Chapter One

1. *InsiderNJ*, *New Jersey Globe*, *USA Today*, the *Wall Street Journal*, and others reported on Sherrill's fundraising during the primary season (Fouriezos 2018; Hook 2018; Pizarro 2018; Wildstein 2018).

2. A significant number of studies have documented these patterns. For several notable examples, see Bronars and Lott (1997), Fouirnaies and Hall (2014), Grenzke (1989), Grier and Munger (1986), Hall and Wayman (1990), Kalla and Broockman (2016), and Powell and Grimmer (2016) (but see also Stratmann 1998, 2002). Powell's (2012) pathbreaking analysis of state legislatures instead turns the attention from whether contributions have influence to when and where they do. Powell (2013) and Weschle (2023) provide helpful reviews of this research.

3. There is growing interest in the role of early money (e.g., Bonica 2017; Hassell 2018; Porter and Steelman 2023), but data collection is more challenging for primaries than for general elections.

4. The fundraising data are described in detail in the appendix. Additional information about the interviews is provided in the appendix as well.

5. One candidate said the targets are "by design beyond what they reasonably think you're going to be able to raise. They are there to increase the pressure and get you to spend more time on the phone."

6. Fundraising totals are also incorporated in leading forecasting models. Fundraising is one of the "fundamentals" in *FiveThirtyEight*'s models, and the Cook Political Report similarly uses fundraising data in their reputable ratings. In fact, in a postelection report about why House ratings missed the mark in 2020, Cook analyst David Wasserman cited the Republican Party's minimal financial investment in two upset races as indications that the districts were not expected to be in play.

7. Another was similarly told not to enter until he was able to report $100,000 in his first quarter.

8. A brief history of campaign finance regulation is included in the concluding chapter.

9. Scholars would also lament any shift away from transparency. Indeed, this book is only possible because of the collection and maintenance of campaign finance records by the FEC.

10. Nor does public funding seem to help: Kilborn and Vishwanath (2022) find that candidates who use public financing are even less representative of their districts than non–publicly financed candidates.

Chapter Two

1. Previous research on candidate quality is premised on the idea that although quality is unobservable, we can measure characteristics that tap into quality. For example, prior experience is a surrogate for characteristics that are associated with winning, such as personal appeal and campaign skills. There is, as Squire (1995, 894) writes, "an element of tautology in this reasoning—individuals have the requisite candidate qualities because they have held elective office, and they have held elective office because they have the requisite qualities." A similar concern is evident with respect to fundraising.

2. A full discussion of the influence of money on election outcomes is provided in chapter 6. Most agree that challenger spending is positively associated with House and Senate outcomes (but see Levitt 1994), though there has been considerable debate over the effect of incumbent spending, with Jacobson (1980, 1990) finding minimal returns and others showing positive effects (Gerber 1998; Green and Krasno 1988, 1990; Krasno and Green 1988).

3. For a few notable examples, see Bianco (1984), Bond et al. (1985), Hassell (2018), Jacobson and Kernell (1983), Pearson and McGhee (2013), Pettigrew et al. (2014), and Porter and Treul (2025).

4. Only several states have preprimary party endorsements, and candidates prioritize fundraising in the same way. Indeed, this candidate expected to win in part because of her campaign's finances. She explained, "I really didn't feel I was losing through all of this because we had strong indicators. Our money was good. And then it came to these delegates saying, 'Well, money doesn't matter. Money isn't really a big deal.'" She was contacted by the national party afterward who "supposedly would've helped" if she had run without the party endorsement, but she declined to do so.

5. Not all candidates have positive experiences with campaign personnel. One said, "My early advisors said one of the first things you need to do is hire a campaign consultant. They gave me names, and [the one I chose] turned out to be one of the biggest rip-offs of my entire campaign. It's turned into a cottage industry for crooks. It's very, very hard to hire somebody who is any good and have them stick with you. I hired multiple people and either ended up firing them with cause, or they left my campaign and went to another campaign and just kept campaign hop-

ping. I found out that one of [my field directors] was actually quietly working for another campaign and taking money from both."

6. In addition, the error around fundraising may be larger in some cycles if expectations are amiss. In 2020, for example, Cook listed twenty-seven House races in their toss-up category. The Democratic candidate outraised the Republican in twenty-one of these but did not win a single one.

7. The FEC had research fees of $4.50 per one hundred pages copied by staff. In 1981, copying fees brought in $40,944 to the FEC, or $123,000 in 2021 dollars (FEC 1981).

8. As one candidate explained, "The traditional bedrock of political fundraising is 'call time,' which is just dialing people who are reliable party donors and asking them to give money. The issues there are a) people don't answer their phones anymore because of all the spam calls that come in, and b) the data is so good that everyone knows exactly who gives money so these people get thirty calls a day without exaggerating." This candidate raised over a million dollars before the primary but did not have much success with this approach. Another agreed, "It's such a small percentage of people that actually answer the phone, and people just don't donate very much."

9. A candidate's source of donations can become symbolic of their values, but it is rare. For example, Senator Bernie Sanders (D-VT) used his twenty-seven-dollar contribution average in his 2016 presidential campaign to convey his integrity, the reach of his support, and the characteristics of his supporters. Senator Elizabeth Warren (D-MA) and Representative Alexandria Ocasio-Cortez (D-NY) have made their rejection of corporate money a large part of their political personas. Republican candidates draw less attention to how they raise money, though President Trump's success in attracting small-dollar donations was used as an indicator of his support. But these cases are more the exception than the rule.

10. Only Louisiana has primaries in the fourth quarter, as they are held on the day of the general election. Louisiana has an additional runoff in December for winners who garner less than 50 percent of the vote.

11. Fundraising reports in the 1980s and 1990s more commonly included midyear reports, which cover the first half of the year rather than one quarter. Most incumbents report fundraising totals in the first reporting period, but the length of these periods was different in the pre- and post-2000 periods. The values for incumbents thus includes the first and second quarters of the year before the election, so the time periods cover the same number of months.

12. Of the 25,200 all-or-nothing fundraisers, 13,300 raised more than 90 percent of receipts, and 11,900 raised less than 10 percent. Of the 13,300 at the top, 58 percent are incumbents, and 38 percent are in challenger-party primaries; 73 percent of the incumbents and 76 percent of the challengers were unopposed in the primary. Of course, the amount raised by unopposed incumbents is far higher than the amount raised by unopposed challengers, but here I am just looking at fundraising shares.

13. If opposed and unopposed incumbents are included, 98.9 percent won the primary in the 1980s, compared to 98.5 and 97.3 percent in the 2010s and 2020s.

14. Some observers may disagree about whether specific races were upsets or expected defeats, but fundraising allows for a more systematic measure that is less subject to interpretation.

15. The share of primary candidates with nonzero independent expenditures made against them before the primary has increased over time, but it is still low, at 5 percent in the 2010s and 8 percent in the 2020s (with median amounts of $5,200 and $800, respectively).

16. Of the 16,977 general election candidates from 1982 to 2022, independent expenditures either for or against candidates (combined) only exceeded $20,000 for 2,776, or 16 percent, of candidates. Forty-two percent of general election candidates had zero outside expenditures either for or against them; the remaining 42 percent had less than $20,000 in independent expenditures either for or against them.

17. A handful of studies that look beyond the ballot show that on-ballot measures miss others who could have run but chose not to (Fowler and McClure 1989; Kazee 1994; King 2017).

18. For a brief history of federal campaign laws, see https://transition.fec.gov /info/appfour.htm.

Chapter Three

1. We used fundraising numbers from FEC reports filed as of the first quarter of 2022. The sample includes candidates running in 250 primaries.

2. There were 1,500 candidates running in the primaries in our sample. We were unable to find email addresses for 300 of them. Our full sample included an additional 70 incumbents, but they are not included here because only four responded. For Texas, the survey was sent before their runoff.

3. Thirty-three percent of experienced candidates in the full sample won the primary, compared to 30 percent of experienced candidates who responded to the survey.

4. The breakdown in where candidates receive their early money is similar for experienced and inexperienced candidates.

5. A larger share of candidates use donors to assess their viability in open seats than in nonopen seats (44 versus 35 percent, respectively), which is perhaps even more noteworthy because most newly elected lawmakers enter from open seats. We should be cautious, however, due to the small sample size.

6. Respondents in open seats rated their top competitors' fundraising ability at 3.35, compared to 3.17 in nonopen seats.

7. These options were taken from the National Candidate Survey, a national survey of state legislators conducted by David Broockman, Nicholas Carnes, Melody Crowder-Meyer, and Christopher Skovron (Broockman et al. 2012). See also Carnes (2018, 280).

8. Candidates who raised over $100,000 in preprimary receipts spend an average of twenty hours per week on fundraising, compared to eight hours for those who raised less than $100,000 in preprimary receipts.

Chapter Four

1. At the end of the fourth quarter of the year before the election, Rogers had raised 57 percent of Blum's total, and Taylor had raised 11 percent of the eventual winner's total (Randy Perkins). In both primaries, there were zero prior officeholders on the ballot.

2. The total number of nonincumbents, with and without dropouts, is provided in the appendix. The number of candidates on the ballot is similar to the number of candidates including dropouts in the 1980s and 1990s.

3. Others have conducted in-depth case studies of the decisions of candidates and near-candidates during the cycle, but they are limited to one year or one race (Fowler and McClure 1989; Kazee 1994).

4. About one-fourth of candidates who raised money but were not on the ballot did not file two fundraising reports. There are other differences between these studies as well. For example, Hassell's analyses include incumbents and nonincumbents, while Bonica's are limited to nonincumbents.

5. See, for example, Banks and Kiewiet (1989); Canon (1993); Carson et al. (2007); Cox and Katz (1996); Fowler et al. (2023); Hirano and Snyder (2019); Jacobson (1989); Jacobson and Kernell (1983); Rohde (1979); Thomsen (2017).

6. I include dropouts who raised at least $1,000 in total receipts. The sample sizes differ slightly across thresholds, but the results are the same with a nonzero threshold (n=2,500), a $5,000 threshold (n=2,000), and the $1,000 threshold used here (n=2,300). Additional discussion of the data and measures is provided in the appendix. Dropouts comprise 9 percent of the 24,334 nonincumbents on the primary ballot across this period, but the proportion of dropouts has increased over time.

7. I used other measures of early money as well. See the appendix for a full discussion. I also examined other time cutoffs in light of the Republican takeover in 1994, the passage of the McCain-Feingold Act in 2002, and the *Citizens United* decision in 2010, and the results are the same.

8. In other analyses, I incorporated Bonica's (2014) ideology scores. Moderates are more likely to drop out, but about one-fourth of on-ballot candidates do not have CFscores, so the sample size decreases.

9. The states included in each sample are discussed in more detail in the appendix.

10. Approximately 15 percent of the sample dropped out and 85 percent were on the congressional ballot.

11. In terms of numbers, there are 362 safe or competitive primaries with no same-party incumbent and an experienced dropout; of these, 87 races had no

experienced candidate on the ballot, and 140 had one experienced candidate on the ballot. In the 200 safe or competitive open-seat primaries with an experienced dropout, 17 had no experienced candidate on the ballot, and 74 had one.

Chapter Five

1. In May 2023, Min was arrested for driving under the influence of alcohol. OCIndependent.com wrote that his future fundraising numbers would show the damage done to his campaign, noting "If his next quarterly campaign fundraising report is anemic, it will be taken as a sign by Democratic-powers-that-be that Min's campaign is too badly wounded to hold CA47 for the Democrats" (OCIndependent 2023).

2. Dropouts are excluded because they may have dropped out during their second reporting period. Candidate loans and candidate contributions are not included in the second report total, but they are included in the first report total, as I am interested in how the top line matters for future donor support. The total from the preprimary period is used as the second-quarter total if they started raising money in the quarter prior to that period.

3. YouGov used the respondents' name, birth date, and address, and verified they were in the L2 voter records as 2016 primary voters.

4. The question on the CES asked whether respondents donated during the past year, whereas respondents in this survey were asked whether they had ever donated money. This difference may account for the slightly higher percentage of donors in the sample of primary voters here. In the CES, 51 percent of Democratic primary voters had donated, compared to 35 percent of Republican primary voters.

5. I also randomized the general election candidate (bipartisan incumbent, partisan incumbent) but it had no effect on vote choice; this attribute is included in the models but not discussed.

6. There was no coverage of either the top two fundraisers or vote-getters in Newspapers.com in 9 primaries (1.8 percent) and only postprimary coverage for 6 of them (1.2 percent). Of the 485 primaries with coverage, 265 are Republican primaries, 185 are Democratic primaries, and 35 primaries are nonpartisan primaries. Duplicate articles in the Newspapers.com database are not included in the dataset.

Chapter Six

1. See, for example, Abramowitz (1988), Ansolabehere and Gerber (1994), Erikson and Palfrey (2000), Gerber (1998, 2004), Green and Krasno (1988, 1990), Levitt (1994), and Jacobson (1978, 1980, 1990).

2. The results in the replication are consistent with those in Jacobson (1990) and Green and Krasno (1988). I similarly use the incumbent's expenditures from the previous election cycle to instrument for incumbent spending. I also use the previous challenger's vote share to examine spending effects over time, but I instead use district presidential vote share to examine the effect of challenger-party strength since it is closer to the concept of interest. An additional note is that my interest is in fundraising as a metric, but here I draw on expenditures for consistency with Jacobson (1990) and Green and Krasno (1988). The findings are very similar with receipts, and more recent work on this topic has drawn on receipts (Bonica 2017).

3. In analyses by year, the relationship has not been significantly different from zero in most years since 1994 (the three exceptions are 2010, 2012, and 2022). This pattern is consistent with Bonica and Cox's (2018) finding that the party-centered nature of voting abruptly increased after 1994.

4. The values reflect those in models 2 and 4 in table 6.1, but the interaction between money and experience is not included, so the R-squared decreases by 0.01 in safe or competitive open seats.

5. Dropouts are not included in the analyses as they did not receive primary votes. They are also not included in the construction of the average and relative income measures.

Chapter Seven

1. I use this time period because party contributions were uncommon until the mid-1990s (see figure 7.1).

2. There are vast differences in fundraising across members, with party leaders and committee chairs expected to raise the most. In 2020, for example, Speaker Nancy Pelosi (D-CA) and Minority Leader Kevin McCarthy (R-CA) raised $28 million and $29 million, respectively. Minority Whip Steve Scalise (R-LA) was the top House fundraiser in 2020 and raised a staggering $38 million.

3. The only difference with the Grimmer and Powell (2013) measure is the exclusion of the Rules Committee. Some studies include Appropriations, Rules, and Ways and Means, but I use the broader measure because few first-term members are assigned to these three committees.

4. Totals include contributions to the member's leadership PAC as well as candidate committees, whereas the other analyses in the book are limited to contributions to candidate committees.

5. There are 447 members per congress, on average. The sample sizes vary slightly across years because the number of MCs varies by Congress and because members are occasionally missing contribution data for a sector. There are 43,200 total observations across the time period, but the sample size decreases due to the

inclusion of lagged effectiveness scores and the exclusion of committee chairs and party leaders.

6. For the most part, the same patterns emerge with both measures of sector contributions (total and logged contributions). The one exception is that the marginal effect is lower for the health sector with total contributions than with logged contributions. With logged contributions, the marginal effect for the health sector is similar to that for the energy sector.

Chapter Eight

1. In what ended up being an unexpectedly good year for the GOP, 14 of the 18 winners in the "Likely Democrat" races won narrowly, compared to only 2 of the 12 winners in the "Likely Republican" races. All 18 winners in the "Lean Democratic" races won narrowly, compared to only 6 of the 14 winners in the "Lean Republican" races. Similarly, Republicans won in all 26 races that were considered to be "Lean Republican" or "Likely Republican," while Democrats won in 29, or 86 percent, of the 36 "Lean Democrat" or "Likely Democrat" races.

2. There were actually 12 winners, but Jimmy Gomez beat another Democrat in the general election so the district was not in play for Republicans.

3. A series of influential articles studied the "vanishing marginals" and the increase in the incumbency advantage that unfolded over the late twentieth century (e.g., Abramowitz 1991; Abramowitz, Alexander, and Gunning 2006; Alford and Hibbing 1981; Ansolabehere, Brady, and Fiorina 1992; Cox and Katz 1996; Erikson 1971, 1972; Ferejohn 1977; Fiorina 1977; Gelman and King 1990; Jacobson 1987; Mayhew 1974b; Tufte 1973; see Jacobson 2015 for a recent update).

4. By the 60 percent threshold, about 40 percent of seats were marginal between 1952 and 1964, but this figure decreased in the decades since, reaching exceptionally low levels of 15 percent in 1988 and 17 percent in 2002 and 2004 (Abramowitz et al. 2006; Jacobson 2006). Since 2010, the share of general elections won by less than 20 points has rebounded to around 30 percent, or similar to levels in the 1990s.

5. By decade, the share is 13 percent in the 1980s, 16 percent in the 1990s, 10 percent in the 2000s, 14 percent in the 2010s, and 17 percent in the 2020s.

6. The measure is the same as previous chapters: districts where the party received more than 57.5 percent of the district vote in the current or previous presidential election.

7. Whereas 42 percent of House members were elected from safe districts in the 1980s, this figure rose to 70 percent from 2012 to 2022. Among winners in open seats, 50 and 63 percent came from safe districts in the 1980s and from 2012 to 2022, respectively.

8. Similarly, at the race level, the difference between the top two fundraisers is larger than that between the top two vote-getters. In opposed races, the average

difference between the top two fundraisers is 65 points, compared to 35 points between the top two vote-getters; in the full sample, the average difference between
the top two fundraisers and vote-getters is 84 points and 72 points, respectively.

9. Eight percent of candidates who raised less than 10 percent of preprimary
receipts won the primary (if primaries with two winners are excluded, this value
is lower at 5 percent). In safe open seats, this figure is lower yet at 3 percent. Of
the 778 primary winners who won with less than 10 percent of receipts, 400 won in
challenger-party primaries, 258 won in incumbent-contested races (of which 244, or
95 percent, won in nonpartisan primaries with two winners); and 120 won in open
seats. Only 0.5 percent of general election winners from 1980 to 2022 raised less than
10 percent of preprimary receipts (51 in total). It is therefore appropriate to describe these candidates as long shots.

10. Vote totals also understate the advantage of fundraisers at the top. Opposed candidates who raise more than 90 percent of receipts receive an average of
72 percent of the vote, and the correlation is 0.13. Yet 74 percent of candidates
who raise more than 90 percent of receipts are unopposed. When unopposed candidates are included, the average vote share is 93 percent. Most of the difference
between measures of competition is driven by long shots because the vote share
and fundraising values are the same in unopposed races.

11. Unlike traditional scatter plots, binned scatter plots are not a visualization
of the entire dataset (Cattaneo et al. 2024). Figure 8.1 does not effectively convey
the distribution of candidates at the low and high ends of fundraising, but the distribution matters for our expectations of where vote share and fundraising measures are likely to differ. Histograms of receipt shares are provided in Thomsen
(2023).

12. The top two vote-getters received an average of 47 and 27 percent of the vote,
and the top two fundraisers raised an average of 54 and 25 percent of receipts. The
disparity between the top two vote-getters and the top two fundraisers is smaller in
open seats than it is in challenger-party and incumbent-contested races, but both fundraising and vote share measures are well above the thresholds of competitiveness in
the vast majority of challenger-party and incumbent-contested races.

13. The 57.5 percent threshold follows from Hirano and Snyder (2019). Ninety-
five percent of candidates who raised at least 57.5 percent of preprimary receipts
won the primary. Ninety-one percent of candidates whose receipt share was more
than twenty points lower than the top fundraiser's share lost the primary; of the
9 percent whose receipt share was more than twenty points lower than the top
fundraiser's share but won, three-fourths lost in the general election. I also examined a measure of whether the winner raised less than 57.5 percent of receipts
and whether the winner's fundraising margin was within twenty points of the top-
raising loser. The results are the same, but I use preelection data here for the fundraising measures. In addition, I use Herfindahl measures of competition calculated
with vote and receipt shares, and the results are the same.

14. The average victory margin for a winner who wins with less than 57.5 percent of the primary vote is sixteen points. Nearly 30 percent of those who won with less than 57.5 percent of the primary vote won by more than twenty points. Even in opposed open-seat primaries in safe districts, the winner's average victory margin is nineteen points.

15. Scholars of comparative politics have given significant attention to what counts as a political party (e.g., Cox 1997; Laakso and Taagepera 1979; Lijphart 1994; Molinar 1991; Taagepera and Shugart 1993) as well as how to measure competition across electoral systems (e.g., Blais and Lago 2009; Folke 2014; Grofman and Selb 2009, 2011, see also Cox et al. 2020). Yet this line of research similarly draws on vote or seat shares, whereas I use preelection resource disparities. One recent exception is a measure of effective spending in UK elections by Fouirnaies (2021) that is similar to the one here.

16. This is a commonly used formula in the weighting literature (see Kish 1965).

17. All Republicans and Democrats on the ballot are included in the ballot-based measures (write-ins are excluded); Republicans and Democrats who raised money but were not on the ballot are included in the fundraising measures in addition to the on-ballot candidates, though the results are the same if dropouts are excluded. Like Hirano and Snyder (2019, 39), primaries in which no candidate ran for the nomination are counted as uncontested, with zero candidates on the ballot and zero effective candidates. Unlike them, I include cases where a nomination was made by convention and count them as uncontested; however, they note that the patterns are similar when conventions are excluded or counted as uncontested. The thirteen cases in which the general election winner or future general election winner (e.g., Bernie Sanders in 1988) is an Independent are also excluded. Unopposed primaries with missing values of receipts are coded as uncompetitive with one candidate in the race. It is unclear how Hirano and Snyder (2019) code nonpartisan primaries; here they are considered by party in order to account for district partisanship. Because vote totals are tabulated at the primary level in nonpartisan primaries, the total number of candidates is calculated at the primary level as well so the average number of candidates is higher. The results are the same if nonpartisan primaries are excluded.

18. Hirano and Snyder (2019) label these disadvantaged-party, parties-balanced, and advantaged-party, respectively. Hopeless, competitive, and safe district labels are consistent with previous chapters. I use Gary Jacobson's presidential vote share data to measure district partisanship.

19. Like Hirano and Snyder (2019, 39), I exclude safe challenger-party primaries and hopeless incumbent-contested primaries. The full sample of 19,140—two primaries in 435 districts over 22 cycles—diminishes by 1,697 as a result; another twenty-six primaries with Independent general election winners are excluded; two primaries in South Dakota's Second District in 1980 are excluded because the district was abolished in 1982; and an additional forty duplicate primaries when

districts were redrawn (e.g., Texas in 1996 and 2006) are included. The total number of observations in the vote share models is thus 17,455.

20. There is no agreed upon victory margin at the primary stage. Boatright (2013) uses a lower threshold of whether the incumbent received less than 75 percent of the vote. I use Hirano and Snyder's (2019) threshold because they provide the most comprehensive account of primary competition to date, but a ten- or twenty-point margin is most common in studies of general elections.

21. The total number of candidates is slightly lower than that in Hirano and Snyder (2019, 181) because disadvantaged-party primaries are excluded from their figures.

22. Of the 8,155 incumbent-contested primaries, 511 and 233 are competitive with the 57.5 percent vote share and fundraising measures, respectively. Of the 7,476 challenger-party primaries, 1,418 and 521 are competitive with the vote share and fundraising measures, respectively. Of the 1,824 open-seat primaries, 1,005 and 730 are competitive with the vote share and fundraising measures, respectively. In the full sample of 17,455 primaries, 2,934 are competitive with the vote share measures, compared to 1,484 with the fundraising measures (or 17 and 9 percent of primaries, respectively). The number of competitive primaries is low with vote shares, but it is significantly lower with fundraising measures.

23. I also ran the analyses without dropouts, and the results are the same. Dropout candidates are included because candidates can amass resources without appearing on the ballot. In other analyses, I accounted for party and group activity in the race. I use Hassell's (2023) data to control for the number of party-connected donors and FEC data to control for party coordinated expenditures and independent expenditures before the primary. The insignificant relationships are unsurprising. As Hassell (2023) shows, factors like seat type and district partisanship influence party engagement.

24. The graphs follow the format in Hirano and Snyder (2019, 200). The main comparisons are with the top right (percent of competitive races) and bottom left (number of candidates) graphs. Their two other measures—whether the race was contested and the total vote percentage to losing candidates—are not incorporated here. The measure of whether there is any candidate in the race is an exceedingly low standard. The measure of the total vote percentage to losing candidates also reveals higher levels of competition than a similar measure based on fundraising, but I focus on the top candidate's advantage and the number of competitors. The values on the number of candidates in open seats are slightly lower in their graphs, which is likely due to differences in the time periods of study. Their data extend from 1950 to 2016, whereas the data here are from 1980 to 2022 when the number of candidates in open-seat primaries is higher (Hirano and Snyder 2019, 183). However, the patterns are clearly similar. I focus on the expected difference between the measures, but the predicted values in tables 8.1 and 8.2 are provided in the appendix. I also examined the difference between fundraising and vote

share measures when either individual or PAC contributions are used, instead of total preprimary receipts, and the results are the same. I use total receipts because contribution type is less central to the material and symbolic benefits of fundraising emphasized here.

25. Of the 509 open-seat primaries in safe districts, 359 are competitive with the 57.5 percent vote share measure, compared to 294 with the 57.5 percent fundraising measure. Of the 806 open seats in competitive districts, 446 are competitive with the 57.5 percent vote share measure, versus 324 with the 57.5 percent fundraising measure.

26. In fact, 366 of these 1,574 mismatches, or 23 percent, are not competitive with the 20-point victory margin measure either. In these races, the top fundraiser's margin is sixty-six points, and the top vote-getter's margin is twenty-seven points, ranging from twenty to forty-five points.

27. Open seats constitute 10 percent of the full sample but 22 percent of the mismatches.

28. Nor is it the case that long shots are more likely to run again and are thus setting the stage for a subsequent congressional bid. Among nonincumbents who ran from 1980 to 2016, 24 percent of long shots ran again, compared to 31 percent of non–long shots.

29. More specifically, we are interested in the number of long-shot candidates whose vote share is higher than their receipt share. Ninety-six percent of long shots outperform their receipt share, so I use this simpler measure of the number of candidates who raise less than 10 percent of receipts. Similarly, the total number of long shots and the total number of long shots who outperform their receipt share are correlated at 0.98.

30. However, the high price tag deters some potential candidates more than others (Carnes 2018).

31. A total of 1,086 primaries are competitive with the dollar amount and the fundraising share measure, and a total of 14,632 primaries are uncompetitive with both. Again, following Hirano and Snyder (2019), incumbent-contested primaries in hopeless districts and challenger-party primaries in safe districts are excluded from this sample.

32. Long shots in general elections matter in different ways for the competition variables because there are only two candidates. In particular, they are likely to increase the difference between the number of candidate measures, but general elections with long shots are unlikely to be competitive with either the vote share or fundraising measure. Our main interest is in overall differences.

Chapter Nine

1. Prior to this decision, two state courts struck down limitations on campaign expenditures and contributions in 1974 and 1975 (*Bare v. Gorton* and *Deras v.*

Meyers, respectively). Each case found no government interest to justify the infringement on First Amendment rights (Schneider 1976, 853).

2. In the US, soaring fundraising demands have not been accompanied by a decline in candidates or higher incumbent reelection rates, but the sheer amount of money in American politics is in a league of its own (Thompson 2012).

Appendix to Chapter One

1. An additional one hundred candidates who were appointed as general election nominees but did not run in a primary also have missing values on their share of primary receipts.

Bibliography

Abramowitz, Alan I. 1988. "Explaining Senate Election Outcomes." *American Political Science Review* 82 (2): 385–403.

Abramowitz, Alan I. 1991. "Incumbency, Campaign Spending, and the Decline of Competition in U.S. House Elections." *Journal of Politics* 53 (1): 34–56.

Abramowitz, Alan I., Brad Alexander, and Matthew Gunning. 2006. "Incumbency, Redistricting, and the Decline of Competition in U.S. House Elections." *Journal of Politics* 68 (1): 75–88.

Acquired. 2022. "From NFL to Startup COO to Congressman Regulating Crypto (with Rep. Anthony Gonzalez)." *Acquired* (podcast), August 1, 2022. https://www.acquired.fm/episodes/from-nfl-to-startup-coo-to-congressman-regulating |-crypto-with-rep-anthony-gonzalez.

Adkins, Randall E., and Andrew J. Dowdle. 2002. "The Money Primary: What Influences the Outcome of Pre-Primary Presidential Nomination Fundraising?" *Presidential Studies Quarterly* 32 (2): 256–275.

Ahler, Douglas J., Jack Citrin, and Gabriel S. Lenz. 2016. "Do Open Primaries Improve Representation? An Experimental Test of California's 2012 Top-Two Primary." *Legislative Studies Quarterly* 41 (2): 237–268.

Aldrich, John H. 1980. *Before the Convention: Strategies and Choices in Presidential Nomination Campaigns.* Chicago: University of Chicago Press.

Alford, John R., and John R. Hibbing. 1981. "Increased Incumbency Advantage in the House." *Journal of Politics* 43 (4): 1042–1061.

Anderson, Sarah E., Daniel M. Butler, and Laurel Harbridge-Yong. 2020. *Rejecting Compromise: Legislators' Fear of Primary Voters.* New York: Cambridge University Press.

Ansolabehere, Stephen, David Brady, and Morris Fiorina. 1992. "The Vanishing Marginals and Electoral Responsiveness." *British Journal of Political Science* 22 (1): 21–38.

Ansolabehere, Stephen, John M. de Figueiredo, and James M. Snyder, Jr. 2003. "Why Is There So Little Money in U.S. Politics?" *Journal of Economic Perspectives* 17 (1): 105–130.

Ansolabehere, Stephen, and Alan Gerber. 1994. "The Mismeasure of Campaign Spending: Evidence from the 1990 U.S. House Elections." *Journal of Politics* 56 (4): 1106–1118.

Ansolabehere, Stephen, and James M. Snyder, Jr. 1998. "Money and Institutional Power." *Texas Law Review* 77 (7): 1673–1704.

Arceneaux, Kevin, Johanna Dunaway, Martin Johnson, and Ryan J. Vander Wielen. 2020. "Strategic Candidate Entry and Congressional Elections in the Era of Fox News." *American Journal of Political Science* 64 (2): 398–415.

Avis, Eric, Claudio Ferraz, Frederico Finan, and Carlos Varjão. 2017. "Money and Politics: The Effects of Campaign Spending Limits on Political Competition and Incumbency Advantage." Technical Report w23508, National Bureau of Economic Research, Cambridge, MA.

Bafumi, Joseph, and Michael C. Herron. 2010. "Leapfrog Representation and Extremism: A Study of American Voters and Their Members in Congress." *American Political Science Review* 104 (3): 519–542.

Banks, Jeffrey S., and D. Roderick Kiewiet. 1989. "Explaining Patterns of Candidate Competition in Congressional Elections." *American Journal of Political Science* 33 (4): 997–1015.

Barber, Michael. 2016. "Donation Motivations: Testing Theories of Access and Ideology." *Political Research Quarterly* 69 (1): 148–159.

Barber, Michael J., Brandice Canes-Wrone, and Sharece Thrower. 2017. "Ideologically Sophisticated Donors: Which Candidates Do Individual Contributors Finance?" *American Journal of Political Science* 61 (2): 271–288.

Bartels, Larry M. 2008. *Unequal Democracy: The Political Economy of the New Gilded Age*. Princeton, NJ: Princeton University Press.

Bawn, Kathleen, Martin Cohen, David Karol, Seth Masket, Hans Noel, and John Zaller. 2012. "A Theory of Political Parties: Groups, Policy Demands and Nominations in American Politics." *Perspectives on Politics* 10 (3): 571–597.

Beckel, Michael. 2017. "The Price of Power: A Deep-Dive Analysis into How Political Parties Squeeze Influential Lawmakers to Boost Campaign Coffers." Technical report, Issue One, Washington, DC.

Berkowitz, Bonnie, and Chris Alcantara. 2019. "How to Run for Congress." *Washington Post*, November 15, 2019.

Berry, Christopher R., and Anthony Fowler. 2018. "Congressional Committees, Legislative Influence, and the Hegemony of Chairs." *Journal of Public Economics* 158: 1–11.

Bianco, William T. 1984. "Strategic Decisions on Candidacy in U.S. Congressional Districts." *Legislative Studies Quarterly* 9 (2): 351–364.

Biersack, Robert, Paul S. Herrnson, and Clyde Wilcox. 1993. "Seeds for Success:

Early Money in Congressional Elections." *Legislative Studies Quarterly* 18 (4): 535.

Blais, André, and Ignacio Lago. 2009. "A General Measure of District Competitiveness." *Electoral Studies* 28 (1): 94–100.

Boatright, Robert G. 2013. *Getting Primaried: The Changing Politics of Congressional Primary Challenges*. Ann Arbor: University of Michigan Press.

Boatright, Robert G. 2020. *Routledge Handbook of Primary Elections*. New York: Routledge.

Bond, Jon R., Cary Covington, and Richard Fleisher. 1985. "Explaining Challenger Quality in Congressional Elections." *Journal of Politics* 47 (2): 510–529.

Bonica, Adam. 2014. "Mapping the Ideological Marketplace." *American Journal of Political Science* 58 (2): 367–386.

Bonica, Adam. 2017. "Professional Networks, Early Fundraising, and Electoral Success." *Election Law Journal: Rules, Politics, and Policy* 16 (1): 153–171.

Bonica, Adam. 2020. "Why Are There So Many Lawyers in Congress?" *Legislative Studies Quarterly* 45 (2): 253–289.

Bonica, Adam, and Gary W. Cox. 2018. "Ideological Extremists in the U.S. Congress: Out of Step but Still in Office." *Quarterly Journal of Political Science* 13 (2): 207–236.

Bonica, Adam, and Jacob M. Grumbach. 2023. "Old Money: Campaign Finance and Gerontocracy in the United States." Working paper.

Bonica, Adam, Nolan McCarty, Keith T Poole, and Howard Rosenthal. 2013. "Why Hasn't Democracy Slowed Rising Inequality?" *Journal of Economic Perspectives* 27 (3): 103–124.

Bronars, Stephen G., and John R. Lott Jr. 1997. "Do Campaign Donations Alter How a Politician Votes? Or, Do Donors Support Candidates Who Value the Same Things That They Do?" *Journal of Law and Economics* 40 (2): 317–350.

Broockman, David A., Nicholas Carnes, Christopher Skovron, and Melody Crowder-Meyer. 2012. "The 2012 National Candidate Study."

Bucchianeri, Peter, Craig Volden, and Alan E. Wiseman. 2025. "Legislative Effectiveness in the American States." *American Political Science Review* 119 (1): 21–39.

Canes-Wrone, Brandice, and Kenneth M. Miller. 2022. "Out-of-District Contributors and Representation in the US House." *Legislative Studies Quarterly* 47 (2): 361–395.

Canon, David T. 1990. *Actors, Athletes, and Astronauts: Political Amateurs in the United States Congress*. Chicago: University of Chicago Press.

Canon, David T. 1993. "Sacrificial Lambs or Strategic Politicians? Political Amateurs in U.S. House Elections." *American Journal of Political Science* 37 (4): 1119–1141.

Carnes, Nicholas. 2018. *The Cash Ceiling: Why Only the Rich Run for Office–and What We Can Do about It*. Princeton, NJ: Princeton University Press.

Carson, Jamie L., Erik J. Engstrom, and Jason M. Roberts. 2007. "Candidate Quality, the Personal Vote, and the Incumbency Advantage in Congress." *American Political Science Review* 101 (2): 289–301.

Carson, Jamie L., and Jason M. Roberts. 2005. "Strategic Politicians and U.S. House Elections, 1874–1914." *Journal of Politics* 67 (2): 474–496.

Cattaneo, Matias D., Richard K. Crump, Max H. Farrell, and Yingjie Feng. 2024. "On Binscatter." *American Economic Review* 114(5): 1488–1514,

Chappell, Henry W. 1982. "Campaign Contributions and Congressional Voting: A Simultaneous Probit-Tobit Model." *Review of Economics and Statistics* 64 (1): 77–83.

Cohen, Marty, David Karol, Hans Noel, and John Zaller. 2008. *The Party Decides: Presidential Nominations Before and After Reform*. Chicago: University of Chicago Press.

Corasaniti, Nick, and Shane Goldmacher. 2018. "Rodney Frelinghuysen, Powerful House Republican, Announces He Will Not Seek Re-Election." *New York Times*, January 29, 2018.

Cox, Gary W. 1997. *Making Votes Count: Strategic Coordination in the World's Electoral Systems*. New York: Cambridge University Press.

Cox, Gary W., Jon H. Fiva, and Daniel M. S1mith. 2020. "Measuring the Competitiveness of Elections." *Political Analysis* 28 (2): 168–185.

Cox, Gary W., and Jonathan N. Katz. 1996. "Why Did the Incumbency Advantage in U.S. House Elections Grow?" *American Journal of Political Science* 40 (2): 478–497.

Cox, Gary W., and Eric Magar. 1999. "How Much Is Majority Status in the U.S. Congress Worth?" *American Political Science Review* 93 (2): 299–309.

Cox, Gary W., and Mathew D. McCubbins. 2005. *Setting the Agenda: Responsible Party Government in the U.S. House of Representatives*. New York: Cambridge University Press.

Crowder-Meyer, Melody, and Rosalyn Cooperman. 2018. "Can't Buy Them Love: How Party Culture among Donors Contributes to the Party Gap in Women's Representation." *Journal of Politics* 80 (4): 1211–1224.

Curry, James M. 2015. *Legislating in the Dark: Information and Power in the House of Representatives*. Chicago Studies in American Politics. Chicago: University of Chicago Press.

Dahl, Robert A. 1956. *A Preface to Democratic Theory*. Chicago: University of Chicago Press.

Dahl, Robert A. 1971. *Polyarchy: Participation and Opposition*. New Haven, CT: Yale University Press.

Dittmar, Kelly. 2020. "Urgency and Ambition: The Influence of Political Environment and Emotion in Spurring US Women's Candidacies in 2018." *European Journal of Politics and Gender* 3 (1): 143–160.

Doherty, David, Conor M. Dowling, and Michael G. Miller. 2019. "Do Local Party

Chairs Think Women and Minority Candidates Can Win? Evidence from a Conjoint Experiment." *Journal of Politics* 81 (4): 1282–1297.

Dominguez, Casey B. K. 2011. "Does the Party Matter? Endorsements in Congressional Primaries." *Political Research Quarterly* 64 (3): 534–544.

Dulio, David A. 2004. *For Better or Worse? How Political Consultants Are Changing Elections in the United States*. Albany: State University of New York Press.

Erikson, Robert S. 1971. "The Advantage of Incumbency in Congressional Elections." *Polity* 3 (3): 395–405.

Erikson, Robert S. 1972. "Malapportionment, Gerrymandering, and Party Fortunes in Congressional Elections." *American Political Science Review* 66 (4): 1234–1245.

Erikson, Robert S., and Thomas R. Palfrey. 2000. "Equilibria in Campaign Spending Games: Theory and Data." *American Political Science Review* 94 (3): 595–609.

Federal Election Commission. 1981. "Annual Report 1981." https://www.fec.gov/resources/cms-content/documents/ar81.pdf.

Fenno, Richard F. 1977. "U.S. House Members in Their Constituencies: An Exploration." *American Political Science Review* 71 (3): 883–917.

Fenno, Richard F. 1978. *Home Style: House Members in Their Districts*. New York: Harper Collins.

Ferejohn, John A. 1977. "On the Decline of Competition in Congressional Elections." *American Political Science Review* 71 (1): 166–176.

Fiorina, Morris P. 1977. "The Case of the Vanishing Marginals: The Bureaucracy Did It." *American Political Science Review* 71 (1): 177–181.

Folke, Olle. 2014. "Shades of Brown and Green: Party Effects in Proportional Election Systems." *Journal of the European Economic Association* 12 (5): 1361–1395.

Fouirnaies, Alexander. 2018. "When Are Agenda Setters Valuable?" *American Journal of Political Science* 62 (1): 176–191.

Fouirnaies, Alexander. 2021. "How Do Campaign Spending Limits Affect Elections? Evidence from the United Kingdom 1885–2019." *American Political Science Review* 115 (2): 395–411.

Fouirnaies, Alexander, and Andrew B. Hall. 2014. "The Financial Incumbency Advantage: Causes and Consequences." *Journal of Politics* 76 (3): 711–724.

Fouirnaies, Alexander, and Andrew B. Hall. 2018. "How Do Interest Groups Seek Access to Committees?" *American Journal of Political Science* 62 (1): 132–147.

Fouirnaies, Alexander, and Andrew B. Hall. 2022. "How Do Electoral Incentives Affect Legislator Behavior? Evidence from U.S. State Legislatures." *American Political Science Review* 116 (2): 662–676.

Fouriezos, Nick. 2018. "Mikie Sherrill Flew Helicopters for the U.S. Now She Wants to Turn D.C. Blue." *USA Today*, May 24, 2018.

Fowler, Anthony, Seth J. Hill, Jeffrey B. Lewis, Chris Tausanovitch, Lynn Vavreck, and Christopher Warshaw. 2023. "Moderates." *American Political Science Review* 117 (2): 643–660.

Fowler, Gareth, and Daniel I. Weiner. 2019. "Understanding H.R.1's Public Financing Provisions." Technical report, Brennan Center for Justice, Washington, DC.

Fowler, Linda L., and Robert D. McClure. 1989. *Political Ambition: Who Decides to Run for Congress*. New Haven, CT: Yale University Press.

Gelman, Andrew, and Gary King. 1990. "Estimating Incumbency Advantage without Bias." *American Journal of Political Science* 34 (4): 1142–1164.

Gerber, Alan. 1998. "Estimating the Effect of Campaign Spending on Senate Election Outcomes Using Instrumental Variables." *American Political Science Review* 92 (2): 401–411.

Gerber, Alan S. 2004. "Does Campaign Spending Work?: Field Experiments Provide Evidence and Suggest New Theory." *American Behavioral Scientist* 47 (5): 541–574.

Gilens, Martin. 2012. *Affluence and Influence: Economic Inequality and Political Power in America*. Princeton, NJ: Princeton University Press.

Gimpel, James G., Frances E. Lee, and Joshua Kaminski. 2006. "The Political Geography of Campaign Contributions in American Politics." *Journal of Politics* 68 (3): 626–639.

Gimpel, James G., Frances E. Lee, and Shanna Pearson-Merkowitz. 2008. "The Check Is in the Mail: Interdistrict Funding Flows in Congressional Elections." *American Journal of Political Science* 52 (2): 373–394.

Goff, Michael J. 2005. *The Money Primary: The New Politics of the Early Presidential Nomination Process*. Lanham, MD: Rowman and Littlefield.

Goffman, Erving. 1959. *The Presentation of Self in Everyday Life*. New York: Knopf Doubleday.

Graber, Doris A., and Johanna Dunaway. 2017. *Mass Media and American Politics*. Washington, DC: CQ Press.

Green, Donald Philip, and Jonathan S. Krasno. 1988. "Salvation for the Spendthrift Incumbent: Reestimating the Effects of Campaign Spending in House Elections." *American Journal of Political Science* 32 (4): 884–907.

Green, Donald Philip, and Jonathan S. Krasno. 1990. "Rebuttal to Jacobson's 'New Evidence for Old Arguments.'" *American Journal of Political Science* 34 (2): 363–372.

Grenzke, Janet. 1988. "Comparing Contributions to U.S. House Members from Outside Their Districts." *Legislative Studies Quarterly* 13 (1): 83–103.

Grenzke, Janet M. 1989. "PACs and the Congressional Supermarket: The Currency Is Complex." *American Journal of Political Science* 33 (1): 1–24.

Grier, Kevin B., and Michael C. Munger. 1986. "The Impact of Legislator Attributes on Interest Group Campaign Contributions." *Journal of Labor Research* 7 (4): 349–361.

Grim, Ryan. 2022. "Senate Races That Could Tip The Balance." *Deconstructed*, October 14, 2022.

Grimmer, Justin, and Eleanor Neff Powell. 2013. "Congressmen in Exile: The Politics and Consequences of Involuntary Committee Removal." *Journal of Politics* 75 (4): 907–920.

Grofman, Bernard, and Peter Selb. 2009. "A Fully General Index of Political Competition." *Electoral Studies* 28 (2): 291–296.

Grofman, Bernard, and Peter Selb. 2011. "Turnout and the (Effective) Number of Parties at the National and District Levels: A Puzzle-Solving Approach." *Party Politics* 17 (1): 93–117.

Groseclose, Tim, and Charles Stewart III. 1998. "The Value of Committee Seats in the House, 1947–91." *American Journal of Political Science* 42 (2): 453–474.

Grossmann, Matt, and David A. Hopkins. 2015. "Ideological Republicans and Group Interest Democrats: The Asymmetry of American Party Politics." *Perspectives on Politics* 13 (1): 119–139.

Grumbach, Jacob M., and Alexander Sahn. 2020. "Race and Representation in Campaign Finance." *American Political Science Review* 114 (1): 206–221.

Hacker, Jacob S., and Paul Pierson. 2010a. *Winner-Take-All Politics: How Washington Made the Rich Richer—and Turned Its Back on the Middle Class*. New York: Simon and Schuster.

Hacker, Jacob S., and Paul Pierson. 2010b. "Winner-Take-All Politics: Public Policy, Political Organization, and the Precipitous Rise of Top Incomes in the United States." *Politics & Society* 38 (2): 152–204.

Hainmueller, Jens, Dominik Hangartner, and Teppei Yamamoto. 2015. "Validating Vignette and Conjoint Survey Experiments against Real-World Behavior." *Proceedings of the National Academy of Sciences* 112 (8): 2395–2400.

Hainmueller, Jens, Daniel J. Hopkins, and Teppei Yamamoto. 2014. "Causal Inference in Conjoint Analysis: Understanding Multidimensional Choices via Stated Preference Experiments." *Political Analysis* 22 (1): 1–30.

Hall, Andrew B., and James M. Snyder Jr. 2015. "Candidate Ideology and Electoral Success." Working paper, Harvard University.

Hall, Richard L., and Alan V. Deardorff. 2006. "Lobbying as Legislative Subsidy." *American Political Science Review* 100 (1): 69–84.

Hall, Richard L., and Frank W. Wayman. 1990. "Buying Time: Moneyed Interests and the Mobilization of Bias in Congressional Committees." *American Political Science Review* 84 (3): 797–820.

Hassell, Hans J. G. 2018. *The Party's Primary: Control of Congressional Nominations*. New York: Cambridge University Press.

Hassell, Hans J. G. 2023. "Party Elite Engagement and Coordination in House Primary Elections: A Test of Theories of Parties." *American Journal of Political Science* 67 (2): 307–323.

Hayes, Danny, and Jennifer L. Lawless. 2015. "As Local News Goes, So Goes Citizen Engagement: Media, Knowledge, and Participation in US House Elections." *Journal of Politics* 77 (2): 447–462.

Hayes, Danny, and Jennifer L. Lawless. 2021. *News Hole: The Demise of Local Journalism and Political Engagement*. New York: Cambridge University Press.

Heberlig, Eric, Marc Hetherington, and Bruce Larson. 2006. "The Price of Leadership: Campaign Money and the Polarization of Congressional Parties." *Journal of Politics* 68 (4): 992–1005.

Heberlig, Eric S., and Bruce A. Larson. 2012. *Congressional Parties, Institutional Ambition, and the Financing of Majority Control*. Ann Arbor: University of Michigan Press.

Hill, Seth J., and Gregory A. Huber. 2017. "Representativeness and Motivations of the Contemporary Donorate: Results from Merged Survey and Administrative Records." *Political Behavior* 39 (1): 3–29.

Hirano, Shigeo, and James M. Snyder Jr. 2014. "Primary Elections and the Quality of Elected Officials." *Quarterly Journal of Political Science* 9 (4): 473–500.

Hirano, Shigeo, and James M. Snyder Jr. 2019. *Primary Elections in the United States*. New York: Cambridge University Press.

Holzberg, Melissa. 2021. "ActBlue Still Outraises WinRed, but the GOP Platform Is Catching Up." *OpenSecrets News*, August 4, 2021.

Hook, Janet. 2018. "How Tough Is the GOP's Midterm Challenge? Just Ask Rodney Frelinghuysen." *Wall Street Journal*, January 24, 2018.

Hopkins, Daniel J. 2018. *The Increasingly United States: How and Why American Political Behavior Nationalized*. Chicago: University of Chicago Press.

Jacobson, Gary C. 1978. "The Effects of Campaign Spending in Congressional Elections." *American Political Science Review* 72 (2): 469–491.

Jacobson, Gary C. 1980. *Money in Congressional Elections*. New Haven, CT: Yale University Press.

Jacobson, Gary C. 1987. "The Marginals Never Vanished: Incumbency and Competition in Elections to the U.S. House of Representatives, 1952–82." *American Journal of Political Science* 31 (1): 126–141.

Jacobson, Gary C. 1989. "Strategic Politicians and the Dynamics of U.S. House Elections, 1946–86." *American Political Science Review* 83 (3): 773–793.

Jacobson, Gary C. 1990. "The Effects of Campaign Spending in House Elections: New Evidence for Old Arguments." *American Journal of Political Science* 34 (2): 334–362.

Jacobson, Gary C. 2006. "Competition in U.S. Congressional Elections." In *The Marketplace of Democracy: Electoral Competition and American Politics*, 27–52. Washington, DC: Brookings Institution.

Jacobson, Gary C. 2015. "It's Nothing Personal: The Decline of the Incumbency Advantage in US House Elections." *Journal of Politics* 77 (3): 861–873.

Jacobson, Gary C., and Samuel Kernell. 1983. *Strategy and Choice in Congressional Elections*. New Haven, CT: Yale University Press.

Jones, Athena. 2012. "Political Newcomers Face High Costs and Difficult Odds." *CNN*, January 22, 2012.

Kalla, Joshua L., and David E. Broockman. 2016. "Campaign Contributions Facilitate Access to Congressional Officials: A Randomized Field Experiment." *American Journal of Political Science* 60 (3): 545–558.

Kang, Hannah. 2023. "Who Has Raised, and Spent, the Most for Katie Porter's Congressional Seat?" *Orange County Register*, April 23, 2023.

Kazee, Thomas A. 1994. *Who Runs for Congress?: Ambition, Context, and Candidate Emergence.* Washington, DC: CQ Press.

Key, V. O., Jr. 1949. *Southern Politics in State and Nation.* New York: A. A. Knopf.

Kilborn, Mitchell, and Arjun Vishwanath. 2022. "Public Money Talks Too: How Public Campaign Financing Degrades Representation." *American Journal of Political Science* 66 (3): 730–744.

King, Aaron S. 2017. *Unfolding Ambition in Senate Primary Elections: Strategic Politicians and the Dynamics of Candidacy Decisions.* Lanham, MD: Lexington Books.

Kirkland, Patricia A., and Alexander Coppock. 2018. "Candidate Choice without Party Labels: New Insights from Conjoint Survey Experiments." *Political Behavior* 40 (3): 571–591.

Kish, Leslie. 1965. *Survey Sampling.* New York: Wiley.

Kistner, Michael. 2022. "Fighting for Majorities? Explaining the Development of Caucus Fundraising in American Legislatures." *Journal of Politics* 84 (1): 321–334.

Klarner, Carl. 2018. "State Legislative Election Returns, 1967–2016."

Koerth, Maggie. 2018. "How Money Affects Elections." *FiveThirtyEight*, September 10, 2018.

Krasno, Jonathan S., and Donald Philip Green. 1988. "Preempting Quality Challengers in House Elections." *Journal of Politics* 50 (4): 920–936.

Krasno, Jonathan S., Donald Philip Green, and Jonathan A. Cowden. 1994. "The Dynamics of Campaign Fundraising in House Elections." *Journal of Politics* 56 (2): 459–474.

La Raja, Raymond J. 2007. "Sunshine Laws and the Press: The Effect of Campaign Disclosure on News Reporting in the American States." *Election Law Journal: Rules, Politics, and Policy* 6 (3): 236–250.

La Raja, Raymond J., and Brian F. Schaffner. 2015. *Campaign Finance and Political Polarization: When Purists Prevail.* Ann Arbor: University of Michigan Press.

Laakso, Markku, and Rein Taagepera. 1979. "'Effective' Number of Parties: A Measure with Application to West Europe." *Comparative Political Studies* 12 (1): 3–27.

Lee, Frances E. 2009. *Beyond Ideology: Politics, Principles, and Partisanship in the U.S. Senate.* Chicago: University of Chicago Press.

Lee, Frances E. 2016. *Insecure Majorities: Congress and the Perpetual Campaign.* Chicago: University of Chicago Press.

Lessig, Lawrence. 2011. *Republic, Lost: How Money Corrupts Congress—and a Plan to Stop It.* New York: Twelve.

Lessig, Lawrence. 2014. "The Plan to Take Our Democracy Back." https://www.youtube.com/watch?v=i3X2eDCmPRY.

Levitt, Steven D. 1994. "Using Repeat Challengers to Estimate the Effect of Campaign Spending on Election Outcomes in the U.S. House." *Journal of Political Economy* 102 (4): 777–798.

Levitt, Steven D., and Catherine D. Wolfram. 1997. "Decomposing the Sources of Incumbency Advantage in the U.S. House." *Legislative Studies Quarterly* 22 (1): 45–60.

Lijphart, Arend. 1994. *Electoral Systems and Party Systems: A Study of Twenty-Seven Democracies, 1945–1990*. New York: Oxford University Press.

Lublin, David Ian. 1994. "Quality, Not Quantity: Strategic Politicians in U.S. Senate Elections, 1952–1990." *Journal of Politics* 56 (1): 228–241.

Maestas, Cherie D., Sarah Fulton, L. Sandy Maisel, and Walter J. Stone. 2006. "When to Risk It? Institutions, Ambitions, and the Decision to Run for the U.S. House." *American Political Science Review* 100 (2): 195–208.

Magleby, David B., Jay Goodliffe, and Joseph A. Olsen. 2018. *Who Donates in Campaigns?: The Importance of Message, Messenger, Medium, and Structure*. New York: Cambridge University Press.

Masket, Seth. 2009. *No Middle Ground: How Informal Party Organizations Control Nominations and Polarize Legislatures*. Ann Arbor: University of Michigan Press.

Mason, Lilliana. 2018. *Uncivil Agreement: How Politics Became Our Identity*. Chicago: University of Chicago Press.

Mayer, William G. 2003. "Forecasting Presidential Nominations or, My Model Worked Just Fine, Thank You." *PS: Political Science & Politics* 36 (2): 153–157.

Mayhew, David R. 1974a. *Congress: The Electoral Connection*. New Haven, CT: Yale University Press.

Mayhew, David R. 1974b. "Congressional Elections: The Case of the Vanishing Marginals." *Polity* 6 (3): 295–317.

Medvic, Stephen K. 2001. *Political Consultants in U.S. Congressional Elections*. Columbus: Ohio State University Press.

The Miller Center. 2020. "President Theodore Roosevelt, December 6, 1904: Fourth Annual Message." Technical report, University of Virginia, Charlottesville.

Miller, Michael G. 2016. "The Power of an Hour: Effects of Candidate Time Expenditure in State Legislative Elections." *Legislative Studies Quarterly* 41 (2): 327–359.

Molinar, Juan. 1991. "Counting the Number of Parties: An Alternative Index." *American Political Science Review* 85 (4): 1383–1391.

Niven, David. 2006. "Throwing Your Hat Out of the Ring: Negative Recruitment and the Gender Imbalance in State Legislative Candidacy." *Politics & Gender* 2 (4): 473–489.

Noble, Jason. 2013. "Congressional Candidates Face Deadline, Seek Cash." *Des Moines Sunday Register*, September 29, 2013.

Norrander, Barbara. 2006. "The Attrition Game: Initial Resources, Initial Contests and the Exit of Candidates During the US Presidential Primary Season." *British Journal of Political Science* 36 (3): 487–507.

OCIndependent. 2023. "CA47: Dave Min Decides to Quit Drinking instead of Campaign." *OCIndependent.com*, June 20, 2023.

Oklobdzija, Stan. 2024. "Dark Parties: Unveiling Nonparty Communities in American Political Campaigns." *American Political Science Review* 118 (1): 401–422.

OpenSecrets. 2020. "Did Money Win?" *OpenSecrets*. Accessed September 29, 2021.

OpenSecrets. 2022. "Top Interest Groups Giving to Members of Congress." *OpenSecrets*. Accessed December 28, 2022.

OpenSecrets. 2023a. "Cost of Election." *OpenSecrets*. Accessed April 17, 2024.

OpenSecrets. 2023b. "Georgia Senate 2022 Race." *OpenSecrets*. Accessed August 28, 2023.

OpenSecrets. 2023c. "PAC Profile: ActBlue." *OpenSecrets*. Accessed April 17, 2023.

Page, Benjamin I., Larry M. Bartels, and Jason Seawright. 2013. "Democracy and the Policy Preferences of Wealthy Americans." *Perspectives on Politics* 11 (1): 51–73.

Page, Benjamin I., and Martin Gilens. 2020. *Democracy in America?: What Has Gone Wrong and What We Can Do About It*. Chicago: University of Chicago Press.

Pearson, Kathryn, and Eric McGhee. 2013. "What It Takes to Win: Questioning "Gender Neutral" Outcomes in U.S. House Elections." *Politics & Gender* 9 (4): 439–462.

Peterson, Erik. 2021. "Paper Cuts: How Reporting Resources Affect Political News Coverage." *American Journal of Political Science* 65 (2): 443–459.

Pettigrew, Steven, Karen Owen, and Emily Wanless. 2014. "U.S. House Primary Election Results (1956–2010)."

Pew. 2018. "The Public, the Political System, and American Democracy." Technical report, Pew Research Center, Washington, DC.

Pildes, Richard H. 2021. "How to Keep Extremists Out of Power." *New York Times*, February 25, 2021.

Pizarro, Max. 2018. "With Frelinghuysen's Retirement Announcement Official, Surging Sherrill Raises Half a Million for Second Straight Quarter." *Insider NJ*, January 29, 2018.

Porter, Rachel, and Tyler S. Steelman. 2023. "No Experience Required: Early Donations and Amateur Candidate Success in Primary Elections." *Legislative Studies Quarterly* 48 (2): 455–466.

Porter, Rachel A., and Sarah A. Treul. 2025. "The Increasing Value of Inexperience in Congressional Primaries." *American Journal of Political Science* 69 (1): 284–298.

Powell, Eleanor Neff, and Justin Grimmer. 2016. "Money in Exile: Campaign Contributions and Committee Access." *Journal of Politics* 78 (4): 974–988.

Powell, Lynda W. 2012. *The Influence of Campaign Contributions in State Legisla-tures: The Effects of Institutions and Politics*. Ann Arbor: University of Michi-gan Press.

Powell, Lynda W. 2013. "The Influence of Campaign Contributions on Legislative Policy." *Forum* 11 (3): 339–355.

Primo, David M., and Jeffrey D. Milyo. 2020. *Campaign Finance and American De-mocracy: What the Public Really Thinks and Why It Matters*. Chicago: Univer-sity of Chicago Press.

Ragsdale, Lyn, and Timothy E. Cook. 1987. "Representatives' Actions and Chal-lengers' Reactions: Limits to Candidate Connections in the House." *American Journal of Political Science* 31 (1): 45–81.

Robinson, Jonathan, and Sean Trende. 2022. "When Your Vote Doesn't Matter, Try Switching Ballots." *Atlantic*, May 24, 2022.

Rohde, David W. 1979. "Risk-Bearing and Progressive Ambition: The Case of Members of the United States House of Representatives." *American Journal of Political Science* 23 (1): 1–26.

Romer, Thomas, and James M. Snyder Jr. 1994. "An Empirical Investigation of the Dynamics of PAC Contributions." *American Journal of Political Science* 38 (3): 745–769.

Schaffner, Brian, Stephen Ansolabehere, and Sam Luks. 2022. "Cooperative Elec-tion Study Common Content, 2020."

Schickler, Eric. 2001. *Disjointed Pluralism: Institutional Innovation and the Devel-opment of the U.S. Congress*. Princeton, NJ: Princeton University Press.

Schickler, Eric. 2016. *Racial Realignment: The Transformation of American Liber-alism, 1932–1965*. Princeton, NJ: Princeton University Press.

Schlesinger, Joseph A. 1966. *Ambition and Politics: Political Careers in the United States*. Chicago: Rand MacNally.

Schnakenberg, Keith E., Collin T. Schumock, and Ian R. Turner. 2023. "Dark Money and Voter Learning." Working paper.

Schneider, Willys. 1976. "Buckley v. Valeo: The Supreme Court and Federal Cam-paign Reform." *Columbia Law Review* 76 (5): 852–891.

Schumpeter, Joseph A. 1942. *Capitalism, Socialism, and Democracy*. New York: Harper and Bros.

Schwarz, Susanne, and Alexander Coppock. 2022. "What Have We Learned about Gender from Candidate Choice Experiments? A Meta-Analysis of Sixty-Seven Factorial Survey Experiments." *Journal of Politics* 84 (2): 655–668.

Scott, Jamil, Kesicia Dickinson, Nazita Lajevardi, and Shayla Olson. 2019. "Supply and Demand in 2018." Paper presented at the 2019 Politics of Race, Immigra-tion, and Ethnicity Consortium (PRIEC), St. Louis, MO.

Sheingate, Adam. 2016. *Building a Business of Politics: The Rise of Political Con-sulting and the Transformation of American Democracy*. New York: Oxford University Press.

Sides, John, Chris Tausanovitch, and Lynn Vavreck. 2022. *The Bitter End: The 2020 Presidential Campaign and the Challenge to American Democracy*. Princeton, NJ: Princeton University Press.

Sides, John, Michael Tesler, and Lynn Vavreck. 2018. *Identity Crisis: The 2016 Presidential Campaign and the Battle for the Meaning of America*. Princeton, NJ: Princeton University Press.

Skelley, Geoffrey. 2021. "Why Candidates with Little Hope of Winning Are Raising More Money Than Ever." *FiveThirtyEight*, August 26, 2021.

Squire, Peverill. 1989. "Challengers in U.S. Senate Elections." *Legislative Studies Quarterly* 14 (4): 531–547.

Squire, Peverill. 1991. "Preemptive Fund-raising and Challenger Profile in Senate Elections." *Journal of Politics* 53 (4): 1150–1164.

Squire, Peverill. 1995. "Candidates, Money, and Voters—Assessing the State of Congressional Elections Research." *Political Research Quarterly* 48 (4): 891–917.

Stewart, Charles, III. 1989. "A Sequential Model of U.S. Senate Elections." *Legislative Studies Quarterly* 14 (4): 567–601.

Stewart, Charles, III, and Jonathan Woon. 2017. "Congressional Committee Assignments, 103rd to 115th Congresses, 1993–2017: House, 2017."

Stone, Walter J., and L. Sandy Maisel. 2003. "The Not-So-Simple Calculus of Winning: Potential U.S. House Candidates' Nomination and General Election Prospects." *Journal of Politics* 65 (4): 951–977.

Stratmann, Thomas. 1998. "The Market For Congressional Votes: Is Timing of Contributions Everything?" *Journal of Law & Economics* 41 (1): 85–114.

Stratmann, Thomas. 2002. "Can Special Interests Buy Congressional Votes? Evidence from Financial Services Legislation." *Journal of Law and Economics* 45 (2): 345–373.

Taagepera, Rein, and Matthew Soberg Shugart. 1993. "Predicting the Number of Parties: A Quantitative Model of Duverger's Mechanical Effect." *American Political Science Review* 87 (2): 455–464.

Teele, Dawn Langan, Joshua Kalla, and Frances Rosenbluth. 2018. "The Ties That Double Bind: Social Roles and Women's Underrepresentation in Politics." *American Political Science Review* 112 (3): 525–541.

Tesler, Michael. 2016. "Views about Race Mattered More in Electing Trump than in Electing Obama." *Washington Post*, November 22, 2016.

Thompson, Nick. 2012. "International Campaign Finance: How Do Countries Compare?" *CNN*, January 24, 2012.

Thomsen, Danielle M. 2014. "Ideological Moderates Won't Run: How Party Fit Matters for Partisan Polarization in Congress." *Journal of Politics* 76 (3): 786–797.

Thomsen, Danielle M. 2017. *Opting Out of Congress: Partisan Polarization and the Decline of Moderate Candidates*. New York: Cambridge University Press.

Thomsen, Danielle M. 2020. "Ideology and Gender in U.S. House Elections." *Political Behavior* 42 (2): 415–442.

Thomsen, Danielle M. 2021. "Women Running, Women Winning: Voter Preferences in 2018." In *Congress Reconsidered, 12th Edition*, edited by Lawrence C. Dodd, Bruce I. Oppenheimer, and C. Lawrence Evans, 133–166. Washington, DC: CQ Press.

Thomsen, Danielle M. 2023. "Competition in Congressional Elections: Money versus Votes." *American Political Science Review* 117 (2): 675–691.

Thomsen, Danielle M., and Michele L. Swers. 2017. "Which Women Can Run? Gender, Partisanship, and Candidate Donor Networks." *Political Research Quarterly* 70 (2): 449–463.

Tufte, Edward R. 1973. "The Relationship between Seats and Votes in Two-Party Systems." *American Political Science Review* 67 (2): 540–554.

Volden, Craig, and Alan E. Wiseman. 2014. *Legislative Effectiveness in the United States Congress: The Lawmakers*. New York: Cambridge University Press.

Wamp, Weston. 2021. "Swamp Stories Episode 29: The Power of Megadonors." *Issue One*, June 25, 2021.

Wawro, Gregory. 2001. "A Panel Probit Analysis of Campaign Contributions and Roll-Call Votes." *American Journal of Political Science* 45 (3): 563–579.

Welch, W. P. 1982. "Campaign Contributions and Legislative Voting: Milk Money and Dairy Price Supports." *Western Political Quarterly* 35 (4): 478–495.

Weschle, Simon. 2022. *Money in Politics: Self-Enrichment, Campaign Spending, and Golden Parachutes*. New York: Cambridge University Press.

Weschle, Simon. 2023. "Campaign Finance." In *The Political Economy of Lobbying: Channels of Influence and Their Regulation*, edited by Karsten Mause, and Andreas Polk. New York: Springer Studies in Public Choice.

Wildstein, David. 2018. "Sherrill Has $1.6 Million Cash on Hand." *New Jersey Globe*, April 10, 2018.

Wood, Abby K. 2021. "Learning from Campaign Finance Information." *Emory Law Journal* 70 (5): 1091–1142.

Wood, Abby K. 2023. "Voters Use Campaign Finance Transparency and Compliance Information." *Political Behavior* 45 (4): 1553–1579.

Wood, Abby K., and Christian R. Grose. 2022. "Campaign Finance Transparency Affects Legislators' Election Outcomes and Behavior." *American Journal of Political Science* 66 (2): 516–534.

Woon, Jonathan. 2018. "Primaries and Candidate Polarization: Behavioral Theory and Experimental Evidence." *American Political Science Review* 112 (4): 826–843.

Wright, John R. 1985. "PACs, Contributions, and Roll Calls: An Organizational Perspective." *American Political Science Review* 79 (2): 400–414.

Zeleny, Jeff. 2006. "Of Party Dues and Deadbeats on Capitol Hill." *New York Times*, October 1, 2006.

Index

Page numbers in italics refer to figures and tables.

CHICAGO STUDIES IN AMERICAN POLITICS

A series edited by Susan Herbst, Lawrence R. Jacobs, Adam J. Berinsky, and Frances Lee; Benjamin I. Page, editor emeritus

www.ingramcontent.com/pod-product-compliance
Lightning Source LLC
Chambersburg PA
CBHW032132020426
42334CB00016B/1139